THE EIGHTEENTH CENTURY PULPIT

THE
Eighteenth Century Pulpit

A STUDY OF THE SERMONS OF
BUTLER, BERKELEY, SECKER, STERNE
WHITEFIELD AND WESLEY

JAMES DOWNEY

CLARENDON PRESS · OXFORD
1969

*Oxford University Press, Ely House, London W.*1

GLASGOW NEW YORK TORONTO MELBOURNE WELLINGTON
CAPE TOWN SALISBURY IBADAN NAIROBI LUSAKA ADDIS ABABA
BOMBAY CALCUTTA MADRAS KARACHI LAHORE DACCA
KUALA LUMPUR SINGAPORE HONG KONG TOKYO

MADE AND PRINTED IN GREAT BRITAIN BY
WILLIAM CLOWES AND SONS, LIMITED
LONDON AND BECCLES

LIST OF PLATES

facing page

1. JOSEPH BUTLER   30
   (Courtesy the Lord Bishop of Durham, Dr. Ian Ramsey)

2. GEORGE BERKELEY   58
   (Courtesy The National Portrait Gallery)

3. THOMAS SECKER   89
   (Courtesy The National Portrait Gallery)

4. LAURENCE STERNE   114
   (Courtesy The National Portrait Gallery)

5. GEORGE WHITEFIELD   155
   (Courtesy The National Portrait Gallery)

6. JOHN WESLEY   189
   (Courtesy The National Portrait Gallery)

The pulpit . . .
Must stand acknowledg'd, while the world shall stand,
The most important and effectual guard,
Support, and ornament, of Virtue's cause.
There stands the messenger of truth: there stands
The legate of the skies!—His theme divine,
His office sacred, his credentials clear.
By him the violated law speaks out
Its thunders; and by him, in strains as sweet
As angels use, the gospel whispers peace.

(Cowper, *The Task*, bk ii)

I

PULPIT ORATORY

A General View

THE TENDENCY of modern scholarship to neglect the contribution of pulpit oratory to English literary history arises from a failure to appreciate the importance that sermons once had in secular as well as religious life. In an age of mass media, compulsory education, professional men of letters, highly-specialized entertainments, and the ubiquitous paperback, many former functions of the pulpit have been taken over by other agencies. Its sole *raison d'être* is now religious; and even as a means of spiritual enlightenment its authority has been weakened and its sphere of influence restricted.

This diminution in the authority and influence of preaching is related to a decline in oratory generally. 'Dirtied by political dictators, sullied with the taint of glib hypocrisy, and linked with herd-psychology',[1] oratory in the twentieth century has fallen into disrepute and 'rhetorical' become a disparaging term. The orator in Victorian England was under no such cloud. He held forth with an air of authority and indulged in verbal pyrotechnics with an *élan* his modern counterpart may well envy. Not that he was personally more flamboyant, but the oratorical tradition as he inherited it allowed him—almost forced him—to be aggressive and authoritative. In the case of the preacher it also, *ipso facto*,

[1] H. Davies, *Varieties of English Preaching 1900–1960* (1963), p. 21.

placed him in a position to wield extraordinary influence in social and intellectual, as well as religious, affairs. And, as E. D. Mackerness has pointed out,[1] it was not the pulpit haranguer who made the most telling impression upon Victorian society, but men of exceptional literary talent such as J. H. Newman, H. P. Liddon, F. W. Robertson, Charles Kingsley, W. C. Magee, and Benjamin Jowett.

When, during the second half of the nineteenth century, the Church began to lose its place at the centre of intellectual and social activity,[2] the sermon was stripped of much of its former power and influence. This, along with a growing mistrust of epideictic oratory, has seemed to mark the end for preaching of a long period of great authority and influence—secular as well as religious—a period which can be said to include medieval monks and friars.

Before this present century it was generally assumed that preaching, having flourished in the early Christian Church, had seriously declined during the Middle Ages. The publication by G. R. Owst of his two celebrated works, *Preaching in Medieval England* (1926) and *Literature and Pulpit in Medieval England* (1933), corrected this misconception. Owst demonstrated that, far from becoming effete, preaching had flourished in medieval England and the preacher had enjoyed enormous popularity and power.

In a world devoid alike of the newspaper and the printed book, of the means of rapid communication by land or sea, the itinerant orator had surely an opportunity which any man of ambition might envy. . . . Modern preachers, eyeing the spoilt children of the modern pew, may well envy the prospect that lay before our medieval friar. Traveller, friend of the outcast, master alike of the ecclesiastical and the popular tongue, with intimate knowledge of the world as well as of books, he could mingle in his discourse the latest 'narration' with the mysteries of nature, 'to please in method and invent by rule'—'joculator Dei' of St. Francis and sacred pedlar rolled into one—for ever bringing forth out of his treasure things new and old.[3]

[1] *The Heeded Voice* (1959), p. xv.
[2] Ibid., p. 102.
[3] *Preaching in Medieval England* (1926), pp. 81–2.

Both the content and the style of preaching underwent change during the Reformation, but the sermon's importance in sacred and secular society was undiminished. It was at this time, principally, that the sermon as a literary, and not just a homiletic exercise received its greatest impetus. For the first time in the history of preaching the written and read discourse gained ascendancy over the straightforward extempore address with a direct appeal to the audience. Clergy of the Church of Rome who wished to remain loyal found their manuscript sermons a defence against charges of heresy which might subsequently be preferred against them. For Protestants, the written discourse was favoured because a corpus of doctrine was essential if the principles and beliefs of the Reformation were to be handed down to future generations. And what better materials than the vituperative rhetoric of the proto-reformers themselves?

In the seventeenth century pulpit oratory achieved a pre-eminence which has not since been equalled. The sermon in every age has revealed men of intellect and integrity reflecting upon eternal verities. But no other age has produced so many astute and articulate preachers as the seventeenth century. The sermons of Lancelot Andrewes, John Donne, Jeremy Taylor, Richard Baxter, Isaac Barrow, Robert South, and John Tillotson, to name only the most famous, are as remarkable for their literary excellence as for their spiritual unction. This indeed was the golden age of English pulpit oratory.

For the century in question the sermon, besides its strictly religious function, took in large measure the place of the journalistic press at the present day, and enjoyed the enormous influence, reinforced by a tremendous sanctity of authority, of a modern broadcasting company. For one person who witnessed a play or ten who happened to read it, thousands may, without exaggeration, be said to have attended sermons, or afterwards studied them from shorthand notes or in printed copies.[1]

[1] W. F. Mitchell, *English Pulpit Oratory From Andrewes To Tillotson*, 2nd ed. (1962), pp. 3-4.

In his study of the Paul's Cross pulpit Millar MacLure confirms this statement. 'THE PAUL's CROSS PULPIT', he contends, 'was nothing less than the popular voice of the Church of England during the most turbulent and creative period in her history.'[1] The ingredients of the sermon, like the functions it was called upon to fulfil, were multifarious.

The public sermon, like the editorial page of a great city newspaper (this one, said Carlyle, *The Times*, 'edited by Heaven'), was at once an arrangement of commonplaces varied in their application to the events of the day, a forum for the great and the would-be great to express their views, and a collection of remembrances. There was enough art in it to satisfy the dilettante, enough sameness to please the sober citizen who did (and does) not like to be startled by new ideas, enough passion for the zealot, enough theology for the Puritan (and Catholic) intellectuals.[2]

In 1644 Milton had remarked on the preponderance of sermons in the book trade:

But as for the multitude of Sermons ready printed and pil'd up, on every text that is not difficult, our London trading St. *Thomas* in his vestry, and adde to boot St. *Martin*, and St. *Hugh*, have not within their hallow'd limits more vendible ware of all sorts ready made: so that penury he need never fear of Pulpit provision, having where so plenteously to refresh his magazin.[3]

The century which followed the publication of *Areopagitica* witnessed considerable change in sermon taste and style, but little diminution in supply. Though it lacked some of the elegance and influence it had enjoyed in the preceding age, the sermon in the eighteenth century was still a power to be reckoned with. Throughout the period it continued to be a best-seller. Publishers vied with one another for copyright to the discourses of the more celebrated divines. In 1742, when Fielding published *Joseph Andrews*, the market was glutted, or so a bookseller informs Parson Adams:

[1] *The Paul's Cross Sermons, 1534–1642* (1958), p. 167.
[2] Ibid., p. 168.
[3] *Areopagitica*, p. 28.

The trade is so vastly stocked with [sermons], that really, unless they come out with the name of Whitefield or Wesley, or some other such great man, as a bishop, or those sort of people, I don't care to touch; unless now it was a sermon preached on the 30th of January; or we could say in the title-page, published at the earnest request of the congregation, or the inhabitants; but truly, for a dry piece of sermons, I had rather be excused; especially as my hands are so full at present.[1]

For men who had a name on which to trade no other *genre* was so lucrative. Profitable as *Tristram Shandy* had proved, Sterne foresaw still greater gains from a volume or two of sermons. In a typically Shandean letter written to David Garrick, 16 March 1765, he sets out his plan:

I have had a lucrative winter's campaign here—Shandy sells well—I am taxing the publick with two more volumes of sermons, which will more than double the gains of Shandy—It goes into the world with a prancing list of *de toute la noblesse*—which will bring me in three hundred pounds, exclusive of the sale of the copy—so that with all the contempt of money which *ma façon de penser* has ever impress'd on me, I shall be rich in spite of myself.[2]

Because the sermon was such a popular and lucrative form of literature, sermon piracy was rampant. The stealing of discourses by means of shorthand transcription was a polished art even in the seventeenth century.[3] In the eighteenth century it continued with unabated vigour though generally less skill, often to the embarrassment of the preacher concerned: 'I wish you had advertised against the publisher of my last sermon. It is not *verbatim* as I delivered it. In some places, he makes me to speak false concord, and even nonsense. In others, the sense and connection are destroyed, by the injudicious disjointed paragraphs; and the whole is entirely unfit for the public review.'[4] Piracy of this kind, especially from men like Whitefield and Wesley who, as Parson Adams's bookseller noted, were

---

[1] Bk. i, ch. xvii.
[2] *Letters*, Shakespeare Head ed. (1927), p. 104.
[3] See Mitchell, pp. 36–7.
[4] G. Whitefield, letter MCCCCXL, *Works*, ed. J. Gillies (1771), iii. 406.

much in demand, but who had little time to prepare their sermons for publication, was a very profitable business.

Oddly enough, it was the clergy themselves who did most to foster this nefarious trade. Hard-pressed or lazy parsons frequently resorted to using, without acknowledgement, the homilies of their more industrious brethren. Nor was 'borrowing' of this kind looked upon as a particularly deplorable act. Dr. Johnson's advice to a young clergyman on the composition of sermons typifies the permissive attitude to sermon plagiarism which prevailed in eighteenth-century England: 'Your present method of making your sermons seems very judicious. Few frequent preachers can be supposed to have sermons more their own than yours will be. Take care to register, somewhere or other, the authours from whom your several discourses are borrowed; and do not imagine that you shall always remember, even what perhaps you now think it impossible to forget.'[1] Johnson's counsel has the weight of a bishop behind it. Speaking to the young clergymen of his diocese (*circa* 1708), Bishop George Bull advised them

not to trust at first to their own compositions, but to furnish themselves with a provision of the best sermons, which the learned divines of our church have published; that by reading them often, and by endeavouring to imitate them, they may acquire a habit of good preaching themselves. And where, through poverty, or any other impediment, ministers are incapable of discharging this duty as they ought, he directed them to use the Homilies of the church, and sometimes to read a chapter to the people, out of that excellent book, called *The Whole Duty of Man.*[2]

It would have pleased Bishop Bull to know that there were men of means who stood ready to assist young preachers in this matter. In praising the fine qualities of character of his own clergyman, Sir Roger de Coverley boasts to his friend how, 'At his first settling with me, I made him a Present of all the good Sermons which have been printed in *English*,

[1] *Boswell's Life of Johnson*, ed. G. B. Hill, rev. L. F. Powell (1934–50), iii. 437.
[2] *Works*, ed. E. Burton (1827), vii. 358–9.

and only begged of him that every *Sunday* he would pronounce one of them in the Pulpit. Accordingly, he has digested them into such a Series, that they follow one another naturally, and make a continued System of practical Divinity.'[1] His friend is much impressed:

I could heartily wish that more of our Country-Clergy would follow this Example; and instead of wasting their Spirits in laborious Compositions of their own, would endeavour after a handsome Elocution, and all those other Talents that are proper to enforce what has been penned by greater Masters. This would not only be more easy to themselves, but more edifying to the People.[2]

But most country squires were less thoughtful and munificent than Sir Roger de Coverley. Consequently, most country clergy had somehow to find their own sermons. J. Timbs tells how a group of Lincolnshire parsons used to meet together every Saturday ostensibly to play whist, backgammon, and smoke 'till they could not see, hear or speak'. But the chief reason for their meeting came out when one servant wondered aloud to another why their masters preferred Saturday for their convention. ' "Why! what do'st think, fool," cried Numps, archly, "but to change sarmunts among one another?"—"Neay, then," said Roger, "I am zure as how they uses my measter very badly, for he always has the worst." '[3]

Inevitably, there were those, like the eccentric divine John Trusler, who stood ready to exploit the sermon market. Trusler, having failed to make a profit from his academy for teaching oratory 'mechanically', turned his devious mind to a related scheme. He realized that a parson who was anxious to make a reputation among his congregation as a fine preacher and scholar did not wish to acknowledge the source or sources of his sermon. If, however, he read from a published work he could hardly conceal his indebtedness. To copy sermons from published sources by hand was a

[1] *Spectator*, no. 106 (2 July 1711).
[2] Ibid.
[3] *A Century of Anecdotes (1760–1860)* (1869), p. 470.

laborious discipline. In order to capitalize on this human weakness, Trusler, in 1769, 'sent circulars to every parish in England and Ireland proposing to print in script type, in imitation of handwriting, about a hundred and fifty sermons at the price of one shilling each, in order to save the clergy both study and the trouble of transcribing'.[1] The success of this scheme more than compensated its author for his trouble and investment. But to a man as devout as William Cowper both Trusler and his scheme were abhorrent:

> He teaches those to read, whom schools dismiss'd,
> And colleges, untaught; sells accent, tone,
> And emphasis in score, and gives to pray'r
> Th' *adagio* and *andante* it demands.
> He grinds divinity of other days
> Down into modern use; transforms old print
> To zig-zag manuscript, and cheats the eyes
> Of gall'ry critics by a thousand arts.[2]

So great was the demand for sermon literature in the eighteenth century that even a few of the religious-minded laity were encouraged to try their hand at this type of composition. Dr. Johnson confessed to having written forty discourses for the pulpit, while illustrating the point that sermon-making was not a difficult art: 'I have begun a sermon after dinner, and sent it off by the post that night.'[3] But it was not always men of deep religious conviction like Dr. Johnson who found a ready market for their pulpit wares. Grub Street hacks, like the one in Goldsmith's *Citizen of the World*, found sermons as vendible as bawdy jests: 'Would you think it, gentlemen? ... I have actually written last week sixteen prayers, twelve bawdy jests and three sermons, all at the rate of sixpence a-piece.'[4] Crabbe heaps scorn and contempt upon clergymen who buy and use such drivel:

---

[1] *DNB* lvii. 268.

[2] *The Task*, bk. ii, ll. 358–65, *Poetical Works*, ed. H. S. Milford (1911).

[3] *Boswell's Life*, v. 67.

[4] Letter 30, *The British Essayists*, ed. R. Lynam (1827), xxi. 213.

And lo! with all their learning, when they rise
To preach, in view the ready sermon lies;
Some low-prized stuff they purchased at the stalls,
And more like Seneca's than mine or Paul's.[1]

If some who were not very religious engaged in writing sermons, others, hardly more devout, purchased them. When Topham Beauclerk died it was discovered that among his library of thirty thousand books was an impressive collection of sermons.

Mr. Wilkes said, he wondered to find in it such a numerous collection of sermons; seeming to think it strange that a gentleman of Mr. Beauclerk's character in the gay world, should have chosen to have many compositions of that kind. JOHNSON. 'Why, Sir, you are to consider, that sermons make a considerable branch of English literature; so that a library must be very imperfect if it has not a numerous collection of sermons.[2]

The fact is, as Dr. Johnson suggests, that in eighteenth-century England the sermon maintained a significant position among the classic forms of the national literature. Englishmen prided themselves that their nation possessed the finest preachers in Europe. 'The Sermons of our Divines', boasts John Langhorne, 'are allowed, by the liberal part of Europe, to be the best and purest compositions within the province of Theology.'[3] Once more Dr. Johnson explains why: 'But our own language has, from the Reformation to the present time, been chiefly dignified and adorned by the works of our divines, who, considered as commentators, controvertists, or preachers, have undoubtedly left all other nations far behind them.'[4] Although the rhetorical

---

[1] *The Borough*, letter iv, *Poetical Works*, eds. A. J. and R. M. Carlyle (1914), p. 125.

[2] *Boswell's Life*, iv, 105. It is somewhat ironic that in remarking upon the splendid list of 661 subscribers whose names appeared in Sterne's first published volume of sermons—a list in which Wilkes is included—Wilbur Cross should wonder 'what use could be made of sermons by Wilkes, the profane politician'. *The Life and Times of Laurence Sterne*, i. 218.

[3] *Letters on the Eloquence of the Pulpit* (1765), p. 38.

[4] *Idler*, no. 91, *Works*, ed. R. Lynam (1825), ii. 649.

bent of education was less in evidence in eighteenth-century curricula than it had been in the curricula of the previous century, yet the sermons of Tillotson, Atterbury, Clarke, and others were held up to students as the finest models of lucid reasoning and writing. And according to a master of Magdalene College, Cambridge, 'the entire religious side of the second collegiate year was devoted to the study of Tillotson's sermons'.[1]

The explanation of this seemingly insatiable demand for homiletic literature is to be found in an examination of the protean nature of the eighteenth-century sermon. Whereas the sermon to-day has a strictly religious character and is expected to do nothing more than provide a suitable concomitant to other aspects of public worship, two hundred years ago it had firm and conscious ties with secular society. Politics, education, philosophy, and literature all made demands upon, and in turn created demands for, sermons.

The orientation of the pulpit to the conventions of polite society was a task to which a majority of eighteenth-century clergy applied themselves with zest. The high-pitched notes of dogmatism gave way to the dulcet strains of ethical preaching. As redefined by Archbishop Tillotson and practised by Latitudinarians throughout the eighteenth century, religion ceased to be a *mysterium tremendum et fascinans*. The church seemed almost to become a society for the reformation of manners, a place where kindred spirits met to have their moral sensibilities tuned to a finer pitch. Many preachers, like Pope's 'soft Dean', could not bring themselves to mention 'Hell to ears polite'.[2] The most distinguishing feature of such preaching was its pragmatism: it was aimed at refining and rationalizing the social order.

Votaries of Tillotsonian theology saw the function of religion as being to provide support and sanctions for morality. Addison, whose *Spectator* essays often require only

---

[1] Quoted by E. C. Mossner, *Bishop Butler and the Age of Reason* (1936), p. 22n.
[2] *Moral Essays*, iv. 149-50.

a scriptural text to make them sermons,[1] mused upon the salutary effects Sunday observances in rural England had upon the behaviour of those who participated:

I am always very well pleased with a Country *Sunday*; and think, if keeping holy the Seventh Day were only a human Institution, it would be the best Method that could have been thought of for the polishing and civilizing of Mankind. It is certain the Country-People would soon degenerate into a kind of Savages and Barbarians, were there not such frequent Returns of a stated Time, in which the whole Village meet together with their best Faces, and in their cleanliest Habits, to converse with one another upon indifferent Subjects, hear their Duties explained to them, and join together in Adoration of the supreme Being. *Sunday* clears away the Rust of the whole Week, not only as it refreshes in their Minds the Notions of Religion, but as it puts both the Sexes upon appearing in their most agreeable Forms, and exerting such Qualities as are apt to give them a Figure in the Eye of the Village. A Country-Fellow distinguishes himself as much in the *Church-yard*, as a Citizen does upon the *Change*; the whole Parish-Politicks being generally discuss'd in that Place either after Sermon or before the Bell rings.[2]

Addison, as is here apparent, was caught up in the optimistic belief, shared by many—though by no means all—Augustans, that man and society were about to reach a new plateau of enlightenment and sophistication. Such an ethos is inimical to prophets; men prefer their priest to be a Barnabas (a son of consolation) rather than a Boanerges (a son of thunder). Swift spoke for many when he said that the chief task of the preacher is to tell people what is their duty, and then convince them to do it.[3] Talk of sin, salvation, and eternal punishment seemed somehow to belong to a past, less enlightened age. In *Joseph Andrews* Parson Adams tries to interest the innkeeper in the final destination of his soul, only to receive this complacent reply: 'As for that, master

---

[1] *The Spectator*'s expressed intention was to 'enliven Morality with Wit, and to temper Wit with Morality'. No. 10 (12 March 1711).

[2] *Spectator*, no. 112 (9 July 1711).

[3] 'A Letter to a Young Gentleman Lately Entered into Holy Orders', *Irish Tracts 1720–23 and Sermons*, ed. H. Davis (1948), p. 70.

... I never once thought about it; but what signifies talking about matters so far off?'[1]

'Take a dozen or more of Robert South's sermons,' says Caroline Richardson, 'behead them of their texts, cut off their extremities of perfunctory reminder that souls should be saved, and what remains is a group of essays well worth reading.'[2] Such a statement could be made with equal justification of the sermons of Swift, Butler, Sterne, and many of their less illustrious contemporaries. It was indeed true, as the Rev. William Jones would later record in his diary, that in many pulpit discourses 'the name of Christ is scarce ever heard, nor any of the characteristic doctrines of His holy religion. The watchword, or *catch-word* . . . is "Morality".'[3] But the rationale behind such preaching was all too apparent. If the end of religion was the creation of a more harmonious society, then the sermon—the principal instrument of instruction in the Protestant tradition—had to be made consequential to the needs of social living.

If the religious history of the eighteenth century proves anything it is this:—That good sense, the best good sense, when it sets to work with the materials of human nature and Scripture to construct a religion, will find its way to an ethical code, irreproachable in its contents, and based on a just estimate and wise observation of the facts of life, ratified by Divine sanctions in the shape of hope and fear, of future rewards and penalties of obedience and disobedience. This the eighteenth century did and did well.[4]

Compared with the best sermons of the seventeenth century, much eighteenth-century preaching seems uninspiring. There is little of Barrow's erudition, less of South's satire, and none of the 'wit' of Andrewes and Donne. It is well to remember, however, that the climate of social and religious opinion had changed. New demands were being

---

[1] Bk. ii, ch. iii.

[2] *English Preachers and Preaching 1640–1670* (1928), p. 86.

[3] *The Diary of the Revd. William Jones*, ed. O. F. Christie (1929), p. 158.

[4] M. Pattison, 'Tendencies of Religious Thought in England, 1688–1750', *Essays and Reviews* (1860), p. 296.

made upon the pulpit. If Sterne, for example, would have appeared woefully restrained at St. Paul's Cross, Donne would have seemed just as anachronistic in the rôle of Yorick. There is much truth in the observation that the 'preachers of any period are not to be censured for adapting their style of address and mode of arguing to their hearers. They are as necessarily bound to the preconceived notions, as to the language, of those whom they have to exhort.'[1]

The predisposition of Augustan England towards a theology based upon reason, and a preaching that was un-impassioned, stemmed largely from the desire to avoid the kind of fanaticism and intolerance which had been such a horrific part of the religion of the previous age. Never again must such acts be perpetrated in the name of Christianity. And prohibition in religious practice and preaching of the heady wine of 'enthusiasm' seemed the most effective guard. Pope had his finger on the pulse of his age when he wrote:

> For Modes of Faith, let graceless zealots fight;
> His can't be wrong whose life is in the right:
> In Faith and Hope the world will disagree,
> But all Mankind's concern is Charity:
> All must be false that thwart this One great End,
> And all of God, that bless Mankind or mend.[2]

With faith in the same principle Swift attempts to discourage his young clerical friend from arousing the emotions of his congregation. 'I do not see', he declares, 'how this Talent of moving the Passions, can be of any great Use towards directing Christian Men in the Conduct of their Lives.'[3] This somewhat complacent, though no doubt genuine, sentiment is the characteristic feature of pulpit oratory during the first four decades of the eighteenth century. If preachers went too far along the road of reasoned restraint it was because such a road seemed to lead away from the excesses of Puritanism.

[1] Pattison, p. 276.
[2] *Essay on Man*, iii. 305–10.
[3] 'Letter to a Young Gentleman', p. 69.

The intellectual basis for such preaching was an uncommon belief in the sufficiency of reason to establish both
the reality of God and the essential truths of the Christian
Faith. Christendom has always been divided on the question
of where ultimate authority should lie. For Roman Catholics
the Pope, as head of the Church, has been accorded the final
say on matters of faith and morals. Calvinists, and this
includes the Puritans of the seventeenth century, have
placed all store by the Bible, holding it to be the definitive
and irrefutable word of God. Anglicans of the seventeenth
and early eighteenth centuries, abhorring what seemed to
them the degeneracy of Rome and the intolerance of
Geneva, sought a more responsible basis of faith. Reason
appeared to be the only plausible alternative.

Constructing a rational foundation for revealed religion
was the task to which men like Samuel Clarke, Joseph Butler,
and George Berkeley applied themselves with vigour.
Locke and Tillotson had shown the way: Locke with his
Essay Concerning Human Understanding (1690)[1] and *Reasonableness of Christianity* (1695), and Tillotson with his
sermon, 'His Commandments are not Grievous'. In this
sermon are embodied the quintessential elements of what
has become known as Latitudinarian theology. As in all his
preaching, Tillotson is solicitous to show how reasonable
and beneficial Christianity can be. Mystery and sacrifice are
not so much condemned as set aside as redundant. His
appeal is to common sense and self-interest.

The laws of God are reasonable, that is, suitable to our nature and
advantageous to our interest. It is true God hath a sovereign right over
us as we are his creatures, and by virtue of this right he might without
injustice have imposed difficult tasks upon us, and have required hard
things at our hands. But in making laws for us he hath not made use
of this right. He hath commanded us nothing in the gospel that is
either unsuitable to our reason, or prejudicial to our interest; nay,
nothing that is severe and against the grain of our nature, but when

---

[1] See especially bk. iv, ch. xix.

either the apparent necessity of our interest does require it, or any extraordinary reward is promised to our obedience.[1]

And true to his benevolent nature God has made that reward doubly attractive:

We have the greatest encouragement to the observance of God's commands. Two things make any course of life easy; present pleasure, and the assurance of a future reward. Religion gives part of its reward in hand, the present comfort and satisfaction of having done our duty; and, for the rest, it offers us the best security that Heaven can give. Now these two must needs make our duty very easy; a considerable reward in hand, and not only the hopes but the assurance of a far greater recompence hereafter.[2]

Of this sermon and the theology it expresses, Horton Davies has said: 'Here is an unequalled combination of eudaemonism, utilitarianism, and pelagianism, masquerading as Christianity. It was left to the Latitudinarians to conceive of a contradiction—Christianity without tears!'[3] This is undoubtedly true; but it was just such a form of Christianity which seemed to Augustan churchmen the *via media* between dogmatism on the one hand and 'enthusiasm' on the other.

It is almost impossible to exaggerate the influence of Tillotson upon eighteenth-century theology and preaching. 'His Commandments are Not Grievous' was easily the most popular sermon in eighteenth-century England. Even in

---

[1] *Works*, ed. T. Birch (1820), i. 468.

[2] Ibid., i. 475. Cf. Locke on the same subject: 'The business of men being to be happy in this world by the enjoyment of the things of nature subservient to life health ease and pleasure, and by the comfortable hopes of another life when this is ended: And in the other world by an accumulation of higher degrees of blisse in an everlasting security, we need noe other knowledg for the atteinment of those ends but of the history and observation of the effects and operations of naturall bodys within our power, and of our dutys in the management of our owne actions as far as they depend upon our wills.' Journal, 8 Feb. 1677, *An Early Draft of Locke's Essay together with Excerpts from His Journals*, eds. R. I. Aaron and J. Gibb (1936), p. 88.

[3] *Worship and Theology in England from Watts and Wesley to Maurice, 1690–1850* (1961), p. 56.

the last decade of the century it was being preached *ipsissima verba* by country parsons like James Woodforde.[1]

Just as philosophy during most of the eighteenth century was dominated by the influence of Locke, so orthodox theology was equally dominated by the seventeenth-century divine, Archbishop Tillotson. Three characteristics of his teaching seem to stand out: (*a*) in all matters of religion there must be an appeal to reason; (*b*) claims to spiritual intuition are to be distrusted; (*c*) man's knowledge of truth must always be imperfect.[2]

Tillotson's prudential ethic is ubiquitous not only in the homiletics of the eighteenth century but in the literature as well; Steele, Addison, Richardson, Fielding, Graves, Smollett, Sterne, and Goldsmith had all imbibed it. Such a belief tended to glorify man and his mind rather than God and his grace. Nor did his Catholicism render Pope immune to such infectious rationalism:

> Know then thyself, presume not God to scan;
> The proper study of Mankind is Man.[3]

Others, like Cowper and Crabbe, rebelled against this anthropocentric religion, but even in condemning it they affirmed its widespread influence. As late as 1810, Crabbe felt compelled to write:

> Hark to the Churchman: day by day he cries,
> 'Children of men, be virtuous and be wise;
> Seek patience, justice, temp'rance, meekness, truth;
> In age be courteous, be sedate in youth.'
> So they advise, and when such things be read,
> How can we wonder that their flocks are dead.[4]

Yet for all its reason and common sense the age was one of heated controversy. Pulpits, presses, and coffee-houses reverberated with the sounds of attack and counter-attack:—

---

[1] N. Sykes, 'The Sermons of a Country Parson', *Theology*, xxxviii (Feb. 1939), see especially pp. 98–100.

[2] L. E. Elliott-Binns, *The Early Evangelicals* (1953), p. 90.

[3] *Essay on Man*. ii. 1–2.

[4] *The Borough*, letter iv.

Juror versus Non-Juror; Erastian versus Laudian; Arian versus Orthodox; Trinitarian versus Unitarian; Arminian versus Calvinist; Theist versus Deist. The Bangorian Controversy which started with a sermon by Bishop Hoadly at Bangor in 1717, and is described by Leslie Stephen as 'one of the most intricate tangles of fruitless logomachy in the language',[1] filled the pulpits with disputants. And Goldsmith complained more than forty years after the Controversy was begun, that congregations were still being subjected to its inane debate.[2]

So it was that until the advent of Methodism, that is to say until after 1740, rational, ethical homiletics had only one competitor for pulpit priority, and that was polemical preaching. If, as Addison suggests, parish politics were usually discussed before and after service on a Sunday morning, it was not uncommon for politics on a wider scale to be considered by the preacher during the sermon. It was an age in which religious and political affairs were inseparable. The marriage of Church and State under the Tudors had proved convenient, if not always blissful. In return for support and protection, the Church, where it could, encouraged public acceptance of governmental policies. No monarch, or parliament, could afford to ignore the relationship in which the clergy stood to public opinion, and 'tuning the pulpit' was a favourite stratagem of Tudors and Stuarts alike.

So close was the union of Church and State under the Tudor and Stuart sovereigns, that the bishops and clergy were regarded, and did commonly regard themselves, as officials of the State hardly less than as ministers of the Church. Indeed, Church and State in the established theory of a National Church were but different facets of the same community. The parish clergy received from the Bishops, who formed the regular medium through which the orders of the State were communicated, the directions which in their turn they were required to convey to their parishioners. They stated in their sermons the

---

[1] *History of English Thought in the Eighteenth Century*, Harbinger ed. (1962), ii. 132.
[2] 'Of Eloquence', *The Bee*, no. 7 (17 Nov. 1759).

decisions of the Government, expounded its policy, and exhorted the people to obedience. They were held closely to their secular duty. They might not preach without licence: four times in the year they were required to expound the Royal Supremacy: their sermons were watched by the Churchwardens, who were required to report to the Bishop any political unsoundness or indication of doctrinal aberration, and they might not make their pulpits places of personal controversy with other preachers.[1]

The Non-Jurors, by their refusal to swear an oath of allegiance to William and Mary in 1689, had threatened both Church and State with schism. But the solid, if verbose, defences of the Establishment by such able scholars as Wake,[2] Warburton,[3] and Paley,[4] seemed to most eighteenth-century preachers and writers a sufficient vindication of the *status quo*.

Some clerics were as much politicians as they were priests. 'I never preached but twice in my life,' said Swift, 'and they were not sermons but pamphlets.' When asked what these discourses were about, he replied: 'They were against Wood's Halfpence.'[5] Another Tory, Henry Sacheverell, could also have claimed that many of his sermons were political tracts. Indeed, it was just such a sermon that brought him into the public limelight. 'The Perils of False Brethren in Church and State' was preached at St. Paul's on 5 November 1709 and subsequently sold 40,000 copies. It was a bold indictment of the government of the day. Whig ministers, many of whom were present at the service,[6] were reproved for their failure to safeguard the interests of the Church of England. Sacheverell was impeached and

---

[1] *Selected English Sermons: Sixteenth to Nineteenth Centuries*, ed. H. H. Henson (1939), p. vii.

[2] *The State of the Church and the Clergy of England* (1703).

[3] *The Alliance between Church and State* (1736).

[4] *Moral and Political Philosophy* (1785).

[5] Quoted by R. W. Jackson, *Jonathan Swift, Dean and Pastor* (1939), p. 124.

[6] The 5th of November was doubly significant for Whigs. On that date they celebrated—often by attending a special church service—two great triumphs of parliament: the thwarting of Guy Fawkes in 1605 and the landing of William of Orange on English soil in 1688.

subsequently found guilty of malicious libel. His trial attracted much public attention; Tories carried out protest demonstrations, and the light sentence he received was acclaimed by supporters and sympathizers as a moral victory for their cause.[1]

But if some of the clergy suffered from the vicissitudes of this Church/State alliance, others benefited. Many Church preferments, particularly the more attractive, were political appointments. An ambitious and astute cleric could, if he were not too scrupulous, secure rapid advancement. Benjamin Hoadly is a case in point. By virtue of his faithful advocacy of the Whig cause, he appropriated in succession the sees of Bangor, Hereford, Salisbury, and Winchester.[2]

By the time Atterbury was banished abroad in 1723 for Jacobite intrigue, much of the force of polemical preaching had been spent. Over the next ten years or so politics ceased to be a subject of major importance in the pulpit. Nor can the Deist Controversy be said to have replaced politics as the chief homiletic concern. It is true that Deism tended to unite churchmen in their condemnation of it, but Christian apologists, such as Butler, Berkeley, and Law, for example, chose to make their defence in more scholarly treatises, thus leaving the sermon for exposition and application of the Christian message. Ethical preaching now completely triumphed. The years 1720–40 are the period of greatest vogue for Tillotsonian theology and ethical preaching.

Not surprisingly, however, the nature of the religious experience fostered by such theology and preaching was unable to satisfy the spiritual and psychological needs of the masses. In their desire to make Christianity intellectually respectable, Latitudinarians had robbed it of two of its most

---

[1] Sacheverell's sentence suspended his right to preach for three years, though during that time he was allowed to perform other ecclesiastical offices and to accept preferment if offered. See under 'Henry Sacheverell' in *A Dictionary of English Church History*, eds. S. L. Ollard and others, 3rd ed. (1948).

[2] For an interesting account of the political involvement of eighteenth-century clergy, especially bishops, see G. R. Cragg, 'The Churchman', *Man Versus Society in Eighteenth-Century Britain*, ed. J. L. Clifford (1968), pp. 54–69.

precious possessions, mystery and passion. God became
invested with mechanical attributes, a 'clock-maker deity'
no longer 'involved' in the human predicament. Reaction
was imminent.

'The history of Evangelical Revival', Canon Smyth has
observed, 'is essentially a history of personalities, rather than
of opinions.'[1] The Methodist Movement—the extremest
form the reaction against Latitudinarianism took—gives
support to this statement. It was through the power of
personality and the strength of conviction, and not through
any reformulation of systematic theology, that men like
John Wesley and George Whitefield achieved their success
as preachers. It is neither possible nor necessary in this
study to assess the contribution of eighteenth-century
evangelicals to the religious and social history of England.
Of greater relevance here is their contribution to English
oratorical prose. Just as the Romantic Revival at the end of
the century gave the poet a feeling of emancipation from
the trammels of 'propriety' and 'taste', so the Evangelical
Movement, spearheaded by the Methodists, gave its
preachers a new freedom of thought and expression. Preaching became with Whitefield what poetry would later become
with Wordsworth: 'the spontaneous overflow of powerful
feelings'. The carefully prepared manuscript (the Tillotsonian ideal) and statuesque delivery gave way to a mode of
address more extemporaneous and gesticulatory. Sermons
were frequently preached first and written out later. Thus
it was that the sermon which at the hands of Tillotson and
his votaries 'lost its heroic note, and became a moral essay'[2]
was once more restored to homiletics.

That there was a close and conscious relationship between
sacred and secular literature throughout the eighteenth
century is evidenced by the large number of clergymen who
engaged in other kinds of writing than the purely devotional.

---

[1] *Simeon and Church Order* (1940), p. 6.
[2] Smyth, *The Art of Preaching* (1939), p. 160.

Butler, Berkeley, and Paley made notable contributions to philosophy; Bentley, Warburton, and Hurd distinguished themselves as literary critics; Lowth and Crabbe earned praise as poets; John Wesley demonstrated the versatility of his genius by writing criticism, translating, compiling a dictionary and grammatical handbooks, and keeping a truly magnificent journal; Hoadly and Law were gifted polemicists; Swift and Sterne hardly need elaboration. Such earnest involvements by these and others in such varying *genres* could not but strongly influence the style and structure of pulpit oratory. In no other period have the preacher and the man of letters shared more in common. In no other period has the sermon been more responsive to the rules of literary criticism.

The idea that the sermon should be made to conform to a canon of literary criticism was conceived and given impetus in the previous century. The second half of the seventeenth century had witnessed a remarkable change in attitude towards prose, the upshot of which was a determined effort at stylistic reform. And as part of this larger movement an attempt was made to chasten pulpit oratory. During this period can be seen developing the reciprocity of thought, taste, and style of writing which would hold true for the sermon and literature in the Augustan age and beyond.

In the first half of the seventeenth century preaching had been dominated by three figures: Lancelot Andrewes, John Donne, and Jeremy Taylor. Though as preachers they differed markedly in temperament and technique, there was a quality of abstruseness about the sermons of all three. Andrewes tended to confound his audience by his immense learning and verbal analyses of scripture; Donne by his clever conceits and hermeneutics; and Taylor by his magniloquent periods. The intellectual climate of Restoration England was inimical to such seemingly precious oratory. Cartesian rationalism, with its emphasis upon clarity of thought and simplicity of expression, was already exerting an influence upon English philosophy. At the same

time, the New Science was insisting upon a prose style for
scientific reporting that was lucid, immediate, and un-
adorned. It was, furthermore, the published intention of the
Royal Society, of whose membership the clergy constituted a
significant part, to set up a severely practical standard for
prose and at the same time discredit the more fulsome style
of the past. According to Thomas Sprat, the Society had
resolved 'to reject all the amplifications, digressions, and
swellings of style: to return back to the primitive purity, and
shortness, when men deliver'd so many *things*, almost in an
equal number of *words*'.[1] To achieve this end 'they [the
Society] have exacted from all their members, a close, naked,
natural way of speaking; positive expressions; clear senses;
a native easiness: bringing all things as near the Mathe-
matical plainness as they can'.[2]

In this campaign the Church of England, collectively as
well as through individual clerics, played a major rôle. As
early as 1644 the Westminster Assembly had registered its
protest against the meretricious manner of preaching and
writing, and thereby struck one of the most telling blows for
the cause of stylistic reform. This was followed in 1646 by
John Wilkins's *Ecclesiastes*, an *ars concionandi* which went
through eight editions by 1704, and which argued for a
'plain and natural' manner of preaching. By the time Sprat,
a clergyman, published his *History of the Royal Society*
victory had almost been won for the plain style. This did not
prevent him, however, from censuring once more the
'fantastical terms' and 'outlandish phrases' which characterized the writing and preaching of the past age.

After 1660 the argument for abandoning fustian rhetoric
gained strength from the fact that oratory of this kind was
being associated more and more with Puritan preachers.
' "Fine preaching" soon became the rhetorical counterpart

---

[1] *History of the Royal Society* (1667), p. 113.

[2] Ibid. Swift takes the Royal Society's theory of language to its logical conclusion and beyond when Gulliver visits the Academy of Lagado in bk. iii, ch. v of
Gulliver's Travels and finds that some of the projectors have dispensed with words
entirely.

of fanatical religion; enthusiasm was detected as quickly in the first as in the second.'[1] In a sermon entitled 'The Scribe Instructed' given at St. Mary's, Oxford, 29 July 1660, Robert South fulminated against Puritan preaching. He ridiculed those who practised 'strange new postures', like 'shutting the eyes, distorting the face, and speaking through the nose'. He attacked them also for their 'whimsical cant of *issues, products, tendencies, breathings, indwellings, rollings, recumbencies,* and scriptures misapplied'.[2]

All vain, luxuriant allegories, rhyming cadencies of similary words, are such pitiful embellishments of speech, as to serve for nothing but to embase divinity. . . . And as this can by no means be accounted divinity, so neither indeed can it pass for wit . . . for true wit is a severe and manly thing. Wit in divinity is nothing else, but sacred truths suitably expressed. It is not shreds of Latin or Greek, nor a *Deus dixit,* and a *Deus benedixit,* nor those little quirks, or divisions into the ὅτι, the διότι, and the καθότι, or the *egress, regress,* and *progress,* and other such stuff, (much like the style of a lease,) that can properly be called wit. For that is not wit which consists not with wisdom.[3]

In a second sermon on this subject, preached at Christ Church, Oxford, 30 April 1668, South is somewhat more restrained, perhaps because by then it was apparent that the cause he supported was winning. He lists the three elements essential to a good sermon: '1. Great clearness and perspicuity. 2. An unaffected plainness and simplicity. And, 3. A suitable and becoming zeal or fervour.'[4] South, it must be confessed, was not always true to his ideal of style: of zeal he possessed an abundance, but his prose does not always have the unaffected plainness and simplicity he demanded of others. This bit of inconsistency aside, it is still true that he lent considerable weight to the movement for sermon reform.

There were others, of course, who joined in the attack on pulpit eloquence and who were instrumental in achieving

[1] R. F. Jones, 'The Attack on Pulpit Eloquence', *The Seventeenth Century* (1951), p. 116.

[2] *Works* (1823), iii. 34–5.

[3] Ibid., iii. 32–3.

[4] Ibid., iv. 149.

the new ideal of style. A more detailed discussion of this subject would include an appraisal of the contributions of Simon Patrick, John Eachard, Joseph Parker, and perhaps others.[1] But of greater importance to this study than any of those previously mentioned is Archbishop John Tillotson (1630–94). Something of his influence upon eighteenth-century theology has already been seen. It remains now to consider his contribution to pulpit oratory.

Tillotson's importance to the development of English prose has sometimes been exaggerated because of the extravagant compliment paid him by Dryden. Birch records that Dryden 'frequently owned with pleasure, that if he had any talent for English prose . . . it was owing to his having often read his Grace's writings'.[2] But as James Sutherland has noted, 'Dryden's prose style, indeed, was already formed before Tillotson could have had much influence on him'.[3] It would be more difficult, however, to exaggerate Tillotson's importance in the development of pulpit oratory. Such was the fame he achieved during his lifetime that after his death his wife is believed to have been offered £2,000 for the copyright of his sermons.[4]

Wherein his greatness as a preacher lay is not now apparent. It is generally felt that in intellect he was inferior to his two great contemporaries, South and Barrow. Certainly his preaching is less arresting and lively than the former's and less profound and scholarly than the latter's. In reading his sermons today one is struck by the lack of any imaginative richness in either their thought or expression. It is only as the critical norms and standards of his own day are applied to him that the reasons for his greatness reveal themselves.

He struck the key-note which in his own day, and for two generations or more afterwards, governed the predominant tone of religious

---

[1] See R. F. Jones, pp. 111 ff.
[2] *Works*, i. ccxxxv.
[3] *On English Prose* (1957), p. 66.
[4] *Term Catalogues, 1668–1709*, ed. E. Arber (1905), ii. ix.

reasoning and sentiment. In the substance no less than in the form of his writings men found exactly what suited them—their own thoughts raised to a somewhat higher level, and expressed just in the manner which they would most aspire to imitate. His sermons, when delivered, had been exceedingly popular. We are told of the crowds of auditors and the fixed attention with which they listened, also of the number of clergymen who frequented his St. Laurence lectures, not only for the pleasure of hearing, but to form their minds and improve their style. He was, in fact, the great preacher of his time.[1]

His sermons are addressed to reason and couched in a diction that is, above all, precise. Appeals to emotion he regarded as both dangerous and unnecessary. He usually begins a discourse with a short proem which seeks to introduce his subject, impress its high seriousness upon his hearers, and prejudice them in his favour. As though outlining a problem in logic, he makes every sentence count; there are no embellishments and no redundant phrases. In turn he considers the several divisions into which his subject logically falls. There is no peroration; no impassioned pleading with sinners; no final 'call'. When the argument is concluded, the counsel for the Prosecution rests his case.

In the celebrated funeral sermon preached for him by his friend and colleague, Gilbert Burnet, an attempt is made to explain the secret of his success as a preacher.

His joining with Bishop *Wilkins* in pursuing the Scheme of an Universal Character, led him to consider exactly the Truth of Language and Stile, in which no Man was happier, and knew better the Art of preserving the Majesty of things under a Simplicity of Words; tempering these so equally together, that neither did his Thoughts sink, nor his Stile swell: keeping always a due Mean between a low Flatness and the Dresses of false Rhetorick. Together with the Pomp of Words he did also cut off all Superfluities and needless Enlargements: He said what was just necessary to give clear Idea's [sic] of things, and no more: He laid aside all long and affected Periods: His Sentences were short and clear; and the whole Thread was of a piece, plain and distinct. No affectations of Learning, no

---

[1] C. J. Abbey and J. H. Overton, *The English Church in the Eighteenth Century* (1902), p. 115.

squeezing of Texts, no superficial Strains, no false Thoughts nor bold Flights, all was solid and yet lively, and grave as well as Fine.[1]

Allowing for the panegyric of funeral sermons, there is still much truth in this assessment. The attributes of Tillotson's oratory which most impressed hearers and readers were the lucidity of his language and the sinewy strength of his argument. Take, for example, this passage from 'The Folly of Scoffing at Religion':

But if we suppose this apprehension of a Deity to have no foundation in nature, but to have had its rise from tradition which hath been confirmed in the world by the prejudice of education, the difficulty of removing it will almost be as great as if it were natural, that which men take in by education being next to that which is natural. And if it could be extinguished, yet the advantage of it will not recompence the trouble of the cure. For, except the avoiding of persecution for religion, there is no advantage that the principles of atheism, if they could be quietly settled in a man's mind, can give him. The advantage indeed that men make of them is to give themselves the liberty to do what they please, to be more sensual and more unjust than other men; that is, they have the privilege to surfeit themselves, and to be sick oftner than other men, and to make mankind their enemy by their unjust and dishonest actions, and consequently to live more uneasily in the world than other men.

So that the principles of religion, the belief of a God, and another life, by obliging men to be virtuous do really promote their temporal happiness. And all the privilege that atheism pretends to is to let men loose to vice, which is naturally attended with temporal inconveniences. And if this be true, then the atheist cannot pretend this reason of charity to mankind (which is the only one I can think of) to dispute against religion, much less to rally upon it. For it is plain, that it would be no kindness to any man to be undeceived in these principles of religion, supposing they were false; because the principles of religion are so far from hindering, that they promote a man's happiness even in this world, and as to the other world there can be no inconvenience in the mistake; for when a man is not, it will be no trouble to him that he was once deceived about these matters.[2]

[1] *A Sermon preached at the Funeral of ... John ... Lord Archbishop of Canterbury* (1694), pp. 13–14.
[2] *Works*, i. 397–8.

Here the reasoned design is obvious; the logic, as everywhere, relentless. Nothing in the vocabulary or sentence structure calls attention to itself. Bishop Warburton described Tillotson's style as 'simple, elegant, candid, clear, and rational'.[1] Such prose, it must be confessed, is devoid of any power to excite the imagination or warm the heart. But it is well to remember that Tillotson regarded appeals to the heart and imagination as a dangerous flirtation with 'enthusiasm'. It would be unfair therefore to condemn him for failing to achieve a goal he did not aim at. He deserves to be judged in the light of his success in attaining the ends he postulated and the effect of that success upon others.

Tillotson was in fact doing for pulpit oratory what Dryden was doing for prose in general: pruning, selecting, refining, creating an architectonic design, imbuing it with clarity and directness. In a word, he was evolving a more efficient vehicle of communication.

Ultimately, it is not Tillotson's excellence as a preacher which is chiefly responsible for his eminent position in the development of English oratorical prose. It is rather his influence upon succeeding generations of preachers. Above all, and herein lies the reason for his influence, Tillotson was imitable. In both structure and language his sermons are easy to emulate. Barrow, South, Burnet, and Stillingfleet were all perhaps better preachers; but none of them was really imitable. Lesser men attempting to emulate their styles were in danger of falling victims to bombast, or bathos, or both. It was, as Fraser Mitchell has remarked, 'Tillotson whose pulpit manner first attracted universal admiration, and persuaded men that a plain, equable, yet judiciously modulated prose was not only possible but was also the most proper for the sermon'.[2]

Tillotson died in 1694. His mantle of succession in the pulpit tradition fell upon the shoulders of a young man of zealous heart and astute mind, Francis Atterbury

---

[1] *Letters from a Late Eminent Prelate to One of his Friends*, 2nd ed. (1809), p. 127.
[2] *English Pulpit Oratory*, p. 336.

(1662–1732). Atterbury's career conveniently spans the period between Tillotson and Joseph Butler,[1] but he is of interest here for a more important reason. In him can be discerned the three major strains of eighteenth-century preaching.

Aristotle, in his *Rhetoric*, posited three principal kinds of proofs: the ethical, the pathetic, and the logical. Each of these could well be used to designate a school of preaching in the eighteenth century, and all three are discernible in the sermons of Atterbury. The most insistent emphasis in his preaching is upon morality, the result equally of his own exacting moral code and the influence of Tillotsonian theology. Yet, temperamentally, he is akin to Wesley, and though he would have been appalled by Methodist 'enthusiasm', his own sermons are often charged with feeling. It was into the main stream of political debate that Atterbury chose to channel his zeal, and there he distinguished himself as one of the most gifted polemicists of his time.

Tillotson—deliberative, dispassionate, cerebral—had made his appeal to man's intellect and self-interest. Though outwardly reserved, Atterbury was by nature more passionate than that. This is apparent not only from the more evangelical bent of his theology, but also in his choice and use of language. He had accepted the Tillotsonian discipline of a plain and malleable prose style, and he shares the same propensity towards fluency and exactness. But there is in his sermons a quality that is for the most part absent from his acknowledged exemplar, a quality more easily illustrated than described.

The first Step towards an *Acquaintance with God*, is, a due *Knowledge* of him: I mean not a Speculative Knowledge, built on abstracted Reasoning about his Nature and Essence; such as Philosophical Minds often busy themselves in, without reaping from thence any advantage towards regulating their Passions, or improving their Manners: But I mean a Practical Knowledge of those Attributes of his, which, invite us nearly to approach him, and closely to unite our selves to him; a thorough Sense, and Vital Experience of his Paternal Care over us, and

---

[1] Butler's *Fifteen Sermons* was first published in 1726.

Concern for us; of his unspotted Holiness, his inflexible Justice, his unerring Wisdom, and his diffusive Goodness; a Representation of him to ourselves, under those affecting Characters of a *Creator*, and a *Redeemer*, an *Observer*, and a *Pattern*, a *Law-giver*, and a *Judge*; which are aptest to incline our Wills, and to raise our Affections toward him, and either to awe, or allure us into a stricter Performance of every Branch of our Duty.[1]

Atterbury's style had been forged through a careful apprenticeship to Tillotson, and the master's influence is never hard to find. But at times one senses in Atterbury's prose a tautness, as though he were being forcibly restrained by stylistic conventions.

Though less influential than Tillotson, it is important to see Atterbury for what he is in himself and what he represents in the development of pulpit oratory. He is not just a lesser Tillotson, though he has often been so regarded. Both as a man and a preacher he was highly individual. His relevance to such a study as this springs from the fact that in him can be observed the major stylistic trends of eighteenth-century preaching—the lucidity and immediacy of the moralists, the aggressiveness of the polemicists, and the passion of the evangelicals.

With Atterbury, the man whom Doddridge once called 'the glory of our English orators'[2] and whose sermons Dr. Johnson said were among the best in the language,[3] the transition from seventeenth- to eighteenth-century preaching is complete. His exile abroad in 1723 coincides with the emergence of England's most profound ethical preacher, Joseph Butler.

---

[1] *Sermons and Discourses on Several Subjects* (1740), ii. 189–90.
[2] Quoted by Mitchell, p. 341.
[3] *Boswell's Life*, iii. 247.

II

JOSEPH BUTLER
(1692–1752)

The Rhetoric of Restraint

Joseph Butler's place in English philosophy and Church history is due entirely to his two major works: *Fifteen Sermons Preached at the Rolls Chapel* (1726) and *The Analogy of Religion Natural and Revealed to the Constitution and Course of Nature* (1736).

During his lifetime, and for the rest of the eighteenth century, it was the *Analogy* for which Butler was best known. Its publication seemed to silence the opponents of Christianity and put an end to the Deist Controversy.[1] There was, to be sure, little originality in the work, its key points having been made previously by other apologists. But its great virtue lay in its organization, or the manner in which the author had marshalled all the most telling arguments against deism. So impressive was his method and so exhaustive his research, that many thought the work unanswerable. It was

---

[1] Opinion is divided on just what part Butler played in bringing the Deist Controversy to an end. Norman Sykes contends that the *Analogy* 'not only achieved a rapid pre-eminence in the contemporary contest, but established its claim as a classic of orthodox apologetic. The victory over Deism thereby won for orthodox Christianity was of astonishing completeness.' *Church and State in England in the Eighteenth Century* (1934), p. 346. But E. C. Mossner, in *Bishop Butler and the Age of Reason*, argues that deism had already spent its force before 1736, and that Butler had less to do with terminating the Controversy than is commonly thought.

JOSEPH BUTLER
From a portrait in the possession of the Bishop of Durham at Auckland Castle.

immediately hailed as a classic defence of Christianity, and
some, Queen Caroline included, rated its importance
second only to that of the Bible.[1]

Most of the references to Butler in eighteenth-century
works are made with the *Analogy* in mind. John Wesley,
Dr. Johnson, David Hume, Edmund Burke, and the
Scottish philosophers Thomas Reid and James Beattie all
acknowledged their debt to Butler and his closely-reasoned
polemic. By the end of the century, however, there were
indications that it was the *Sermons*, and not the *Analogy*,
which would prove to be his most lasting contribution to
English thought.

The reason for this is not far to seek. The *Analogy*,
massive and awe-inspiring though it was, was dated. It had
been written for a particular generation and to answer the
objections of a specific group of Christian detractors. It had
met the deists on their own ground; its argument was a
masterful *tu quoque*. Butler demonstrated that most of the
intellectual objections to Christianity the deists were putting
forward could as easily be turned against deism itself. For,
like Christians, deists argued from the assumption that there
is a God.[2] But the strength of Butler's argument proved
eventually to be its weakness. When, as was the case in the
nineteenth century, Christianity was faced with other foes—
atheism and agnosticism—the *Analogy*, whose basic assumption about a deity this new generation of doubters denied,
was no longer an effectual defence.

Let us, then, confess it to ourselves plainly. The *Analogy*, the great
work on which such immense praise has been lavished, is, for all real
intents and purposes now, a failure; it does not serve. It seemed once

---

[1] Butler was a favourite of the Queen. As clerk of the closet, an office to which he
was appointed in 1736, he was expected to spend two hours each evening with her,
discussing philosophy and theology, until her death the following year. Among
notable divines sometimes invited by the Queen to take part in these discussions
were George Berkeley, Thomas Secker, and Thomas Sherlock.

[2] Unlike Christians, of course, they denied both the veracity and necessity of
revelation, claiming that reason alone was sufficient to discover the nature and will
of God.

to have a spell and a power; but the *Zeit-Geist* breathes upon it, and we rub our eyes, and it has the spell and the power no longer. It has the effect upon me, as I contemplate it, of a stately and severe fortress, with thick and high walls, built of old to control the kingdom of evil;—but the gates are open, and the guards gone.[1]

Here, as was frequently true, Arnold spoke not just for himself, but for his generation. Both William Pitt the Younger and James Mill claimed the *Analogy* had raised more doubts for them than it had answered.[2] Leslie Stephen also found its arguments ungermane to the kind of doubts that assailed his mind:

Meanwhile, Butler passes lightly over the ultimate problem. He takes it 'for proved, that there is an intelligent Author of nature, and natural Governor of the world'. He accepts the validity of all the ordinary reasonings upon which this doctrine has been based; the arguments, that is, from analogy, from final causes, from abstract reasoning, from tradition, and from general consent. He elsewhere accepts, in particular, the argument of Descartes or Anselm, derived from the necessary existence of an archetype corresponding to our idea of 'an infinite and immense eternal Being'. Butler, therefore, does not address himself to atheists, if such there be, who dogmatically deny the existence of God; nor to the undoubtedly numerous class who, neither denying nor affirming, hold that our vision is limited to this world by a veil of impenetrable mystery.[3]

Long since out of favour with most intellectuals of the age, the *Analogy* was finally dropped from the prescribed reading list at Oxford in 1860.

While the *Analogy*'s star waned, however, that of the *Fifteen Sermons* was in the ascendant. By the end of the eighteenth century some of these discourses, and particularly the first three, were finding their way into collected editions of popular sermons. News of their worth was being passed on in other ways too, and by men skilled in the appreciation

---

[1] M. Arnold, 'Bishop Butler and the *Zeit-Geist*', *Works* (1904), ix. 333.
[2] Mossner, pp. 200-1.
[3] *English Thought*, i. 238.

of homiletic literature. Hazlitt, writing in 1823, tells how he was first introduced to them. In an interview which took place in 1798, Coleridge had said that he 'considered Bishop Butler as a true philosopher, a profound and conscientious thinker, a genuine reader of nature and of his own mind'.[1]

He did not speak of his *Analogy*, but of his *Sermons at the Rolls' Chapel*, of which I had never heard. Coleridge somehow always contrived to prefer the *unknown* to the *known*. In this instance he was right. The *Analogy* is a tissue of sophistry, of wire-drawn, theological special-pleading; the *Sermons* (with the Preface to them) are in a fine vein of deep, matured reflection, a candid appeal to our observation of human nature, without pedantry and without bias.[2]

In 'Memorabilia of Mr. Coleridge' Hazlitt records some further remarks of Coleridge on the *Sermons*: 'He extolled Bishop Butler's *Sermons at the Rolls' Chapel* as full of thought and sound views of philosophy; and conceived that he had proved the love of piety and virtue to be as natural to the mind of man as the delight it receives from the colour of a rose or the smell of a lily.'[3] By 1805 Hazlitt was ready to agree. In *An Essay on the Principles of Human Actions*, written in that year, he remarked: 'After Berkeley's Essay on Vision, I do not know of any work better worth the attention of those who would learn to think than these same metaphysical Discourses at the Rolls' Chapel.'[4]

This discovery by Coleridge and Hazlitt of the charm and value of the *Sermons* was repeated time and again by serious-minded men throughout the nineteenth century. And while it is impossible to determine the influence of Butler on nineteenth-century English thought, it is well within the mark to say that during that period he was considered the best ethical theorist in the history of the Church of England. At Oxford and Cambridge his name was hallowed, his theories

---

[1] *Works*, ed. P. P. Howe (1930–34), xvii. 113.
[2] Ibid.
[3] Ibid., xx. 216.
[4] Ibid., i. 50n.

sacrosanct. Matthew Arnold had been an undergraduate at Oxford when Butler's influence there was at its peak. Later, he reflected upon how it had been:

Your text-book was right; there were no mistakes *there*. If there was anything obscure, anything hard to be comprehended, it was your ignorance which was in fault, your failure of comprehension. Just such was our mode of dealing with Butler's *Sermons* and Aristotle's *Ethics*. Whatever was hard, whatever was obscure, the text-book was all right, and our understandings were to conform themselves to it . . . we at Oxford used to read our Aristotle or our Butler with the same absolute faith in the classicality of their matter as in the classicality of Homer's form.[1]

In the twentieth century the *Analogy* has passed virtually into oblivion. The *Sermons*, on the other hand, have continued to command their share of scholarly attention, as evidenced by the fact that in England, Scotland, the United States, Canada, and Italy detailed studies of Butler's ethical theory have appeared.[2]

It is somewhat ironic that these fifteen discourses should generate research and discussion long after the more erudite *Analogy* had been set aside. Certainly no one would have been more surprised at this turn of events than Butler himself. He entertained little hope of immortality for the *Sermons* when he first offered them to the public in 1726. Not until more than three years later was it found necessary to issue a second edition, and at that time the author prepared a preface to warn the reader not to expect too much from the discourses:

It may be proper just to advertise the reader, that he is not to look for any particular reason for the choice of the greatest part of these Discourses; their being taken from amongst many others, preached in the same place, through a course of eight years, being in great measure accidental. Neither is he to expect to find any other connection between them, than that uniformity of thought and design, which will

---

[1] *Works*, ix. 259–60.
[2] See Mossner, pp. 228–30.

always be found in the writings of the same person, when he writes with simplicity and in earnest.[1]

Obviously, Butler never intended that these sermons should embody a complete system of ethics. Nor do they. There is, certainly, the framework of a theory of ethics which, by virtue of its cogent insights and logical construction, still continues to challenge the student of moral philosophy. But pregnant with meaning though they are, they are much too laconic to answer all the questions that come to mind as one reads them. The first three, 'On Human Nature', are the most important since they supply the theoretical scaffolding for what could have been one of the most elaborate ethical systems in the history of philosophy. The last twelve attempt to apply to practical problems the theory enunciated in the first three. Still further application of this system is to be found in the Preface to the second edition of the Sermons, 1729; the 'Dissertation on Virtue', affixed to the first edition of the *Analogy*; and his 'Six Sermons on Public Occasions', preached between 1738 and 1748, and first published in 1749.

It will not be necessary here to examine Butler's ethical theory or attempt to estimate his contribution to moral philosophy. The manner, not the matter, of the *Sermons* must be the primary consideration. Yet it is extremely difficult, perhaps impossible, to assess the merits of a vehicle of expression without knowing something of the occasion for which it was employed, what it was meant to convey, and to whom. In Butler's case this is particularly true. More than enough irrelevant criticism (some favourable, some unfavourable) has been written about his prose by commentators who have too little understood his intentions in writing. First of all therefore it will be necessary to put the *Sermons* into historical perspective and suggest something of the preacher's design.

It has already been seen that the principal preoccupation

---

[1] *Works*, ed. S. Halifax (1874), ii. xxviii.

of Augustan religion was with ethics. Indeed, Mossner has gone so far as to suggest that 'ETHICAL theory, by and large, was the chief intellectual pursuit of the eighteenth century, coloring even its historiography and its science.'[1] This is reflected in all forms of literature of the period, but particularly in the sermon. A good deal of the preaching was intended not just to articulate the finer points of Christian morality, but to defend them as well.

And the need for solid defence seemed more acute than ever. Hobbes's *Leviathan* (1651) had had iconoclastic effects upon prevailing ethical theories. From his observations of human nature Hobbes concluded that man was utterly selfish in every motive and impulse, and that the ultimate rule of conduct—and thus the final arbiter of right and wrong—was the authority of the state. To men like Cudworth, Locke, and Tillotson, who believed in the innate goodness of man, Hobbes's psychological egoism was anathema. They sprang to the defence of the orthodox position. Others followed their lead, including Dr. Samuel Clarke whose learned treatise on the subject greatly influenced the young Joseph Butler. Like Tillotson, Clarke tried to refute Hobbes by employing *a priori* reasoning. The attempt was unsuccessful. By contrast with Clarke's argument from first causes, Hobbes's empirical method seemed much more germane to the psychological and social contexts in which man had his being. It appeared obvious to a few that if Hobbes were to be successfully countered, he must be engaged on his own ground.

In 1711 Lord Shaftesbury published a collected edition of his own works under the title *Characteristics of Men, Manners, Opinions, Times.* Volume two contained his main ethical treatise, 'Enquiry concerning Virtue and Merit'. Without denying the validity of *a priori* logic, Shaftesbury chose to build his case on empirical observation. His findings were vastly different from those arrived at by Hobbes. Where Hobbes had observed only one class of natural tendencies

[1] *Bishop Butler*, p. 105.

in man, and that purely selfish, Shaftesbury finds two: some directed at the good of self and some at the good of others. Neither of these, he contended, is good or bad in itself, but goodness consists in a proper adjustment of the relations between social and selfish tendencies. As the faculty capable of presiding over these two classes of tendencies and of effecting the proper adjustment between them, Shaftesbury posited his theory of 'moral sense'.

Butler in writing the *Sermons* accepted Shaftesbury's basic approach and some of his conclusions. He was, however, more than a little unhappy with the concept of 'moral sense' and its restrictive utilitarian criteria for determining right and wrong.

The not taking into consideration this authority, which is implied in the idea of reflex approbation or disapprobation, seems a material deficiency or omission in lord Shaftesbury's Inquiry concerning Virtue. He has shewn beyond all contradiction, that virtue is naturally the interest or happiness, and vice the misery, of such a creature as man, placed in the circumstances which we are in this world. But suppose there are particular exceptions; a case which this author was unwilling to put, and yet surely it is to be put: or suppose a case which he has put and determined, that of a sceptic not convinced of this happy tendency of virtue, or being of a contrary opinion. His determination is, that it would be *without remedy*.[1]

The answer to this dilemma, as Butler saw it, lay in the existence of a principle of authority, separate from human drives and tendencies, with the capacity to discern moral goodness without reference to utilitarian criteria. By *a posteriori* reasoning he concluded that man possessed just such a faculty, 'conscience'. In Butler's articulated scheme, man is made up of appetites (physical drives), passions (mental and emotional drives), benevolence (the rational principle of concern for others), self-love (the rational principle of concern for self), and conscience (the reigning principle which formulates concepts of right and wrong).

[1] *Works*, ii. xvi.

Conscience, unlike 'moral sense', is not committed to a utilitarian ethic.

Take in then that authority and obligation, which is a constituent part of this reflex approbation, and it will undeniably follow, though a man should doubt of every thing else, yet, that he would still remain under the nearest and most certain obligation to the practice of virtue; an obligation implied in the very idea of virtue, in the very idea of reflex approbation.[1]

It must appear obvious from all this that Butler's mind, and his purpose in writing the *Sermons*, was essentially philosophical. Attempting, as he was, to meet the challenge of Hobbes and perfect a psychological theory of ethics, Butler could scarcely avoid the dialectic of philosophical debate. That he chose to posit his ethical theory in a series of sermons is to some extent an accident of history; but one which should not be ignored, for it demonstrates once again the versatility of the eighteenth-century pulpit discourse.

As in most other things, tastes in prose style vary considerably. But the diversity of opinion about the prose of Bishop Butler is extraordinary indeed. At one extreme he has been praised for his grace and power; at the other he has been dismissed as intractable. W. H. Hutton, writing in *The Cambridge History of English Literature*, left little doubt about which extreme he favoured:

His prose has a massive force, a sheer weight, to which no English writer of his time approaches. Under its severe restraint burns the fire of a deep and intense conviction. He has been but poorly understood by those who have regarded him as a convincing critic, a master of logical acuteness. He was far more; and what he was is revealed in every paragraph of his writing. On the one hand, his view of life and thought was synthetical, not merely inquisitive or analytic: on the other, he was inspired with a supreme belief, a mastering optimism, a triumphant faith. In the cold marble of his prose, there are veins of colour, touches of rich crimson, caerulean blue, or sunny gold, such as one sees in some beautiful ancient sarcophagus. He is a master of calm

---

[1] *Works*, ii. xviii.

exposition, as well as of irony; but he is, even more notably, a writer of profound and unquenchable passion. His heart no less than his head is in what he has written; and it is this which gives him his place among the masters of English prose.[1]

Here indeed is extravagant praise. There is, of course, as almost every commentator on Butler's style has noted, 'a massive force' and 'a sheer weight' in his prose. But to talk of 'a mastering optimism', 'veins of colour . . . such as one sees in some beautiful ancient sarcophagus', 'irony', and 'unquenchable passion' is wildly inaccurate. Neither 'rich crimson' nor 'caerulean blue' nor 'sunny gold' nor purple patches can be found anywhere in Butler. There is no ostentation of any kind—no flights of fancy, no flashes of wit, no imaginative sallies; all is serious and essential. And nothing is more noticeably absent from his writing than irony and optimism. Admittedly, Archdeacon Hutton was attempting to correct a traditionally accepted, and to some extent erroneous, belief about the intractability of Butler's prose. But in doing so he seems to have fallen victim to a danger Butler himself warned against: 'EVERY body knows . . . that there is such a thing, as having so great horror of one extreme, as to run insensibly and of course into the contrary.'[2]

In juxtaposition to Archdeacon Hutton's panegyric, Walter Bagehot's critique of Butler's prose seems almost vitriolic:

Some men find a compensation in the excitement of writing, for all other evils and exclusions; but it is probable that, if Butler hated anything, he hated his pen. Composition is pleasant work for men of ready words, fine ears, and thick-coming illustrations. . . . But Butler, so far from having the pleasures of eloquence, had not even the comfort of perspicuity. He never could feel that he had made an argument tell by his way of wording it; it tells in his writings, if it tells at all, by its own native and inherent force. In some places the mode of statement is even stupid; it seems selected to occasion a difficulty. . . .

[1] *CHEL*, x. 361.
[2] *Works*, ii. 172.

This awkward and hesitating manner [of Aristotle] is likewise that of Butler. He seems to have an obscure feeling, an undefined perception, of what the truth is; but his manipulation of words and images is not apt enough to bring it out. Like the miser in the story, he has a shilling *about* him somewhere, if people will only give him time and solitude to make research for it. As a person hunting for a word or name he has forgotten, he knows what it is, *only* he cannot say it. The fault is one characteristic of a strong and sound mind wanting in imagination. The visual faculty is deficient.[1]

It is hard to believe that Hutton and Bagehot are describing the same writer. Of the two, Bagehot's, it must be confessed, is the more legitimate criticism. But he too is carried away with his own rhetoric. Lacking in eloquence Butler may have been, but no statement is stupid or selected to occasion difficulty; nor is his command of language so inept as Bagehot suggests. It is true that Butler was not a felicitous writer; thoughts came more easily than words. If his prose is laboured, it is because of too great a compression of thought.

The charge most frequently preferred against Butler as a writer is that he is obscure. It was this objection which was responsible for the disappointing reception accorded to the first edition of the *Sermons*. When, in 1729, a second edition was called for, Butler, at the prompting and with the help of Thomas Secker, made extensive stylistic revisions. Paragraphs were shortened to help the reader distinguish more clearly the main points of the argument. Here and there sentences were altered to read more smoothly or to eliminate ambiguity. In a few places passages were deleted, while whole paragraphs were interpolated in others. Most extensive revision, however, was made to punctuation, where almost every page reveals the author's efforts to inject clarity into his prose.[2] But even with these changes the *Sermons* remained essentially the same, and the charge of

---

[1] *Estimates of Some Englishmen and Scotchmen* (1858), pp. 186–8.

[2] J. H. Bernard, in his edition of Butler's works, footnotes all the changes made to the first edition of the *Sermons*. See *The Works of Bishop Butler* (1900), i, 27, 37, 49, 78, 114, 121, 130, 133, 143, and 160 for telling examples.

obscurity persisted. Not that Butler ever really believed that the revisions would vindicate him in this matter. In the Preface to the second edition he admits as much:

It must be acknowledged, that some of the following Discourses are very abstruse and difficult; or, if you please, obscure; but I must take leave to add, that those alone are judges, whether or no and how far this is a fault, who are judges, whether or no and how far it might have been avoided—those only who will be at the trouble to understand what is here said, and to see how far the things here insisted upon, and not other things, might have been put in a plainer manner; which yet I am very far from asserting that they could not.[1]

Butler, as previously observed, was primarily a philosopher; not a homilist. But even more than that, he was a solitary intellect who enjoyed brooding over difficult metaphysical problems. To a large extent he lost contact with the minds he so earnestly wished to convince. The language they understood was inadequate for his purposes.

His zest for metaphysics was no doubt encouraged by his first congregation, perhaps to the chagrin of his later charges. At twenty-six he was appointed preacher at the Rolls Chapel in London. There he drew his congregation chiefly from the lawyers and magistrates of the nearby inns of court. There, too, the esoteric bent of his genius was encouraged. The *Sermons* constitute only a small, but perhaps representative, sampling of eight years of preaching at the Rolls. The other discourses delivered there, like all his subsequent sermons (except the 'Six Preached on Public Occasions'), were destroyed at his own request after his death.[2] The *Sermons*, then, were obviously not preached for, nor were they meant to be read by, ordinary people, and their reading public in eighteenth-century England must have been small indeed.

Butler's thoughts came thick and fast, clamouring for expression. Parentheses and commas proliferate. Hardly any

---

[1] *Works.* ii. vii.

[2] From Butler's will: 'Lastly, it is my positive and express will, that all my sermons, letters and papers . . . be burnt without being read by any one, as soon as may be after my decease.' T. Bartlett, *Memoirs of Bishop Butler* (1839), pp. 275-6.

statement is allowed to go unqualified, and often even the qualifications are further amended. One cannot but wonder how many readers have been discouraged from going further into the *Sermons* by the first paragraph of the first sermon:

THE Epistles in the New Testament have all of them a particular reference to the condition and usages of the Christian world at the time they were written. Therefore as they cannot be thoroughly understood, unless that condition and those usages are known and attended to: so further, though they be known, yet if they be discontinued or changed; exhortations, precepts, and illustrations of things, which refer to such circumstances now ceased or altered, cannot at this time be urged in that manner, and with that force which they were to the primitive Christians. Thus the text now before us, in its first intent and design, relates to the decent management of those extraordinary gifts which were then in the church, but which are now totally ceased. And even as to the allusion that *we are one body in Christ*; though what the apostle here intends is equally true of Christians in all circumstances; and the consideration of it is plainly still an additional motive, over and above moral considerations, to the discharge of the several duties and offices of a Christian: yet it is manifest this allusion must have appeared with much greater force to those, who, by the many difficulties they went through for the sake of their religion, were led to keep always in view the relation they stood in to their Saviour, who had undergone the same; to those, who, from the idolatries of all around them, and their ill treatment, were taught to consider themselves as not of the world in which they lived, but as a distinct society of themselves; with laws and ends, and principles of life and action, quite contrary to those which the world professed themselves at that time influenced by. Hence the relation of a Christian was by them considered as nearer than that of affinity and blood; and they almost literally esteemed themselves as members one of another.[1]

In this long opening paragraph there are only five sentences. One, the fourth, contains 163 words, 13 commas, 4 semicolons, and a colon. It is true that sentences of such labyrinthine length and nature do not occur often in Butler, but the proliferation of subordinate clauses is indicative of the process of accretion by which his rhetoric grows. That such a

---

[1] *Works*, ii. 1-2.

sentence as this should occur at the beginning of a sermon is further evidence that there was little of either the homilist or the orator in Butler.

Yet his is no derivative mind. The intellect one follows through the tortured and sometimes unwieldy prose is highly original. One never doubts, even when one's own sense of direction fails, that Butler knows where he is going.

Confusion and perplexity in writing is indeed without excuse, because any one may, if he pleases, know whether he understands and sees through what he is about: and it is unpardonable for a man to lay his thoughts before others, when he is conscious that he himself does not know whereabouts he is, or how the matter before him stands. It is coming abroad in disorder, which he ought to be dissatisfied to find himself in at home.[1]

There is no inconsistency here. In the *Sermons* there may frequently be compression and complexity of thought; but never confusion. Butler's fault is, as Leslie Stephen observed, that 'of the lonely thinker who forgets the necessity of expounding with sufficient clearness the arguments which have long been familiar to himself'.[2]

Butler's devotion was deep, but troubled. No one, after reading his works and the scanty biography of him,[3] could seriously claim that he enjoyed a triumphant faith or an optimistic spirit. On the contrary; he knew little of the serenity of Berkeley and Law, and none of Wesley's heart-warming zeal. For Butler the optimism of the age of reason wore thin, possibly because reason itself no longer seemed all-sufficient. In his pessimism he is akin to Swift, Johnson, Cowper, and Smart, in all of whom religious devotion ran deep but whose sanity was at best a 'perilous balance'.[4]

[1] *Works*, ii. vii–viii.

[2] *English Thought*, i. 236.

[3] Of no other leading eighteenth-century divine is so little known. Only Bartlett's *Memoirs* has any claim to be considered original material, and even there much of the information given is of questionable authenticity.

[4] See W. B. C. Watkins, *Perilous Balance* (1939), a study of melancholia in Swift, Johnson, and Sterne.

Butler's moroseness can be demonstrated from both his biography and his works.

Bartlett relates an incident first told by Dean Tucker, one of Butler's closest friends. The conversation would seem equally authentic had the participants been Johnson and Boswell.

The late Dr. Butler, bishop of Bristol, and afterwards of Durham, had a singular notion respecting large communities and public bodies . . . His custom was, when at Bristol, to walk for hours in his garden in the darkest night which the time of the year could afford, and I had frequently the honour to attend him. After walking some time he would stop suddenly and ask the question, 'What security is there against the insanity of individuals? The physicians know of none; and as to divines, we have no data, either from Scripture or from reason, to go upon relative to this affair.' 'True, my lord, no man has a lease of his understanding, any more than of his life; they are both in the hands of the Sovereign Disposer of all things.' He would then take another turn, and again stop short: 'Why might not whole communities and public bodies be seized with fits of insanity, as well as individuals?' 'My lord, I have never considered the case, and can give no opinion concerning it.' 'Nothing but this principle, that they are liable to insanity, equally at least with private persons, can account for the major part of those transactions of which we read in history.'[1]

Such morbid preoccupation would hardly indicate a sanguine spirit. Nor was this an isolated example of the gloom which left its mark on almost everything Butler did or wrote. The truth would seem to be that he lacked faith in the stability of the human mind and human institutions. In 1747, on the death of Archbishop Potter, Butler was invited to become primate of all England. His reply betrays his lack of confidence in the institution dearest to his life, the Church of England. 'He is said to have answered, that, "It was too late for him to try to support a falling Church." '[2]

That Butler despaired of the future of Christianity is apparent from the opening paragraph of his 'Charge to the Clergy at Durham' given in 1751.

[1] *Memoirs*, pp. 92–3.
[2] Ibid., p. 96.

It is impossible for me, my brethren, upon our first meeting of this kind, to forbear lamenting with you the general decay of religion in this nation; which is now observed by every one, and has been for some time the complaint of all serious persons. The influence of it is more and more wearing out of the minds of men, even of those who do not pretend to enter into speculations upon the subject: but the number of those who do, and who profess themselves unbelievers, increases, and with their numbers their zeal. Zeal, it is natural to ask— for what? Why truly *for* nothing, but *against* every thing that is good and sacred amongst us.[1]

Matthew Arnold argued that Butler's pessimism grew out of a *saeva indignatio*, or a righteous indignation against the prevailing expectation of his time that the religious writer should present himself at the bar of public criticism. Nor was it an enlightened and earnest public, but one of 'loose thinkers and loose livers, who might choose to lend half an ear for half an hour to the great argument'.[2] Arnold's argument, though plausible in itself, lacks the strength to support the point it seeks to establish. Certainly Butler himself made absolutely no attempt to popularize philosophy or theology. Others might do as they pleased, he would not be compromised: 'It is very unallowable for a work of imagination or entertainment not to be of easy comprehension, but may be unavoidable in a work of another kind, where a man is not to form or accommodate, but to state things as he finds them.'[3] And no one would wish to deny that as Butler found things, so he stated them. *Saeva indignatio* there may be in Butler against 'the multitudes who read merely for the sake of talking, or to qualify themselves for the world',[4] but this in itself will not explain his lugubrious tendencies.

A more likely explanation lies in the dilemma into which Butler's quest for a system of morals led him. Like Tillotson, Butler was essentially Aristotelian; reason was man's

[1] *Works*, ii. 323.
[2] Arnold, *Works*, ix. 284.
[3] *Works*, ii. vii.
[4] Ibid., ii. v.

highest faculty of appeal. The *Sermons* contain innumerable references to man's mind, and verbs suggesting some form of mental activity are ubiquitous. By contrast, a reference to 'the soul' or 'faith' is almost impossible to discover.

Also like Tillotson, Butler believed that the attributes of God, in so far as they were scrutable at all, were perceived through reason. His appellations for God provide an insight into his concept of religion. Those that occur most often are: 'Almighty God', 'Creator', 'Governor', 'Divine Will', 'Infinite Being', 'Supreme Mind', 'Supreme Being', 'that Mind', 'Divine Presence', and 'the Author and Cause of all things'. God—as the supreme, omniscient Mind of creation—looms large in Butler's theology. The other two Persons of the Trinity are hardly ever mentioned. In two sermons 'Upon the Love of God' (Sermons XIII and XIV) Christ's name appears only once, and even then the reference is an oblique one. In answering the question: 'Why should man love God?' Butler ignores the traditional Christian reply, 'We love Him because He first loved us', in favour of the more rational and humanistic: 'It is reasonable and right so to do.'

Butler is concerned not so much with saving souls as with opening men's eyes to the light of reason. His prose is almost wholly devoid of metaphor. It is significant, however, that on the few occasions when he does call upon his imagination to provide him with an apt figure, it almost invariably has something of reason and light in it. His most sustained flourish, and one of the few expanded figures anywhere in Butler, portrays such an image:

If a man were to walk by twilight, must he not follow his eyes as much as if it were broad day and clear sunshine? Or if he were obliged to take a journey by night, would he not *give heed to* any *light shining in the darkness, till the day should break and the day-star arise?* It would not be altogether unnatural for him to reflect how much better it were to have day-light; he might perhaps have great curiosity to see the country round about him; he might lament that the darkness concealed many extended prospects from his eyes, and wish for the sun to draw away the veil: but how ridiculous would it be to reject with scorn and disdain the guidance and direction which that lesser light might afford him, because it was not the sun itself![1]

There is something sadly revealing in this last sentence. Is it reason that Butler speaks of as 'the lesser light'? Is it not for him, as it was for many of his contemporaries, the sun? The answer is not far to seek.

Butler's concept of conscience has already been alluded to. One very important observation remains to be made on it, which is, that there is within it a partial repudiation of reason. Though not wishing to vitiate reason's importance as a guide to human behaviour, Butler's scrupulous honesty will not permit equivocation:

Reason alone, whatever any one may wish, is not in reality a sufficient motive of virtue in such a creature as man; but this reason joined with those affections which God has impressed upon his heart: and when these are allowed scope to exercise themselves, but under strict government and direction of reason; then it is we act suitably to our nature, and to the circumstances God has placed us in.[2]

To write these words must have pained the essentially rationalistic Butler. Tillotson had preached that reason alone should be the guiding principle in human life and activity. Though not always with the same belief in the infallibility of reason, most poets, writers, and preachers during the first half of the eighteenth century acknowledged it to be the 'one clear, unchanged, and universal light'. The scepticism of Hume and the evangelicalism of Wesley have generally been thought the principal causes of the decline of reason during the second half of the century. And there is much truth in this belief. What is sometimes overlooked, however, is that Butler had, unwillingly perhaps but not unwittingly, dealt reason a severe blow a quarter century before the anti-rationalism of either Wesley or Hume was felt.

As the century wore on it was 'those affections which God

[1] *Works*, ii. 205.
[2] Ibid., ii. 58.

has impressed upon [man's] heart' that in preaching, and religion generally, replaced reason as the guiding light to earthly joy and heavenly bliss. Paradoxically, in Joseph Butler eighteenth-century rational preaching and religion were condemned even while they achieved fruition. Having denied the sufficiency of reason, he was forced to assign to conscience intuitional as well as rational powers. In spite of himself, he had, in theory at least, opened the door to the religious enthusiasm of Methodism.

While reason reigned supreme man's capacity to improve himself and the social order appeared almost limitless. When, for Butler, reason's authority proved unequal to the claims made for it, belief in personal and social eudaemonism was undermined. In Sermon XV, 'Upon the Ignorance of Man', Butler attempts to assess the extent of man's spiritual and intellectual limitations. Perhaps the text itself, from Ecclesiastes viii. 16–17, is sufficient commentary:

When I applied mine heart to know wisdom, and to see the business that is done upon the earth: then I beheld all the work of God, that a man cannot find out the work that is done under the sun: because though a man labour to seek it out, yet he shall not find it; yea farther, though a wise man think to know it, yet shall he not be able to find it.

In the fifteen sermons preached at the Rolls Chapel and the six given on public occasions, Biblical allusions and references are made chiefly to Ecclesiastes, Job, Proverbs, and Psalms in the Old Testament, and to St. Matthew's Gospel in the New Testament. No books in the Bible place greater emphasis upon man's limitations and the brevity and frustrations of life than these four Old Testament books. And of the four gospels, Matthew is certainly the least evangelical and reassuring. By contrast, St. John's Gospel— the most apocalyptic and triumphant of the four—is referred to but once in the *Fifteen Sermons*.

But perhaps the book that most influenced the mood and tenor of the *Sermons* was Ecclesiasticus, of the Apocrypha. Time and again Butler quotes the always solemn, sometimes portentous sayings of Jesus, son of Sirac. Though not as nihilistic as Ecclesiastes, Ecclesiasticus is full of forebodings and moral preachments. In Butler's choice of reference materials can be seen again something of the sombre aspect of his genius. His refusal to be comforted by the more optimistic theories of knowledge of his time links him in spirit with a modern Christian existentialist like Karl Barth.[1]

But perhaps nowhere is his existential 'anguish' more apparent than in his manner of writing. His prose is rigid and tormented, without a glimmer of humour or irony. One feels that in delivering his sermons Butler hardly ever needed to raise his voice or make an emphatic gesture. His questions—and they are common enough in the *Sermons*—are simple rather than rhetorical and one has but to compare them with, say, Atterbury's to realize how unimpassioned they are:

And what if we were acquainted with the whole creation, in the same way and as thoroughly as we are with any single object in it? What would all this natural knowledge amount to? It must be a low curiosity indeed which such superficial knowledge could satisfy. On the contrary, would it not serve to convince us of our ignorance still; and to raise our desire of knowing the nature of things themselves, the author, the cause, and the end of them?[2]

Such questions seem more the property of the university lecturer than the pulpit orator. The case against Butler as a preacher can perhaps be summed up best by saying that he lacked the homiletic mind. Proem, climax, peroration, articulated division, illustration, anecdote, repetition, metaphor, simile—the warp and woof of pulpit oratory—are almost entirely absent from his sermons. Unlike Law, Berkeley, and John Wesley, his genius was not versatile. Throughout the *Sermons* and the *Analogy* the style is fundamentally the same; the prose is all of a piece.

[1] Perhaps in fairness it should be said, however, that Barth's personal temperament (as contrasted with his theology) was far from melancholic.

[2] *Works*, ii. 200.

For all its crabbedness, however, there still remains something about Butler's way of writing that evinces power and leaves a dint on the memory. That something is carefully concealed in his prose, and is discoverable only through a closer look at his style.

The 'Sober, judicious, dignified, weighty, sometimes a little laboured' prose of Butler, as one critic has accurately described it,[1] is built principally on two rhetorical devices: parallelism and antithesis. They form the marrowy backbone of Butler's highly intellectual style. Such devices have traditionally been the property of deliberative and forensic speech. An example of each will elucidate Butler's technique:

And if there be in mankind any disposition to friendship; if there be any such thing as compassion, for compassion is momentary love; if there be any such thing as the paternal or filial affections; if there be any affection in human nature, the object and the end of which is the good of another; this is itself benevolence, or the love of another. Be it ever so short, be it ever so low a degree, or ever so unhappily confined; it proves the assertion, and points out what we were designed for, as really as though it were in a higher degree and more extensive.[2]

The first sentence is a fine example of anaphora. An initial emphatic phrase, 'if there be', holds together and balances the sentence while it builds to a climax. The second sentence is also connected and balanced by an emphatic phrase, 'be it ever so', but here another kind of parallelism is introduced. 'Proves' and 'points' are made parallel not only by the use

---

[1] A. Pollard, *English Sermons*, 'Writers and their Work', no. 158 (1963), p. 32. Such prose is agreeable not only with Butler's theology and personal temperament, but with his appearance and deportment as well: 'He was of a most reverend aspect: His face thin and pale; but there was a divine placidness in his countenance, which inspired veneration, and expressed the most benevolent mind: His white hair hung gracefully on his shoulders, and his whole figure was patriarchal. Officiating in the episcopal duties of the church whilst bishop of Durham, he gave a striking example of piety and holy solemnity, which was of the most serious and fervent, and perhaps somewhat of the ascetic kind.' W. Hutchinson, *The History and Antiquities of the County Palatine of Durham* (1785), i. 578.

[2] *Works*, ii. 5–6.

of the connective 'and', but by reason of the fact that syntactically they are predicates of the same subject.

Butler's antitheses, like his parallelisms, are not bold; he will not sacrifice nuance for the sake of a more striking contrast of words. His antithetical balance is achieved more by a comparison which involves a negative implication than by the juxtaposition of two strong nouns: 'What justifies public executions is, not that the guilt or demerit of the criminal dispenses with the obligation of good-will, neither would this justify any severity; but, that his life is inconsistent with the quiet and happiness of the world.'[1] But it is in the paragraph, not the sentence, that Butler's technique is best observed. And perhaps nowhere in his writings is antithesis more effectively employed than in a paragraph in Sermon II. There is a skilful building up to a climax which culminates in one of Butler's most memorable aphorisms. He is explaining his theory of conscience:

All this is no more than the distinction, which every body is acquainted with, between *mere power* and *authority*: only instead of being intended to express the difference between what is possible, and what is lawful in civil government; here it has been shown applicable to the several principles in the mind of man. Thus that principle, by which we survey, and either approve or disapprove our own heart, temper, and actions, is not only to be considered as what is in its turn to have some influence; which may be said of every passion, of the lowest appetites: but likewise as being superior; as from its very nature manifestly claiming superiority over all others: insomuch that you cannot form a notion of this faculty, conscience, without taking in judgement, direction, superintendency. This is a constituent part of the idea, that is, of the faculty itself: and, to preside and govern, from the very economy and constitution of man, belongs to it. Had it strength, as it had right; had it power, as it had manifest authority, it would absolutely govern the world.[2]

Nothing provides a more revealing insight into Butler's mind than his use of parallelism and antithesis. Such figures

[1] *Works*, ii. 110.
[2] Ibid., ii. 27–8.

require thought to construct; they are the stock-in-trade of the deliberative orator. They are also the rhetorical tools of the logician who, at whatever cost, must have his arguments accurately expressed. Every sentence in Butler, Gladstone aptly remarked, is like a well-considered move in chess.[1] With him there is never any question of whether a word, phrase, or paragraph has literary charm or is rhetorically telling. The tripartite question seems always to be: Is it true? Is it necessary? Does it accurately represent the idea it is meant to communicate?

Despite the frequent complexity of his sentence structure, there is a modesty and simplicity about other features of Butler's prose. A characteristic reserve pervades his writings, as it did his life. Nothing is ever done or said for show. Though one of the most learned divines of the eighteenth century, he took pains to conceal his scholarship. His reading must have been oceanic, but in the *Sermons* and the *Analogy* he studiously avoids parading names and theories either in support or for refutation.

If he built with brick, and not with marble, it was because he was not thinking of reputation, but of utility, and an immediate purpose. Mackintosh wished Butler had had the elegance and ornament of Berkeley. They would have been sadly out of place. There was not a spark of the littleness of literary ambition about him. . . . Though he has rifled their [contemporary apologists'] books he makes no display of reading. In the *Analogy* he never names the author he is answering. In the *Sermons* he quotes, directly, only Hobbes, Shaftesbury, Wollaston, Rochefoucauld, and Fenelon.[2]

Similarly, he avoids all classical quotations and allusions, and his vocabulary is everywhere simple and functional.

Like Tillotson, Butler feared 'imagination', that 'author of all error'.[3] He feared also lest any feature of his preaching

[1] Quoted by W. H. Hutton, *CHEL* x. 361.

[2] Pattison, *Essays and Reviews*, p. 289.

[3] He likewise dreaded religious enthusiasm and felt that the Methodists' claim of special revelation was a 'very horrid thing'. Henry Moore, in his *Life of Wesley* (1824), i, 463–5, records a conversation which transpired between Butler and Wesley while the former was still at Bristol. Moore's source was the original

or writing might be construed as the product of imagination. If ever he were tempted to yield himself up to the claims of rhetoric it must surely have been when discussing the evidences of God in creation, a subject close to his heart. Tempted he may have been; he certainly did not yield:

Thus the scheme of Providence, the ways and works of God, are too vast, of too large extent for our capacities. There is, as I may speak, such an expense of power, and wisdom, and goodness, in the formation and government of the world, as is too much for us to take in, or comprehend. Power and wisdom and goodness are manifest to us in all those works of God, which come within our view: but there are likewise infinite stores of each poured forth throughout the immensity of the creation; no part of which can be thoroughly understood, without taking in its reference and respect to the whole: and this is what we have not faculties for.[1]

Butler's aversion to ostentatious writing is best exhibited in his determination never to exaggerate the truth. A strict discipline of meiosis is maintained throughout his work. No one has offered a more accurate comment on this facet of Butler's style than R. W. Church:

We feel in every page and every word the law that writer and thinker has imposed upon himself, not only to say nothing for show or effect, but to say nothing that he has not done his best to make clear to himself, nothing that goes a shade beyond what he feels and thinks; he is never tempted to sacrifice exactness to a flourish or an epigram. . . . If only as a lesson in truth—truth in thought and expression—Butler is worth studying. He is a writer who, if there is any reason for it, always *understates* his case; and he is a writer, too, from whom we learn the power and force, in an argument, of understatement, the

---

manuscript in Wesley's hand. Part of the exchange ran as follows: 'B[utler]. Mr. Wesley, I will deal plainly with you. I once thought you, and Mr. Whitefield, well-meaning men; but I cannot think so now. For I have heard more of you: matters of fact, Sir. And Mr. Whitefield says in his Journal, "There are promises still to be fulfilled in me." Sir, the pretending to extraordinary revelations and gifts of the Holy Ghost, is a horrid thing, a very horrid thing!' Wesley counters the Bishop's arguments, but Butler is adamant: 'Well, Sir, since you ask my advice, I will give it you very freely. You have no business here. You are not commissioned to preach in this diocese. Therefore, I advise you to go hence.'

[1] *Works*, ii. 201-2.

suggestion which it carries with it both of truthfulness and care, of strength in reserve. He never wastes a word in fine writing, but he never spares one when it would make him more intelligible. His writing bears the impress of that severe economy and thriftiness of material which comes from a man having taken great trouble to arrange and prepare his work.[1]

Though he offers no direct evidence from the *Sermons* to support his appraisal, Church had obviously read Butler with discernment.

Butler's economy of expression and his tendency towards understatement often produced aphorisms worthy of Swift.

Though a man hath the best eyes in the world, he cannot see any way but that which he turns them.[2]

But after all, the same account is to be given, why we were placed in these circumstances of ignorance, as why nature has not furnished us with wings; namely, that we were designed to be inhabitants of this earth.[3]

Likewise in his definitions thought is compressed and words sparing. Yet he never leaves the reader to guess at the meaning of important terms; he never begs the question. So painstakingly are his definitions woven into the fabric of his argument that one seldom pauses to reflect upon the intellectual *tour de force* they represent. In one pregnant sentence he can summarize his own elaborate theory of morals: 'That mankind is a community, that we all stand in a relation to each other, that there is a public end and interest of society which each particular is obliged to promote, is the sum of morals.'[4] Occasionally his definitions are charged as much with feeling as with meaning:

Devotion is retirement, from the world he has made, to him alone: it is to withdraw from the avocations of sense, to employ our attention wholly upon him as upon an object actually present, to yield ourselves up to the influence of the Divine presence, and to give full scope to the affections of gratitude, love, reverence, trust, and dependence; of

---

[1] *Paschal and Other Sermons* (1895), p. 30.
[2] *Works*, ii. 122.
[3] Ibid., ii. 204.
[4] Ibid., ii. 146–7.

which infinite power, wisdom, and goodness is the natural and only adequate object.[1]

For all his compression of thought, however, there is little in Butler which can be described as sententious; his genius was not of that kind. He found little profit or delight in either semantics or speculation for its own sake. His occasional aphorisms are the sparks inevitably struck by a serious and penetrating mind.

As a prose stylist Butler possessed strength in abundance, but he lacked that simple grace and ease which characterized Augustan writing at its best. If, as James Sutherland has suggested, good prose, like Swift's, is that which 'allows the writer's meaning to come through with the least possible loss of significance and nuance, as a landscape is seen through a clear window',[2] then Butler's cannot be called good. Though he sacrificed all for clarity and preciseness, he failed to achieve that transparency of meaning which is characteristic of good writing.

Nothing is known of Butler as an orator, except what is suggested by the sermons themselves. It is difficult to believe that the tools and techniques of oratory were of any concern to him. Perhaps finally it was Butler's own exacting honesty which prevented him from being a more effective orator. His refusal to exaggerate, even slightly, tended to enervate even those rhetorical figures he attempted to employ. One obvious example is the manner in which he used the technique of 'imaginary objector'. This device enables the speaker to construct a hypothetical figure—a devil's advocate—who, at appropriate moments during the argument, poses objections which the speaker wishes to answer. For maximum effect, these objections must be phrased in such a manner as to allow the speaker dramatically and conclusively to dismiss them. Wesley and Whitefield would later use this device with great skill. But Butler's objectors

---

[1] *Works*, ii. 188.
[2] *On English Prose*, p. 77.

are never men of straw; the questions they ask are embarras-
singly difficult. Sometimes indeed the preacher is hard-put
to answer the objections he poses for himself in this way:

But allowing that mankind hath the rule of right within himself, yet
it may be asked, 'What obligations are we under to attend to and
follow it?' I answer: it has been proved that man by his nature is a law
to himself, without the particular distinct consideration of the positive
sanctions of that law; the rewards and punishments which we feel, and
those which from the light of reason we have ground to believe, are
annexed to it. The question then carries its own answer along with it.
Your obligation to obey this law, is its being the law of your nature.[1]

It is questionable whether such an answer gave much
emotional satisfaction to those who first heard it, or subsequently read it. What is not questionable, however, is the
honesty and courage of the preacher to face up to such
problems. Leslie Stephen once said of Butler: 'We can but
honour him as an honest and brave man—honest enough to
admit the existence of doubts, and brave enough not to be
paralysed by their existence.'[2] Deception, however seemingly
harmless, or for whatever good purpose was anathema to
him.[3] With characteristic candour he once summarized his

[1] *Works*, ii. 33.

[2] *English Thought*, i. 260.

[3] Two letters by Butler to the Duke of Newcastle are sufficient to show that his
probity was indeed a way of life for him. Each letter is a polite but unequivocal
rebuff to Newcastle for presuming that his patronage of Butler entitled him to
decide who should be appointed to certain offices in Butler's diocese. The first
letter is dated Bristol, 5 August 1750: 'I have this afternoon the honour of your
grace's Letter informing me of my nomination to the Bishoprick of Durham, wch
I am sensible is the greatest Instance of Favour I could receive from the King. As I
read your Letter, my Lord, my answer to it in my own Thoughts say, to return
your grace my humble Thanks for all your Favours, particularly for your kind
Concurrence and Assistance upon this Occasion, & the obliging Satisfaction you
take in the Success of them. But when I came to the Postscript and found a
Command accompanying that nomination it gave me greater Disturbance of
Mind than I think I ever felt ... My Lord the Bishops as well as the inferior
Clergy take the Oath against Simony and as I should think an express Promise of
Preferment to a Patron *beforehand* an express Breach of that Oath, & would deny
Institution upon it, so I should think a tacit Promise a tacit Breach of it. I am afraid
your grace may think I have already said too much, but as this Affair, that I am
to give Dr. Chapman the first Prebend of Durham, is common Talk at Cambridge,

own existential view of life: 'Things and actions are what they are, and the consequences of them will be what they will be: why then should we desire to be deceived?'[1]

'The sermons of Andrewes', T. S. Eliot has said, 'are not easy reading. They are only for the reader who can elevate himself to the subject.'[2] The same can be said of Butler's sermons. Their stolid, rather austere style notwithstanding, they still have a power to challenge, stimulate, even inspire such a reader. They are the record of one of the most devout, profound, and honest thinkers the English Church can boast. Even Bagehot, whose mordant criticism of Butler's prose has already been cited, was forced finally to pay tribute to his piety and achievement:

The vehement temperament, the bold assertion, the ecstatic energy of men like St. Augustine or St. Paul, burn, so to speak, into the minds and memories of men, and remain there at once and for ever. . . . Such are the men who move the creeds of mankind, and stamp a likeness of themselves on ages that succeed them. But there is likewise room for a quieter class, who partially state arguments, elaborate theories, appreciate difficulties, solve doubts; who do not expect to gain a hearing from the many—who do not cry in the streets or lift their voice from the hill of Mars—who address quiet and lonely thinkers like themselves, and are well satisfied if a single sentence in all their writings remove one doubt from the mind of any man. Of these was Butler. *Requiescat in pace*, for it was peace that he loved.[3]

& consequently will be so, if it be not already, wherever I am known, I think myself bound, whatever be the Consequences of my Simplicity and Openness to add, that it will be impossible for me to do it consistently with my Character & Honour, since if I should, it would be understood (tho your grace & I know the contrary) to be done in Consequence of some *previous* Promise, either express or tacit.' The second letter was written at Hampstead and dated 1 December 1751: 'I shall pay all the Regard to your grace's Recommendation that, I am persuaded, you yourself will think reasonable. But as I am altogether unacquainted wth the Character of the Person recommended, I must desire a little time to inquire into it; especially as I am inclined to think he is a Stranger to your grace.' (British Museum, Add. MSS. 32722, ff. 56–7 and 32725, f. 457.)

[1] *Works*, ii. 90.
[2] *Selected Essays*, 3rd ed. (1951), p. 344.
[3] *Estimates*, pp. 220–1.

III

GEORGE BERKELEY
(1685–1753)

Proleptic Preaching

BECAUSE so few of his sermons have survived, it is difficult to determine accurately Bishop Berkeley's place in the history of English pulpit oratory. Though he preached hundreds—perhaps thousands—of sermons, only ten, not all of them complete, and fourteen sets of pulpit notes are extant.[1] Of these ten only one—'Anniversary Sermon before the Society for the Propagation of the Gospel'—appeared in print during Berkeley's lifetime.[2]

In an age when the sermon trade was flourishing, it is inconceivable that a divine of Berkeley's reputation as a thinker and writer could not, had he so desired, have found a publisher for his homilies. It would appear safe to conclude,

[1] The MSS. of the sermons and notes have been preserved. All, except a draft copy of 'On the Will of God', which is in the Chapman MS. in Trinity College Library, Dublin, are now in the British Museum: Add. MS. 39306, ff. 28–245, and Add. MS. 39304, ff. 5–33. They have all been edited and published by A. A. Luce in vol. vii of *The Works of George Berkeley* (1948–57), hereafter referred to as *Works*.

[2] That is, in sermon form. His treatise on *Passive Obedience* (1712) originated as three sermons preached in Trinity College chapel between 1709 and 1712. It is more than probable that the 'Anniversary Sermon' would not have found its way into print had it not been the practice of the S. P. G. to publish all such discourses. The sermon, which Berkeley preached before the Society at St. Mary-le-Bow, 18 February 1732 (N.S.), offers a general defence of foreign missions and includes a report on conditions in Rhode Island, where he had spent the previous three years.

GEORGE BERKELEY
From a portrait by J. Smibert in the National Portrait Gallery, London.

therefore, that Berkeley had no wish to publish them, though it is impossible to do more than guess at the reasons why. Given his humility, he may have felt he had nothing new or worth while to contribute to the sermon literature of the day. Perhaps he believed that all his best ideas could be more effectively expressed in philosophical, sociological, and ethico-political treatises. Or, again, he may have felt that sermons were to be preached and heard, not written and read. Whatever the reason, the student of eighteenth-century preaching can only regret that Berkeley did not take the trouble to publish his sermons. Those discourses which have come down indicate that he was not just an interesting but a powerful and significant preacher.

These manuscript sermons lack of course the literary refinement of discourses prepared for the press. But this is not altogether a disadvantage. Because they have not been redacted they represent the more accurately what the preacher said, and thus bring one closer to the actual oral presentation. They have also the virtue of being representative of Berkeley the preacher. They span the whole of his ministry: the first, 'On Immortality', was preached in the College Chapel, Dublin, 11 January 1708, and the last in St. Colman's Cathedral, Cloyne, on Whit Sunday 1751. They indicate both the scope of his theology and the extent of his travels: 'And what a traveller the preacher was! ... Here are sermons preached as far to the east as the British Consulate church at Leghorn, and as far to the west as Trinity Church, Rhode Island, and King's Chapel, Boston, Mass.'[1]

A glance at his first and last sermons will indicate how much Berkeley improved as a preacher. Leaving aside for the moment the quality of the prose, there is a difference in theological emphasis and in the attitude of the preacher towards his audience. In the first sermon he exhibits a certain complacency—almost a smugness—which the more

---

[1] *Works*, vii. 5.

mature Berkeley avoided. His argument for belief in immortality is blatantly crass. One must play the odds:

> Whatever effect brutal passion may have on some or thoughtlessness & stupidity on others yet I believe there are none amongst us that do not at least think it as probable the Gospel may be true as false. Sure I am no man can say he has two to one odds on the contrary side. But wn life & immortality are at stake we should play our part with fear & trembling tho 'twere an hundred to one but we are cheated in the end.[1]

Granted, in suggesting that belief in life after death is the only safe way, Berkeley is employing a technique of argument commonly used by preachers of the time to counter free-thinkers. Nevertheless, actually to quote the odds on immortality does represent a breach of good taste and was going further than most Latitudinarians were willing to go.

When in a much later sermon Berkeley treats the same subject, his attitude and approach have undergone considerable change. An unaffected humility, a respect for his audience's intelligence, and an implicit faith in immortality are all apparent. He argues first from the 'light of nature' and then from 'the prevailing consent and general authority of all mankind'. Ultimately, however, it is the assurance of Christian faith and experience which proves most telling.

> To conclude I shall only observe that as in all other things we see a gradual progress to perfection, even so in the oeconomy of Religion, the first dawning thereof in the Jewish nation was like the infancy of a child, weak and sensual, taken up with rites and ceremonies, and types of things to come. But the Christian religion enlargeth our view and extends our prospect. It raiseth our hopes from sensible things to things spiritual, from this life to that which is to come, from earth to heaven. That light which in its original was glimmering and obscure still shineth forth more and more unto perfect day. God grant this doctrine we have preached unto you may so thoroughly affect your minds, and sink so deep in your hearts as to produce those vertuous habits and Christian graces, which may finally make you partakers of eternal life.[2]

[1] *Works*, vii. 12–13.
[2] Ibid., vii. 113.

Gone is the slight impatience, the inability to understand why in the light of reason people persist in sinning, which is discernible not only in 'On Immortality' but his other early sermons as well.[1] This is not to suggest that the younger Berkeley was intolerant. On the contrary; throughout his life he showed himself to be one of the most tolerant men of his century. What his later sermons reveal is an expansion of spirit, a greater sympathy for those who had fallen from grace or who found the ways of God less apparent or less easy to observe than he.

Though it serves well enough as an indication of Berkeley's early attitude to his hearers, it would prove misleading to place very much store by his first sermon in assessing his early belief. When he delivered it in Trinity College chapel he had not yet been admitted to holy orders, and the discourse itself was almost certainly prepared to fulfill a College requirement.[2] It has been used as evidence to support the spurious claim that in his youth Berkeley was an unconfessed deist.[3] The truth is that he had very early in life decided to reject deism and come down squarely on the side of the angels. Though no mystic, he had too profound a respect for religious mystery to deny the supremacy of faith in Christian experience. While still a junior fellow at Trinity he wrote in his notebook: 'There may be Demonstrations used even in Divinity . . . Hence 'twere no very hard matter for those who hold Episcopacy or Monarchy to be establish'd jure Divino. to demonstrate their Doctrines if they are true. But to pretend to demonstrate or reason any

---

[1] Cf. this passage from a sermon on religious zeal: 'We have now done with the object, principle and degree of religious zeal. Whether You will be the better or the worse for what has been said, whether it will sink into your hearts and influence your practice or else pass only for an idle entertainment of your ears, is now at your own determination. But surely if you are gathered here with the latter of these views, your solemn attendance in the House of God will serve only to aggravate your sins and make your punishment more speedy and severe.' *Works*, vii. 24.

[2] Resident masters, whether in orders or not, were required by the statute *De Baccalaureorum et Magistrorum Exercitus* to prepare and preach a sermon, or 'commonplace', as it was called.

[3] See J. D. Wild, *George Berkeley*, 2nd ed. (1962), pp. 154–62.

thing about the Trinity is absurd here an implicit Faith becomes us.'[1] And in his sermon, 'On Religious Zeal', which A. A. Luce dates between 1709 and 1712,[2] he begins by rejecting a purely rational approach to religion: 'RELIGION must not be thought to consist in a lazy inactive contemplation of virtue and morality, of God and his attributes, of the rewards or punishments he has annexed to the good or evil actions of men. Religion, I say, is no such speculative knowlege which rests merely in the understanding. She makes her residence in the heart, warms the affections and engages the will.'[3]

It seems reasonable, then, to treat Berkeley's first sermon more as an academic exercise than as a statement of faith. When this is done, the other sermons, spread though they are over forty years, reveal no very great change in theology. This of course is not surprising to anyone familiar with Berkeley's philosophy. The concept of immaterialism, first propounded in *A Treatise Concerning the Principles of Human Knowledge* (1710), remained the underlying assumption of every philosophical work he subsequently wrote. As a thinker he matured early, and the fundamental tenets of his theology were well thought out by the time he preached 'On Religious Zeal'.

In his attitude towards the church, as in his theology generally, Berkeley seems to belong to the second, rather than the first half of the eighteenth century. The Augustans tended to view the church as the temporal custodian of virtue and a bulwark for morality. To Berkeley, however, it was much more than this. He saw it, as Wesley and Simeon would later rediscover it, as the mystical body of Christ:

This society of regenerate persons into whom new life is put by the Spirit of Christ residing and dwelling in them is linked together by the internal bond of charity (an outward sign or badge whereof is the holy communion of the Lord's supper) and they being animated by one

---

[1] *Works*, i. 73.

[2] 'Two Sermons by Bishop Berkeley', *Hermathena* xlvii (1932), 3.

[3] *Works*, vii. 16.

Spirit drawing grace and life from the same fountain, become members of one body of which Christ is the head.

I say the regenerate and elect of God, though living in different ages and different parts of the world are yet joined and knit together by professing the same faith, by submitting to the same laws, by entertaining the same hope, by being inwardly moved by the same spirit of love and reliance on Christ Jesus.

Which society of Christian men in holy Scripture goeth by various denominations and is put in several lights. It is said to be a chosen generation, a royal priesthood, an holy nation, a peculiar people: it is spoken of sometimes as a kingdom whereof Christ is king: sometimes as a building aptly fitted together whereof Christ is the foundation or corner stone: at other times, as a body whereof he is the head.

All which emblemes and allusions agree in this, that they set forth the Messiah as a Prince and ruler of a great people: a people holy and chosen, wch from sinners he has made pure, from slaves he has made free, from dead he has made alive: whose hearts and affections he hath renewed, which he hath reconciled and dedicated a living temple to God. A people to whom he gives laws, whom he instructs and governs, and will finally lead to a state of glory and happiness.[1]

Because he saw the church in such a light he resisted the temptation to make his sermons political diatribes, on the one hand, or ethical essays, on the other. The content of his oratory is devotional and hortatory, with a strong current of evangelism running through it.

It may be said of Berkeley that more than any other leading divine of his day he anticipates the evangelicals. This he does in a number of ways. In the first place his theology is much taken up with the rôle of the heart in religious experience. It is not that he attempts to disparage reason, or even diminish its importance. No less perhaps than Butler does he insist that reason is man's highest faculty. In *Alciphron* Euphranor speaks for his creator when he says: 'Reason, therefore, being the principal part of our nature, whatever is most reasonable should seem most natural to man.'[2] But like Butler, if not quite for the same

[1] *Works*, vii. 89–90.
[2] Ibid., iii. 86.

reasons, Berkeley held that the mind of man could not 'prove' God, but that 'faith alone is required'.[1] Further, he would argue that the modern cult of reason has worked against the best interest of Christianity.

The Christian religion was calculated for the Bulk of Mankind, and therefore cannot reasonably be supposed to consist in subtle and nice Notions. From the Time that Divinity was considered as a Science, and human Reason inthroned in the Sanctuary of God, the Hearts of its Professors seem to have been less under the Influence of Grace. From that Time have grown many unchristian Dissensions and Controversies, of men *knowing nothing, but doting about Questions and Strifes of words, whereof cometh Envy, Strife, Railings, evil Surmises, perverse Disputings of Men of corrupt Minds and destitute of Truth* (*I Tim. vi.* 4, 5). Doubtless, the making Religion a notional Thing, hath been of infinite Disservice. And whereas its holy Mysteries are rather to be received with Humility of Faith, than defined and measured by the Accuracy of human Reason; all Attempts of this Kind, however well intended, have visibly failed in the Event; and, instead of reconciling Infidels, have, by creating Disputes and Heats among the Professors of Christianity, given no small Advantage to its Enemies.[2]

Religion, then, for Berkeley is more than, as Edward Young thought of it, 'the proof of common sense'.[3] It speaks to the heart as well as to the head. 'Zeal' in eighteenth-century parlance was a slightly odious term, used by Latitudinarians to bludgeon Puritans and fanatics. But for Berkeley, religion was sterile indeed if passion had no place:

Small are the advantages we derive from the dawning of the Sun of righteousness tho we shoud discover by it's light the beauty of Holiness, and the deformity and wretchedness of sin. if withall, the heat thereof be not sufficient to stir our passions, to work in us strong aversion from the one and ardent desires and thirst after the other, if it does not kindle in our hearts the flames of Divine love, if it serves not to quicken our endeavour after christian perfection and inspire us with a

---

[1] See especially the Sixth Dialogue of *Alciphron*.
[2] *Works*, vii. 127–8.
[3] *Night Thoughts*, bk. ix, l. 2050.

jealousy for the honour of God and the prosperity of his Church. In a word if we are not affected with a religious zeal.[1]

This is not of course an endorsement of religious frenzy. To be 'affected with a religious zeal' is one thing; to be inebriated with it, quite another. Here, as in other areas of human experience, reason's rôle is to regulate and, where necessary, restrain: 'But as it is highly needful that all the motions, and passions of the soul shoud be under the regulation and influence of Reason ... So is this in a peculiar manner necessary with regard to religious zeal the impulses whereof are so strong and powerful. Let yr zeal be according to knowlege.'[2] Nevertheless, the fact is significant that so early in the century[3] Berkeley is prepared to encourage an emotional response to religion.

Also significant, because here again his preaching is proleptic, is his insistence upon the disturbing reality of sin and the necessity of salvation. 'But since we are all of us under the slavery of sin, and our best works are defective, insomuch that there is no salvation to be expected by the law, therefore we must make up that imperfection by Faith in Christ Jesus whereby we lay hold on his merits and sufferings who knew no sin but fulfilled all Righteousness.'[4] This theme of sin and salvation is typically revivalistic, and one which Augustan religion, with its optimistic view of man and society, could scarcely accommodate. But just as in philosophy Berkeley's independence of mind kept him from being overawed by the reputation of Locke, so it also caused him to reject the prevailing ethico-rational approach to religion. The danger, as he saw it, was not that men should have too much enthusiasm, but that they should have too little. Indifference to evil was the real spiritual enemy. When expatiating on the consequences of sin, Berkeley could exploit evangelistic rhetoric and imagery with the earnestness of a Whitefield:

[1] *Works*, vii. 16.
[2] Ibid., vii. 16.
[3] By 1712.
[4] *Works*, vii. 19.

Such is the infinite purity and holiness of Almighty God that we could not hope for any reconciliation with him, so long as our souls were stained with the filthiness and pollution of sin. But neither could rivers of the blood of Rams and Bulls or of our own tears, have been sufficient to wash out those stains. It is in the unalterable nature of things that sin be followed by punishment. For crimes cryed aloud to heaven for vengeance, and the Justice of God made it necessary to inflict it. [Behold, then mankind at an immense distance from Heaven and happiness, oppressed with a load of guilt, and condemned to a punishment equal to that guilt, which was infinitely heightened and aggravated by the Majesty of the offended God! Such was our forlorn and hopeless condition] when lo! the Lamb of God, the eternal Son of the Father, cloathed himself with flesh and blood that he may tread the wine-press of the wrath of God and offer himself a ransom for us. He sheds his own blood that he may purge away our sins, & submits to the shameful punishment of the cross, that by his death he may open to us a door to eternal life.[1]

Berkeley's adherence to the Penal Substitutionary Theory of the Atonement[2] sprang from his conviction that reason, though important as a guide, is not efficacious of salvation. Likewise, conformity to an ethical code, regardless of how enlightened that code may appear, is not enough. An 'inner change' is essential:

Let us not flatter our selves, as too many are apt to do, that an outward respect to rites and ceremonies, to sacraments, to hearing and reading the Scripture and frequenting the public worship of God will alone be able to avail us, without the practice of an inward and sincere piety, without cutting off the right hand and plucking out the right eye, that is without mortifying every lust and cultivating every vertue. A practice no less salutary to the soul than disagreeable to flesh and blood.[3]

It was these same theological emphases—the inescapable reality of sin, the efficacy of faith in Christ, and the necessity of 'an inward and sincere piety'—which were to become the dominant themes of the Methodist revival.

---

[1] *Works*, vii. 46. The square brackets are in Berkeley's MS.

[2] The theory that Christ died to satisfy God's justice and to prevent the wrath of God being visited upon man.

[3] *Works*, vii. 90.

Theology apart, a quality of character—a romantic idealism—links Berkeley with the evangelicals. His Bermuda project[1] had more utopianism about it than the American adventures of either Whitefield or the Wesleys.[2] Berkeley saw America as a land where Christianity could have a fresh start, free from the decadence and superstition European history had bred. His proposed college in Bermuda, catering to the spiritual and educational needs of natives and colonists alike, would help to usher in this brave new world. Perhaps only his poem 'America' measures the intensity of his vision:

> The Muse, disgusted at an Age and Clime,
> Barren of every glorious Theme,
> In distant Lands now waits a better Time,
> Producing Subjects worthy Fame:
>
> In happy Climes, where from the genial Sun
> And virgin Earth such Scenes ensue,
> The Force of Art by Nature seems outdone,
> And fancied Beauties by the true:
>
> In happy Climes the Seat of Innocence,
> Where Nature guides and Virtue rules,
> Where Men shall not impose for Truth and Sense,
> The Pedantry of Courts and Schools:
>
> There shall be sung another golden Age,
> The rise of Empire and of Arts,
> The Good and Great inspiring epic Rage,
> The wisest Heads and noblest Hearts.

[1] About May of 1722 Berkeley got the idea of founding a college at Bermuda to meet the educational and spiritual needs of the American Colonies. He received encouragement from many prominent people in London, and a promise from the Prime Minister, Walpole, of financial help. In September 1728 he sailed for Rhode Island, convinced that his plan would be sanctioned by Westminster. When, after two years, word finally came, it was, for various reasons, negative. Disappointed, Berkeley returned to England in the autumn of 1731. For a more detailed account of the project see Luce's *Life of George Berkeley* (1949), pp. 94–114.

[2] Further evidence of Berkeley's idealism is seen in his quest for, and eventual belief that in tar water he had found, a cure for all human illnesses. Wesley too was interested in medicine, but his *Primitive Physic* is a practical handbook, not, as is Berkeley's *Siris*, a paean for a panacea.

> Not such as *Europe* breeds in her decay;
>   Such as she bred when fresh and young,
> When heav'nly Flame did animate her Clay,
>   By future Poets shall be sung.
>
> Westward the Course of Empire takes its Way;
>   The four first Acts already past,
> A fifth shall close the Drama with the Day;
>   Time's noblest Offspring is the last.[1]

Nor is this just a case of poetic licence run rampant. Berkeley could be equally ecstatic in prose about the new world. In a letter to Lord Percival, 4 March 1723, he rhapsodises about the beauties and natural advantages of Bermuda. He had not yet set foot there!

It would take up too much of your Lordship's time minutely to describe the beauties of Bermuda, the summers refreshed with constant cool breezes, the winters as mild as our May, the sky as light and blue as a sapphire, the ever green pastures, the earth eternally crowned with fruits and flowers. The woods of cedars, palmettos, myrtles, oranges &c., always fresh and blooming. The beautiful situations and prospects of hills, vales, promontories, rocks, lakes and sinuses of the sea. The great variety, plenty, and perfection of fish, fowl, vegetables of all kinds, and (which is in no other of our Western Islands) the most excellent butter, beef, veal, pork, and mutton. But above all, that uninterrupted health and alacrity of spirit, which is the result of the finest weather and gentlest climate in the world, and which of all others is the most effectual cure for the cholic, as I am certainly assured by the information of many very credible persons of all ranks who have been there.[2]

Such a rapturous spirit hardly seems compatible with the analytical mind behind the *Essay towards a New Theory of Vision* or *The Principles of Human Knowledge*. But such was the nature of Berkeley's intellectual and spiritual genius that he could be, at one and the same time, cherub and seraph, an angel of light and an angel of fire.

Berkeley's sermons pulsate with feeling; they are instinct

---

[1] *Works*, vii. 373.
[2] Ibid., viii. 128–9.

with evangelistic fervour. The extent to which they differ from the more standard discourses of the day is best seen when Berkeley the preacher is compared with two men who are very much more typical of that age—Joseph Butler, who represents better than anyone else the ethical approach to homiletics, and Jonathan Swift, the arch-polemicist.

The first and most important difference is one of temperament. Butler and Swift, though for different reasons and in different ways, were both pessimists; Berkeley was one of nature's optimists. All three acknowledged, as preachers in every age have done, the waning influence of religion. But Berkeley alone refused to doubt the ultimate victory of good over evil. Having remarked, in his sermon before the Society for the Propagation of the Gospel, on the general decline of religion both at home and in the Colonies, he goes on to reassure his congregation:

Whatever Men may think, the Arm of the Lord is not shortened. In all this Prevalency of Atheism and Irreligion, there is no Advantage gained by the Powers of Darkness, either against God, or godly Men, but only against their own wretched Partisans. The Christian dispensation is a dispensation of Grace and Favour. The Christian Church a Society of Men intitled to this grace, on performing certain Conditions. If this Society is diminished, as those who remain true Members of it suffer no Loss to themselves, so God loseth no Right, suffereth no Detriment, forgoeth no Good; his Grace resisted or unfruitful being no more lost to him, than the Light of the Sun shining on desert Places, or among People who shut their Eyes.[1]

Such confidence is the product of a serene and stalwart faith, a faith neither Butler nor Swift ever enjoyed.

Ultimately, Berkeley and Butler are concerned with the same basic issues: how should man live? what moral laws should govern his behaviour? what should be his ultimate appeal in matters of right and wrong? But where Butler can examine the psychology of human behaviour with an almost scientific detachment, Berkeley is too involved in life to be

[1] *Works*, vii. 124. Cf. the opening paragraph of Butler's 'Charge to the Clergy at Durham', *ante*, p. 45.

objective in this way. As T. E. Jessop put it: 'He looked on
the human scene before him with a longing to mend it.
Expressed summarily, he had a concern for the intellectual,
moral, religious and bodily betterment of his fellows.'[1] For
this reason he is too much a part of the society of men, and
his religion too strongly emotional, to ponder human
problems in the abstract. Butler was perhaps finally more at
home with ideas than with people; Berkeley, extrovert and
stimulating conversationalist, sought wherever he went to be
part of the *vita communis*.[2]

Swift and Berkeley contrast with one another in a very
different way. Luce[3] has enumerated some of the things
they had in common, including the same school and university; the same concern for Ireland and hatred for the
oppressive political system which prevailed there; the same
loyalty to the Church of England and the same willingness
to defend her doctrines against her critics; many of the same
literary friends and some of the same literary gifts, the most
conspicuous of which was a remarkable talent for fluent and
concise prose.

Temperamentally, however, they could hardly have been
more unlike. Swift was volatile and vociferous, with a
tendency towards melancholy. Berkeley was equanimous,
disciplined, and sanguine. Swift rebelled against the social
evils and injustices of the day by joining in the heated
political debate and satirizing his opponents and the ideas
they stood for. Berkeley was no less aware of the inequities
of the social order,[4] but he strove for reparation, not
revolution. Where Swift commanded and demanded, Berkeley sought to persuade. He refused to be drawn into party
politics or to indulge in personal invective. He chose to address himself to public, as distinct from political, issues, and

[1] *George Berkeley*, 'Writers and their Work', no. 113 (1959), p. 7.

[2] This is evidenced by the way in which he entered into London literary
society. Addison, Steele, Swift, Pope, and Prior all sought his company.

[3] *Life*, p. 64.

[4] Berkeley in the *Querist*, as much as Swift in his writings on Irish economics,
demonstrates an awareness of the root problems of Irish government and life.

calmly, but with conviction, warned men against the evils inherent in society.[1]

This difference is nowhere more evident than in their sermons. Those of Swift are as much a vehicle for his social and political theories as are any of his other writings. He never misses an opportunity to fire a philippic at Whigs, dissenters, papists, free-thinkers, or whomever the target of his attack happens to be. Louis Landa has said that 'we can assess the nature of his mind and define his position in the eighteenth century from the sermons as clearly as we can from his other works'.[2] This may seem an inordinate claim for these eleven laconic discourses, but there is ample evidence to justify it:

For example, in *Upon the Martyrdom of King Charles I* are the lineaments of his political theory. Here, and in other sermons as well, are the basic assumptions about kingship, government, and party that gave a particular bias to his interpretation of events, both historical and current. In *On Brotherly Love* is revealed his unquestioning acceptance of a national church, with its implications concerning toleration and schism in the religious life of the country. In certain of his other writings deism drew from Swift irony and ridicule but no reasoned statement of the grounds of his opposition. Such a statement is to be found only in the sermon *On the Trinity*. From two of the sermons, *On the Testimony of Conscience* and *Upon the Excellence of Christianity*, he emerges as an apologist for Christianity, the Christian moralist combating contemporary theories of an ethic divorced from religion. His views of charity, of foreign trade, of reason and the passions, of the Revolution of 1688, of England's treatment of Ireland—these and many others have found their way into the sermons, to such an extent

---

[1] *An Essay towards Preventing the Ruine of Great Britain* (1721) is a good example of this. Berkeley blames the public as a whole, and not a particular political party, for the moral decadence and disorder of Britain. Very early in his career he had attempted to come to grips with the question of the obligation of the citizen to the highest civil authority. His treatise on *Passive Obedience* reveals his pacific nature. He argues that there is 'an absolute unlimited non-resistance, or passive obedience, due to the supreme civil power'. Only in cases of extreme tyranny can this moral law be laid aside. From this it is apparent that for Berkeley rebellion, revolution, or any public upheaval was repugnant.

[2] *Irish Tracts and Sermons*, p. 101.

that it may be said the sermons represent fairly adequately the range of his opinions.[1]

By contrast, Berkeley's sermons are devoid of political comment or criticism. His aim is simply to impress upon men the beauty and reasonableness, as well as the mystery and pathos, of Christianity, so that they will experience the hope and consolation of religion.

It would appear that Swift is more concerned for the social order; Berkeley for the individual. Swift saw man in an almost Hobbesian light—drawn irresistibly by sin and needing the injunctions of scripture and the laws of an enlightened society to stave off the forces of chaos and darkness. The average person, R. W. Jackson has remarked, 'while perhaps agreeing with Article IX that "man is very far gone from original righteousness, and is of his own nature inclined to evil", is optimist enough to add that, on the whole, the world is not too bad.' Swift could not bring himself to do this. 'He must flay the covering of shams from society and show the ugly meanness underneath. He must shock the world into repentance. That was his self-appointed mission.'[2] Berkeley refused to believe that man was controlled by forces outside himself. He held that men made and fashioned society—not vice versa. Because of this his message was intended not so much for social reform as individual conversion. The question which must be asked of every human action or decision was not what will this do to the social order, but how will this look *sub specie aeternitatis*?

But if we are not generous and grateful enough to be affected with the sufferings of our Saviour: Yet at least let us have some regard to our own, and bethink our selves in this our day of the heavy punishment that awaits every one of us, who continues in a course of sin. Let us bethink our selves that in a few years the healthiest and bravest of us all shall lie mingled with the common dust, and our souls be disposed of by an irreversible decree. No tears, no humiliation, no repentance

---

[1] *Irish Tracts and Sermons*, pp. 101–2.
[2] *Jonathan Swift, Dean and Pastor* (1939), p. 31.

can avail on the other side the grave: But it is now in our power to avoid the torments of that place where the worm dieth not, and the fire is never quenched, provided that we repent of our sins, and, for the time to come, denying ungodliness and worldly lusts we live soberly, righteously and godly in this present world, Looking for that blessed hope and the glorious appearance of the great God and our Saviour Jesus Christ, who gave himself for us that he may redeem us from all iniquity, and purify unto himself a peculiar people zealous of good works.[1]

The widely differing temperaments and theologies of Butler, Swift, and Berkeley led them to hold widely differing views of what a sermon should be and do. Some of these differences have already been demonstrated. Further illumination is possible through a closer look at a representative sermon of each preacher. Conveniently, there are extant sermons of all three on the subject of brotherly love.

Butler's two sermons, 'Upon the Love of our Neighbour', can be treated as one; they appear together under the same text in the *Fifteen Sermons*, and were separated only for convenience in preaching. In treating this subject Butler brings all his knowledge of philosophy and psychology to bear. In the first sermon he explores the nature and meaning of self-love. He attempts to establish its spiritual legitimacy by distinguishing it from all other passions. Next, he demonstrates how self-love and benevolence, though commonly believed to be inimical, may be reconciled. He strengthens his case by illustrating how natural benefits accrue when these two forms of love are allowed to complement each other.

In the second sermon he turns to benevolence and considers its object, extent, and effect. Everywhere the reasoning is close and demanding:

As human nature is not one simple uniform thing, but a composition of various parts, body, spirit, appetites, particular passions, and affections; for each of which reasonable self-love would lead men to have due regard, and make suitable provision: so society consists of various

<hr>

[1] *Works*, vii. 51–2.

parts, to which we stand in different respects and relations; and just benevolence would as surely lead us to have due regard to each of these, and behave as the respective relations require. Reasonable good-will, and right behaviour towards our fellow-creatures, are in a manner the same: only that the former expresseth the principle as it is in the mind; the latter, the principle as it were become external, i.e. exerted in actions.[1]

He concludes by describing how such 'reasonable' love leads both to personal happiness and a greater knowledge of God.

Swift's sermon 'On Brotherly Love' is, in spite of its title, a treatise on religious schism and toleration. Under the pretext of inquiring into the reasons for the lack of brotherly love, he strikes out with a two-fisted attack on dissenters and Roman Catholics. His principal concern is to defend the privileged legal position of the Church of England. It is obvious that Swift accepts the doctrines of the Anglican church as a body of revealed and unimpeachable truth, in much the same way as Archbishop Laud had done. Dissenters, precisely because they had rejected the one true church, should have no legal position or privileges. Nor, because of their invidious subterfuges against Church and State, should they be shown any charity. The same holds true for Catholics:

THIS Nation of ours hath for an Hundred Years past, been infested by two Enemies, the Papists and Fanaticks, who each, in their Turns, filled it with Blood and Slaughter, and for a Time destroyed both the Church and Government. The Memory of these Events hath put all true Protestants equally upon their Guard against both these Adversaries, who, by Consequence, do equally hate us: The Fanaticks revile us, as too nearly approaching to Popery; and the Papists condemn us as bordering too much on Fanaticism.[2]

---

[1] Butler, *Works*, ii. 167–8.

[2] *Irish Tracts and Sermons*, p. 172. Cf. a passage from Berkeley's 'Primary Visitation Charge' delivered to the clergy of the diocese of Cloyne sometime between 1734 and 1737. His subject too is religious toleration, and he is speaking of Roman Catholics: 'The main point, therefore, is to bring them to reason and argue: in order to which it should seem the right way to begin with a proper

The papists, Swift thinks, no longer represent a real danger to the Establishment because wise laws have weakened their position. The dissenters, on the other hand, have the 'Power, the Luck, or the Cunning, to divide us among ourselves'.[1] And they have succeeded already to the extent that if any clergyman were to preach against schism many in his congregation would 'censure him as hot and high-flying, an Inflamer of Men's Minds, an Enemy to Moderation, and disloyal to his Prince'.[2]

This hath produced a formed and settled Division between those who profess the same Doctrine and Discipline, while they who call themselves Moderate are forced to widen their Bottom, by sacrificing their Principles and their Brethren to the Incroachments and the Insolence of Dissenters, who are therefore answerable, as a principal Cause of all that Hatred and Animosity now reigning among us.[3]

Of this sermon Landa has written: 'The problems touched on—the status of the established church, comprehension of dissenters, the nature of schism and of toleration—are those that recur again and again in Swift's works; and this sermon is a synthesis of his views.'[4] Certainly it is a typical Swiftian sermon: uninhibited, vitriolic, and as much an expression of political opinion as of theological belief.

Turning from Butler's psychological inquiry and Swift's strident polemics, one is struck by Berkeley's orthodox treatment of the brotherly love subject. His sermon is ethical and devotional; his text can scarcely be developed in any other way: 'By this shall all men know that you are my disciples, if you have love one for another' (John 13: 35).

---

behaviour. We should be towards them charitable gentle obliging returning good for evil, shewing and having a true concern for their interest, not alwaies inveighing against their absurdities and impieties. At least we ought not to begin with taxing them as fools and villains; but rather treat of the general doctrines or morality and religion wherein all Christians agree, in order to obtain their good opinion, and so make way for the points controverted between us, which will then be handled with great advantage.' *Works*, vii. 162.

[1] *Irish Tracts and Sermons*, p. 172.
[2] Ibid.
[3] Ibid., pp. 172-3.
[4] Ibid., p. 118.

The preacher has a threefold objective: 'In treating of which words I shall observe this method. First I shall endeavour to make you sensible of the nature and importance of this duty. Secondly I shall lay before you the good effects it is attended with when duly practised. And in the last place I shall add some further considerations to persuade you to the observation of it.'[1] Berkeley demands more of Christians than civility and good manners: 'There must be an inward, sincere disinterested affection that takes root in the heart and shews it self in acts of kindness and benevolence. My little children, saith St. John, let us not love in word but in deed and truth.'[2] The argument for love is double-barrelled: first, it is man's duty; second, it is in man's best interest to obey God in this as in all matters. Berkeley is careful, however, that his appeal to self-interest not seem too complacent.

As different countries are by ⟨their re⟩spective products fitted to sup⟨ply each⟩ other's wants: so the all-wise ⟨provi⟩dence of God hath ordered ⟨that⟩ different men are endowed w⟨ith⟩ various talents whereby they are mutually enabled to assist and promote the happiness of one another. . . . ⟨Hence⟩ it is that men find it necessary ⟨to⟩ unite in friendships and societies, ⟨to⟩ do mutual good offices, and carry on the same designs in harmony and concert. We relieve one another in distress, we bear with each other's infirmities, we study to promote the advantage of each other: that is in our Saviour's phrase we have love one to the other. And so long as we continue thus disposed peace and plenty abound families live comfortably together our affairs thrive and flourish in the world wch gives a blessing to our endeavours; every one finds his own in⟨terest⟩ in advancing that of his n⟨eighbour.⟩[3]

Then amid a flourish of Pauline metaphor and allusion he concludes with a plea for greater love.

You, Christians, seriously ⟨consider⟩ what has been said. . . . Put on (as the elect of God, Holy & Beloved) bowels of mercy kindness humbleness of mind, meekness long-suffering, forbearing one another

---

[1] *Works*, vii. 28.

[2] Ibid.

[3] Ibid., vii. 35. The brackets have been supplied by the editors to indicate where the MS. has been damaged by water.

& forgiving one another if any man have a quarrel against any: even as Christ forgave you so also do ye. And above all things, put on charity wch is the bond of perfectness. So will the good Providence of God protect & bless you during the course of this mortal life. And at the last day you will be ⟨owned⟩ for true disciples of the kind and merciful Jesus: to whom with Thee, O Father, & the Holy Ghost be all glory.[1]

Throughout his preaching Berkeley deliberately tones down the strains of prudential morality. Although he recognizes that a doctrine of rewards and punishments, relating both to this life and the life hereafter, is a catalyst to good works, he lays greater stress upon love for love's sake.

As a final point of comparison, it is worth noting the similarity between the homiletic techniques of Swift and Berkeley. For both, simplicity, clarity, and immediacy are the essential ingredients of good writing and speaking. Each states his argument as concisely and cogently as he can; there is nothing which can be misconstrued as embellishment. Both were on the side of popular opinion in rejecting the older, more elaborate style of pulpit address, with its manifold divisions and fustian rhetoric. Swift abhorred 'pert Wit and luscious Eloquence'. 'I HAVE lived', he boasts in his 'Letter to a Young Gentleman', 'to see *Greek* and *Latin* almost entirely driven out of the Pulpit; for which I am heartily glad.'[2]

ALTHOUGH, as I have already observed, our *English* Tongue be too little cultivated in this Kingdom; yet the Faults are nine in ten owing to Affectation, and not to the want of Understanding. When a Man's Thoughts are clear, the properest Words will generally offer themselves first; and his own Judgement will direct him in what Order to place them, so as they may be best understood. Where Men err against this Method, it is usually on Purpose, and to shew their Learning, their Oratory, their Politeness, or their Knowledge of the World. In short, that Simplicity, without which no human Performance can arrive to any great Perfection, is no where more eminently useful than in this.[3]

[1] *Works*, vii. 38–9.
[2] *Irish Tracts and Sermons*, p. 75.
[3] Ibid., p. 68.

Berkeley concurred entirely in this sentiment. Very early in life he resolved to avoid everything in composition which might be thought affectation. Entry 300 in his *Philosophical Commentaries* records his intention: 'I abstain from all flourish & pomp of words & figures using a great plainness & simplicity of stile having oft found it difficult to understand those that use the Lofty & Platonic or Subtil & Scholastique strain.'[1]

Like their method of presentation, Swift's and Berkeley's technique of sermon construction is simple and direct. The text merely suggests the theme; detailed exegesis is never attempted. The introduction can hardly be called an exordium; it consists of a few general statements on the nature of the subject being considered. Primary divisions are next announced and each is proceeded to in turn. Under these headings, usually three, and sub-headings, the case is stated and the proofs brought forward. Both preachers argue persuasively, but whereas Swift distrusted the eloquent appeal to the emotions,[2] Berkeley is capable of impassioned pleading with sinners which, as has already been seen, would have done justice to Wesley's evangelical zeal.

The fourteen sets of pulpit notes which have survived throw additional light on Berkeley's homiletic technique. Each set is, of course, only an outline which was later expanded into an oral discourse, but as such it throws into relief the preacher's method of sermon construction. Though his practice of note-making and numbering of points varies from sermon to sermon, yet a common design is discernible in the manner in which a theme is introduced, its importance established and demonstrated, shown to be compatible with both reason and scripture, defended against the arguments of would-be detractors, and brought to an exhortative conclusion. Notes used for a sermon preached at Newport, Rhode Island, 3 August 1729, will serve to illustrate Berkeley's method.

[1] *Works*, i. 37.
[2] See *Irish Tracts and Sermons*, pp. 68–70.

I Tim. 3. 16.

Without controversy great is the mystery of godliness.
God was manifest in the flesh.

St. John I. 14

The Word was made flesh & dwelt among us.

I.

The Divinity of our Saviour a fundamental article of the Christian Faith. We believe in him, pray to him, depend upon him here and hereafter. Omniscience &c.—Denied of late years.—Mystery what.

State, clear up, shew the proofs; answer objections, consider use and importance of the doctrine.

II.

Concerning the soul & body of Christ there is no controversy. but concerning the personal union of the divinity with the manhood.

Some sort of union with the Godhead in prophets, apostles, all true Christians, all men. but with men, Xtians, inspired persons, Xt in different degrees. the latter in kind also contra-distinct as personal.— This explained, and shewn not repugnant to natural reason.

III.

Shewn to be in fact from express words in Scriptures terming Christ God The Word was God, John I. I; My Lord & my God said Thomas to the Saviour Jo 20. 28 From attributions of omnipotence by Him all things consist, Colos. I. 17;—Upholding all things by the word of his power, Heb. I. 3; Whatsoever things the Father doth these also doeth the Son likewise John 5. 19, 21. Omnipresence: John 14. 23, Xt saith if a man love him that the Father & he will come unto him & make their abode with him. and in St. Matthew that wherever two or three are gathered together there he is in the midst of them. 18, 20. & I am with you alway even to the end of the world. 28. 20. Omniscience Now are we sure that Thou knowest all things, John 16, 30. Peter saith to him Lord thou knowest all things. John 21. 17.

From the history & circumstances of his birth, life & resurrection prophecies miracles apparition of angels. From His works: Pardoning sins, giving grace, sending the Holy Spirit, judging the world, distributing rewards & punishments, dooming to final perdition or crowning with life & immortality. From the worship paid to Him: All men are commanded to honour the Son even as they honour the Father, John 5. 23. Baptism In the name of the father & of the son and of the holy Ghost. Apostles' benediction. The grace of our Lord, &c. Doxologies. St. Peter ascribes to Him praise and dominion for ever & ever. and again, to Him be glory for ever and ever, Heb. 13. 21; and in the Apoc: c. 5. v. 13. and every creature wch is in heaven, & on the earth & under the earth and in the sea and all that are in them heard I saying blessing honour glory & power be unto him yt sitteth upon the throne & unto the Lamb for ever & ever

IV.

Obj: from Scripture: The Son can do nothing of himself but what he seeth the father do John; I seek not Mine own will, but the will of the father who hath sent me. ib.: I have not spoken of my self but the father who hath sent Me he gave me a commandment wt I should say and what I should speak. to sit on my right hand or on my left is not Mine to give but it shall be given to them for whom it is prepared of my father. of that hour knoweth no man, not the angels, nor the Son, but the Father. He prayeth is afflicted, tempted, distressed. Answered by acknowledging Xt to be man as well as God whence contradictorys are predicated of his different natures.

V.

Obj: from reason from the meanness of his figure & appearance. Ans: by shewing wherein true greatness and glory consist. more in miracles & sanctity, infinitely more than in pomp & worldly grandeur.

VI.

Objection 2nd from reason, i.e. from substance, personality, &c. The seed of the woman shall break the serpent's head in the daies of Adam. to Abraham, In thee shall all the families of the earth be blessed. by Jacob, Shiloh to whom the gathering of the people shall be. Balaam, There shall come a Star out of Jacob & a sceptre shall rise out of israel. Types Paschal lamb, all sacrifices. From Samuel to Malachi. Luke. 10. 24 many prophets have desired to see those things, which ye have seen & have not seen them & to hear those things which ye have heard & have not heard them.

Hence motives to obedience—faith—hope—joy. This doctrine or mystery, what not intended to produce / what it hath accidentally produced / Simile of the sun & weak eyes, mind dim'd by folly or enflamed with pride; malice envy—rescue from despair, a hopeless case cutts of⟨f⟩ all endeavour, &c. Favour extended / door open'd / sing citizens / endeavours accepted /[1]

Two points are worth making about this sermon. First, it is doctrinal, and Berkeley's concern is to show not only that the divinity of Christ is well-founded in both reason and scripture, but that it is essential to Christianity and relevant to the life of the Christian. Second, Berkeley's proofs from scripture are drawn principally from St. John's Gospel. In contrast to Butler, this was Berkeley's favourite scriptural source and reflects once again his serene and confident faith.

All this is a long way from the suave and polished periods of a Jeremy Taylor or even the carefully woven argument of a John Tillotson. Berkeley seems wholly unmindful of the rules and traditions which in former ages made the sermon a respectable literary *genre*. His attitude to homiletics, as exhibited in both his sermons and sermon notes, is pragmatic. He appears to regard the sermon solely as a method of oral communication—a means whereby the wicked are reproved and the faithful encouraged.

And yet at their best these sermons are not unworthy of Berkeley either as a thinker or writer. This latter recommendation is all the more impressive when it is remembered that Berkeley is one of the great prose artists of the English language. It is not, as Jessop has noted, that he consciously set out to become a fine writer. 'He wrote only to communicate. Nevertheless, almost all that he touched he turned into literature. He was an outstanding stylist in an outstanding age; further, in the entire line of those who have handled English well he emerges as one of the sovereigns of our prose.'[2] Quite apart from their philosophical, theological, or sociological content, his works can be read and enjoyed as literature. For George Saintsbury the awareness of beautiful prose as such was born while reading Berkeley.[3]

[1] *Works*, vii. 61–3.
[2] 'George Berkeley', *Hermathena*, lxxxii (1953), 2–3.
[3] *A History of English Prose Rhythm* (1912), p. 254.

Berkeley, I confess, appears to me to have been almost the greatest *writer*, from our own and the nearest adjacent points of view, whom the new style *post* 1660 had yet produced—greater than Addison, if not so variously agreeable, and though not so great as Dryden, possessing the advantage that, as he only used one harmony (for his few verses are negligible in form) he was able to pour his whole strength into it.[1]

Changes in literary tastes since Saintsbury have not diminished the pleasure Berkeley's prose affords. In a more recent tribute to 'Berkeley as a Man of Letters' Bonamy Dobrée said: 'I am content to abandon myself to the enchantment of the prose of a master, prose that is musical as well as precise, persuasive as well as firm, warm, congenial, humane.'[2]

Perhaps the most striking feature of Berkeley's prose is its perfect naturalness and ease. Nothing is formal or contrived. It is almost impossible to imagine him sitting, with pen poised, searching for the correct word or phrase to round off a period or sharpen an aphorism. He seems too spontaneous for that. His facility for precise and lucid thought is more than matched by his facility for precise and lucid expression.

Another virtue of his prose is its marvellous versatility. Whether describing an eruption of Vesuvius, the concept of immaterialism, the redolent beauties of Rhode Island, the moral degeneracy of Britain, the curative properties of tar water, or the passion of Christ at Calvary, Berkeley's language is perfectly suited to its subject. 'We should say that he is a master of styles rather than of style,' says Jessop, 'for he could be now coolly scientific and then deeply moving, precise and evocative, grave and witty, satirical and quietly gracious. He could frame an epigram as easily as a period.'[3] Because of its malleability there is nothing mannered in Berkeley's style, any more than there is in Swift's.

---

[1] *A History of English Prose Rhythm*, pp. 252–3.

[2] *Hermathena*, lxxxii. 50.

[3] Ibid., lxxxii. 3.

Berkeley had no prose style for his sermons as distinct from that of his other works. The sermon, of course, because its rules of composition are to some extent dictated by the oratorical performance for which it is created, tends to be more rhetorical than most *genres*. Repetition, rhetorical questions, apostrophe, and antithesis are endemic. But, like Swift, Berkeley achieves this rhetorical bent without altering the basic structure of his prose.

There is, as one might expect from sermons spread over almost half a century, an unevenness in the quality of the prose. The early sermons lack some of the fluency and polish of the later, but there can be little doubt that the author of 'On the Will of God' is also the author of 'On Immortality' written forty years before. In the early sermon there are portents of what was to come. The balance, the cadence, and the potency are already apparent: 'But be it never so unfashionable, be it never so painfull & laborious a task. He yt will enjoy heaven in ye next life must think on it in this.'[1] Present too, though not so apparent, is an almost Shakespearean poignancy and simplicity: 'I say is it not equally evident & strange yt at this time of day & in these parts of ye world men go together by the ears about the things of this life, & scramble for a little dirt within sight of heaven.'[2]

It has been noted that Berkeley was particularly skilful in the use of language to create a mood and evoke an emotional response. Nowhere did this aspect of his literary genius prove more useful, and nowhere is it now more easily observed, than in his sermons. With the deft and confident strokes of a master he can paint with moving realism a scene of pathos or anger, ecstasy or fear. The image of a suffering, bleeding, rejected Jesus, groaning out his life upon a cross, was disturbingly poignant for Berkeley. Time and again he returns to this most pathetic of scenes:

Figure to your selves his head dishonoured with an ignominious crown of thorns: his face spit upon and buffeted by an impious and

[1] *Works*, vii. 15.
[2] Ibid., vii. 10.

prophane rabble: his flesh torn with scourges: His hands & feet pierced with nails: blood & water streaming from his side: his ears wounded with taunts and reproaches: And that mouth wch uttered the glad tidings of salvation filled with gall and vinegar: in fine figure to your selves his sacred body hung upon a cross there to expire in lingering torments between thieves and malefactors. But who can figure to himself, or what imagination is able to comprehend the unutterable agony that he felt within, when the cup of the fury of God was poured out upon his soul, and his spirit laboured under the burden of the guilt of all mankind! Can we think on these things which are all the effects of our sins, and at the same time be untouched with any sorrow or compunction for them. Shall the sense of those crimes that made our blessed Saviour sweat drops of blood, be unable to extort a single tear from us? [When the earth quakes, the rocks are rent, the skies are covered with darkness, and all nature is troubled at the passion of the Lord of Life, shall man alone remain stupid and insensible?][1]

Here is pleading and pathos quite unmatched in Augustan preaching. Here again is a prefiguration of revivalistic religion.

But there was a social, as well as an evangelistic, side to Berkeley's gospel. When depicting the scourge and ravages of an evil such as war, he could be equally vivid and intense:

But when the spirit of ambition or Revenge begins to operate, when jealousy of each other's wealth and power divides nations and breaks the bonds of Charity, then all those advantages are interrupted, and men, instead of promoting each others benefit are imploy'd in destroying one another. Whole Provinces are laid waste, Cities, palaces and churches . . . are in an instant demolished & burnt to the ground. Thousands of widows and orphans are made in one fatal day: And he who makes the greatest havock of his fellow-Christians is esteemed most worthy of renown and honour. After an infinity of rapes, murders, rapines, sacrileges, when fire and sword have spent their rage & are glutted with Humane blood, the dreadful scene often ends in Plague or Famine as the natural consequences of War.[2]

Confronted with passages such as these it is difficult to understand how Luce could write: 'One would wish to

---

[1] *Works*, vii. 51. These square brackets are in Berkeley's MS.
[2] Ibid., vii. 34–5.

know something of his pulpit manner; but we have no information, save what we can glean from the sermons themselves; the preacher does not appear to raise his voice, nor scold, nor even argue; but in unemphatic level tones he works out his theme, quietly persuasive.'[1] On the contrary; Berkeley's sermons suggest that he was willing to use any oratorical device which might enable him to impress the high seriousness of his message upon his auditory. He could scold, plead, cajole, exhort, or chastise as the occasion demanded. But of all the infelicities of human behaviour which could arouse his anger, none was more effective than malicious gossip:

We shou'd be slow to believe, displeased to hear and always averse from propagating any scandalous stories to the disparagment of our neighbors. If they are false, to spread or countenance them is the highest injustice and if they are true it may be called the highest cruelty. It is not doing as you wou'd be done by to draw the secret failures of your neighbors into the full view of the world, It is a *barbarous savage joy* that you take in discovering his sins and imperfections, It is a *cruelty* not only to him, but likewise to other men inasmuch as *vicious* examples made public strengthen the party of sinners, spread the *contagion of vice*, and take off from the *horror* of it. And yet by a *base malignity of temper* men are for the most part better pleased with satyr than panegyric, and they can behold with much greater satisfaction the reputation of another *stab'd and torn* by the *venemous tongues of slanderers and detractors*, than sett off to advantage by the recital of his good actions.[2]

The italicized words and phrases show the extent of Berkeley's indignation.

Everything about his sermons suggests that Berkeley was responsive to the claims of oratory: the authoritative injunctions; the measured, rhythmic periods; the epigrammatic thrust; the crescendo of emphasis and emotion; the quiet, insistent pleading; the thunderous, impassioned warning; and the skilful use of Biblical idiom and imagery.

---

[1] *Proceedings of the Royal Irish Academy*, xliii (1936), 274.
[2] *Works*, vii. 29. Italics mine.

All this argues eloquently that the mind and voice which charmed the coffee-house wits of London were not deficient in powers to stir the masses.

Sparse though it is, there is also external evidence to support the claim that Berkeley was a popular and effective preacher. Certainly his physical appearance must have endeared him to his audiences. There is little exaggeration in this devotee's description: 'In person, Berkeley was handsome and robust; very strong, and with a countenance beaming with intelligence and goodness.'[1] He combined with this an amiable and infectious personality, to which Pope ascribed every virtue under heaven[2] and of which Atterbury exclaimed: 'So much understanding, so much knowledge, so much innocence, and such humility, I did not think had been the fashion of any but angels, till I saw this gentleman.'[3]

Ludowick Updike who, as a boy in Newport, Rhode Island, heard Berkeley preach in Trinity Church on more than one occasion, remarked on his unusual popularity with people of other sects: 'All sects rushed to hear him; even the Quakers, with their broad brimmed hats, came and stood in the aisles. In one of his sermons he very emphatically said, "give the devil his due, John Calvin was a great man".'[4] In August 1729 Berkeley wrote to Lord Percival and described his relationship with the Quakers during the period of which Updike writes:

For the first three months I resided at Newport and preached regularly every Sunday, and many Quakers and other sectaries heard my sermons in which I treated only those general points agreed by all Christians. But on Whit-Sunday (the occasion being so proper) I could not omit speaking against that spirit of delusion and enthusiasm which misleads those people: and though I did it in the softest manner and with the greatest caution, yet I found it gave some offence, so bigoted are they to their prejudices. Till then they almost took me for one of their own,

---

[1] K. Thomson, *Memoirs of Viscountess Sundon* (1847), ii. 173.

[2] 'Epilogue to the Satires', dial. ii, l. 73.

[3] *DNB*, iv. 350.

[4] Quoted by W. Updike, *History of the Narragansett Church* (1847), p. 120.

to which my everyday dress, being only a strait-bodied black-coat without plaits on the sides, or superfluous buttons, did not a little contribute.[1]

One suspects that here again Berkeley is being modest. His unassuming dress no doubt helped, but it is more likely that it was his ability to preach with evangelical verve and authority which attracted his large congregations.

This assumption would appear to be borne out by the account of another eye witness, who heard Berkeley preach in Boston: 'On Lord's Day 12 [September, 1731] in ye morn Dean George Berkeley preacht in ye [King's] Chapel from ye 1st Epistle to Timothy ye 3rd Chap., Verse 16, and a fine sermon; according to my opinion I never heard such a one. A very great auditory.'[2] It is a matter of regret that there is not more description of Berkeley's preaching style to draw upon. His sermons themselves and what external evidence there is strongly support the claim that he was a preacher of power and distinction. And certainly no other eighteenth-century divine makes one more aware of the strength and beauty of English oratorical prose.

His sermons generate both heat and light. His greatest contribution to Anglican worship and theology was his attempt to accommodate both reason and emotion within the framework of a genuine religious experience. He more than anyone else of his generation believed that the claims of mind and heart need not militate against each other. His rejection of the belief that reason alone was the way to God stemmed mainly from his study of philosophy. The god he arrived at through metaphysics was singularly unsatisfying: 'The Metaphysical Knowledge of God, considered in his absolute Nature or Essence, is one Thing, and to know him as he stands related to us as Creator, Redeemer, and Sanctifier is another.'[3] It was his desire to know God in this way

[1] *Works*, viii. 202.

[2] Quoted from Benjamin Walker's diary by B. Rand, *Berkeley's American Sojourn* (1932), p. 45.

[3] *Works*, vii. 116. See the *Guardian* no 88 (22 June 1713) for one of Berkeley's most rhapsodic—but altogether sincere—views of God.

which led him early in life to embrace a faith which, while not embarrassing his intellect, warmed his heart. That faith found expression in everything he did or said, and, above all, in the rhythmic warmth and optimism of his sermons. One of Berkeley's most famous fellow countrymen said it best of him: 'Though he could not describe mystery—his age had no fitting language—his suave glittering sentences suggest it; we feel perhaps for the first time that eternity is always at our heels or hidden from our eyes by the thickness of a door. . . . What does it matter when we are in such good company if Michael's trumpet blares on every threshold?'[1]

[1] W. B. Yeats in his Introduction to J. M. Hone's and M. M. Rossi's *Bishop Berkeley: His Life, Writings, and Philosophy* (1931), pp. xxi–xxii.

THOMAS SECKER
From a portrait (after Reynolds) in the National Portrait Gallery, London.

IV

THOMAS SECKER
(1693–1768)

Sermons of 'Discreet Warmth'

IF THE FACTORS which give rise to popularity also gave
rise to greatness, Thomas Secker would have to be considered the most outstanding prelate of the eighteenth
century. His rise to fame was rapid and impressive: chaplain
to the king (1732); rector of St. James's (1733); bishop of
Bristol (1734); bishop of Oxford (1737); dean of St. Paul's
(1750); and Archbishop of Canterbury (1758). But posterity often deals harshly with the popular, and Secker has long
since been relegated to obscurity. Nor is it easy now to
explain the reason for his success and reputation in his own
age.

That he was popular is beyond question. Even Horace
Walpole, who intensely disliked Secker, was forced to
concede: 'It is incredible how popular he grew in his
parish.'[1] Much of that popularity was due to the efficiency
and versatility he displayed in his multi-lateral role of pastor.
Methodical and meticulous, he was an excellent adminis-
trator. A. W. Rowden has remarked on the splendid
manner in which he organized parish accounts at St. James's
and caused matters generally to run more smoothly.[2] And

---

[1] *Memoirs of the Reign of King George the Second* (1846), i. 65.
[2] *Primates of the Four Georges* (1916), pp. 261–2.

one has only to consult the 'Accounts of Archbishop Secker', still in manuscript in Lambeth Palace Library,[1] to realize how competently he dealt with the demanding and uninspiring task of church administration.

The natural dignity and aplomb Secker brought to his several ecclesiastical offices may be considered a second cause of his popular success. Tall, with ruggedly-handsome features, his physical appearance itself commanded attention; his demeanour bespoke a prelate of eminence.[2] 'Secker is decent',[3] said Pope, by which he meant that he was tolerant and moderate. And it was this quality of transparent decency which attracted many people to him.

A third and perhaps chief source of Secker's appeal was his skill as a preacher. James Hervey observed that 'When *Secker* preaches . . . the church is crowded'.[4] And Ralph Churton, in defending the Archbishop against Bishop Hurd's strictures that his sermons were designed merely to popularize the views set forth in Butler's *Analogy*, concludes: 'The truth is, that Dr. Secker's transcendent abilities as a practical preacher were universally acknowledged, were strongly attested by those numerous congregations, consisting of all ranks of people, that constantly attended his sermons.'[5] Those who crowded to hear him were attracted as much by his manner of preaching as by what he had to say. Not that there was anything very unusual about that manner; a man of Secker's temperament and thought could never bring himself either to indulge in or countenance the sensational. His appeal as a pulpit orator was summed up well enough by Christopher Pitt. In a poem 'On the Art of Preaching' he offers advice to those who would improve their style:

---

[1] Secker MS. 1483 ff. 1–275.

[2] For a detailed, though altogether too flattering, account of Secker's appearance see the *Gentleman's Magazine*, xxxviii (1768), 453. A more reliable source is Sir Joshua Reynolds' portrait of Secker which hangs in Lambeth Palace.

[3] 'Epilogue to the Satires', dial. ii, l. 71.

[4] 'Theron and Apasio', *Works* (1805), ii. 24.

[5] *A Letter to the Lord Bishop of Worcester* (1796), p. 32.

Some easy subject choose, within your power,
Or you can never hold out half an hour.
One rule observe: this Sunday split your text;
Preach one part now, and t'other half the next.
Speak, look, and move, with dignity and ease,
Like mitred Secker, you'll be sure to please.[1]

Though not a man of outstanding intellect or wit, Secker enjoyed those traits of mind and character which facilitate popularity in almost any age. Perhaps Viscount Percival came closest to describing the impression Secker made upon his contemporaries: 'His agreeable person and outward behaviour, civility of manners, and discreet behaviour, together with the graceful delivery of his sermons, do all contribute to make him friends and give a lustre to his learning.'[2]

Secker was by nature conservative. He occasionally voted with the minority in the House of Lords,[3] but it was not in him to be even slightly radical. He had no desire to see the *status quo* upset in any way. The extent of his conservatism is evidenced in a sermon preached at the anniversary meeting of the charity schools, 5 May 1743. He is solicitous that the wards of the schools be fitted for their place in society.

Cleanliness should be required of them, as far as ever their Employments allow it: but no extraordinary Provision should be made for it, nor the least Affectation of Nicety tolerated in either Sex. Their Cloaths should be no better, if so good, as they may hope to wear all the rest of their Lives; no Gaiety of Colour, no trifling Ornaments permitted; nor any Distinction between them and other Children, in which they can possibly be tempted to take Pleasure. If they are fed: their Food should be of the coarsest Sort, and not more than enough. If they are lodged: it should be in a manner, that is suitable to every Thing else. For, besides that Frugality is a most important Branch of

---

[1] *Poets of Great Britain*, ed. R. Anderson (1794), viii. 821. 'Split your text' is an allusion to Secker's habit of preaching a series of sermons from the same text. In the collected edition of his sermons 63 of 116 are in series of 2, 3, 4, and sometimes five.

[2] *Diary of the First Earl of Egmont, First Viscount Percival* (1923), ii. 137.

[3] See C. J. Abbey, *The English Church and Its Bishops* (1887), ii. 46.

Faithfulness in the Management of Charities, *it is good that they should bear the Yoke in their Youth*; be inured to the Treatment they must expect to receive: and wrong-judged Indulgence is the greatest Cruelty, that can be exercised towards them.[1]

It is obvious that Secker believed he was living in the best of all possible worlds.

His theology, like his politics and social theory, was pretty much in the main stream of eighteenth-century thought. He was more orthodox than either Butler or Berkeley, and as such is a more representative spokesman for the period. Try as he could he was unable to escape the indigenous rationalism of the age. Nor could he reject the belief, popularized by Tillotson, that it is the primary task of the preacher to show that Christianity is intellectually respectable. For this reason all his sermons, even where his principal theme is ethical, devotional, or doctrinal, are essentially apologetic. His first concern is to defend Christianity (synonymous for him with the Church of England) from its three perennial and perfidious foes—scepticism, enthusiasm, and Roman Catholicism.

The proofs he marshals in support of Christianity are both intrinsic and forensic: intrinsic because they attempt to show that there is nothing in Christian doctrine inimical to reason[2]; forensic because they appear designed to persuade the impartial mind rather than confirm and comfort believers.

Then as to the Evidence in Favour of our Religion: whatever Difficulties may be started concerning particular Points of it, taken singly; as there may, in the same Manner, concerning any Evidence in the World; yet lay together, in one View, the Scripture-Narration of Things from the Beginning; the Consistency and Connection of the Scheme, though carried on for so many thousands of Years; the admirable Temper and Character of the Author of Christianity; the

---

[1] *Fourteen Sermons preached on Several Occasions* (1766), pp. 164–5.

[2] There is no attempt to authenticate by external evidence the historicity of scripture. This task was undertaken by Christian apologists, like Paley, in the second half of the eighteenth century.

Sublimity and Reasonableness of its Doctrines; the Purity and Benevolence of its Precepts; the Excellency of its Means of Improvement and Grace; the eternal and true Felicity of its Rewards; the manifold Attestations of its History and Miracles; the wonderful Propagation of it through the World, and its primitive Influence on the Souls and Lives of Men; the undeniable Completion of many of its Prophecies, and the evident Room there is left for the fulfilling of the rest: all these notorious Facts, thus united and combined, can surely never fail to convince every impartial Examiner, that the System, they support, must be from God, and that the supreme Happiness of Man is to share in its Blessings.[1]

It is to man's reason, then, that Christianity makes its primary appeal. Faith is not, as the writer of the book of Hebrews believed, 'the substance of things hoped for, the evidence of things not seen', but the logical upshot of a thorough examination of the evidence for Christianity.

Accordingly Christianity recommends itself to us at first Sight by this peculiar Presumption of its being the true Religion, that it makes Application to Men as reasonable Creatures, and claims our Assent on Account of the Proofs, which it offers. By these alone it prevailed originally: on these it still relies; and requires Faith for the Principle of our Obedience, only because it produces Evidence for the Ground of our Faith.[2]

The preacher's first task, Horton Davies has observed, is *'to remove objections to his message and to establish its relevance'*.[3] Secker would have agreed. His own approach is to vindicate the Christian faith by obviating difficulties and objections. This is demonstrable from a sermon on faith, where successive paragraphs begin: 'Some indeed have argued . . .', 'But perhaps it will be said . . .', 'Nor must it be objected . . .', 'But it will be said . . .', 'But perhaps it will be urged . . .', 'Once more, however, it may be objected . . .'.[4] Occasionally, however, Secker becomes excessively simple

---

[1] *Sermons on Several Subjects* (1770–1), i, 46–7, hereafter referred to as *Sermons*.
[2] Ibid., i. 1–2.
[3] *Varieties of English Preaching 1900–1960*, p. 29.
[4] *Sermons*, iv. 173 ff.

—even banal—in raising objections that are only obliquely
relevant. Inevitably, at such times, he creates more mis-
givings than he dispels.[1] Such an unremitting apologetic
tenor tends also to detract from the delicate beauty of the
scriptural narrative the preacher is seeking to interpret. A
good example of this occurs in a sermon on Abraham's
intended sacrifice of Isaac.[2] So concerned is Secker to justify
the ways of God to man, and particularly to Abraham, that
he completely misses the poignancy of the story.

Secker, despite his occasional emphasis upon the rational
proofs of Christianity, was not, strictly speaking, a Latitudinarian. In most matters of doctrine he was a high churchman in the Laudian tradition. For him there was but one
true church and that the Church of England. It was not
merely a collection of like-minded people, nor had it come
into being by historical accident. Rather, it was divinely
ordained; its episcopal ministry, liturgy, and sacraments
were God's chosen means of imparting knowledge, salvation, and grace. 'When I mention religion', said Dr.
Thwackum, 'I mean the Christian religion; and not only
the Christian religion, but the Protestant religion; and not
only the Protestant religion, but the Church of England.'[3]
Such were Secker's sentiments, exactly.

His uncompromising faith in the institutes and ordinances
of the Church is apparent in the five sermons he gave in
defence and explication of the liturgy.[4] There he deals in
detail with almost every aspect of Anglican worship:
General Confession; Absolution; Lord's Prayer; doxology;
Psalms; organ music; lessons; hymns; creeds; petitions and
general prayers; collects; litany; and Eucharist. Nothing is
too insignificant to merit attention: 'Another Direction is,
that the Confession be said, *all kneeling* . . . Still they, whose
Infirmities will not permit them to be on their Knees

[1] See *Sermons*, iii, sermon xvi.
[2] Ibid., iv. 343 ff.
[3] *Tom Jones*, bk. iii, ch. iii.
[4] *Sermons*, vi. 165–292.

without Pain or Hurt, may doubtless allowably stand, or even sit: for God *will have Mercy, and not Sacrifice*.'[1] To most eighteenth-century clerics such a qualification would have seemed too obvious to mention. Not so Secker; here, as everywhere, the canon is sacrosanct and no exceptions can be taken for granted.

Church dogma, like church liturgy, he accepts un-equivocally. Many of his sermons are occasional, and consequently doctrinal. His *Sermons* contain a discourse for every significant event in the Christian calendar and a vindication of the doctrine which underlies it. In one sermon he considers in turn the Church's teaching on the Trinity, the Resurrection, Original Sin, and the Atonement, and pronounces it perfect in every detail.[2]

The truth would seem to be that Secker, unlike his close friend, Joseph Butler, did not possess a questioning mind. He was almost prepared to say with Pope that 'whatever is, is right'. In a sermon concerned with sacrifice and suffering he makes no attempt to come to grips with the problem of pain.[3] With complete resignation he accepts life's apparent injustices as the inscrutable, but perfectly good, will of God. By virtue of his omnipotence and the relationship in which he stands to the whole of creation, God may, with perfect fairness, deal in the most arbitrary fashion with man. A charge of injustice against God not only has no grounds, it has no meaning either. The secret of happiness lies in a quiet acceptance of life as one finds it.

And happy would Men always have been made, and happy might they become yet, by the Observance of its Rules. These are

I. That we should never pry into Matters, which infinite Wisdom hath concealed. For *the secret Things belong unto The Lord our God.*

II. That we should receive with attentive Humility whatever it communicates. For *those Things, which are revealed, belong to us and our Children for ever.*

---

[1] *Sermons*, vi. 174.
[2] See Ibid., iii, sermon xv.
[3] Ibid., iv. 346 ff.

III. That we should allow every divine Truth its due Influence on our Behaviour. For we are to learn them, *that we may do all the Words of this Law.*[1]

Here can be glimpsed another facet of Secker's religion—a facet not easily reconciled with the closely-reasoned creed by which ostensibly he lived. At the deepest level of his existence Secker was a man of profound faith. And if that faith had roots in the 'evidences from reason', it had still stronger roots in emotion.

Though apprehensive about the religious ferment taking place in England after 1740, it would be wrong to say that Secker was openly hostile to it. In fact, one can discover in both his sermons and letters an occasional sympathetic reference to the evangelicals and their cause. He realized that it would be detrimental to the Church of England categorically to set itself against this new wave of religious emotion. Some means had to be found of containing, then channelling, its waters into the main stream of Anglican worship and theology.[2]

His sympathies in this matter were occasioned by the fact that he himself was not immune to the warm emotions engendered by evangelical religion. His zeal sometimes breaks through in his sermons, and when it does he sounds remarkably like Wesley.

Let every one therefore of every Degree *fight the good Fight of Faith, and lay hold on eternal Life, whereunto he is called:* for these are *not cunningly devised Fables,* but *the true Sayings of God.* They who have hitherto lived in Sin, (and so far we all have, that *by* his Obedience to *the Law no Man is justified in the Sight of God)* let them *flee* to the merciful Jesus *from the Wrath to come, acquaint themselves with him, and be at Peace.* They that once had a Sense of Religion, but *have left their first Love,* drawn away by vicious Indulgences, or to temporal Interests, or *the Instruction that causeth to err from the Words of Knowledge,* let them remember from whence they are *fallen, and*

---

[1] *Sermons,* iv. 377–8.

[2] Another half-century would pass before the evangelical movement would gain a plaee of respect within Anglicanism. Then it was largely accomplished through the teaching and influence of Charles Simeon.

repent, and do their first Works. They, who have hitherto persevered in Piety, let them form in themselves, as they will always have Room and Need, a still completer Image of Christ. And let us all incessantly study to acquire that constant, that affectionate and influencing Attention to him, for which St. *Peter* celebrates the early Christians, when he saith, *Whom having not seen, ye love: in whom, though now ye see him not, yet believing, ye rejoice with Joy unspeakable and full of Glory, receiving the End of your Faith, even the Salvation of your Souls.*[1]

If such impassioned outbursts are not allowed to dominate his preaching, yet they occur with surprising frequency in one so restrained and orthodox.

It must be said to Secker's credit that he perceived the essential weakness in Augustan worship and belief. Reason, which had formerly been offered as a support for faith, gradually replaced it. In consequence of this, morality replaced mystery as the chief religious preoccupation. Secker saw this marriage of ethics and religion as detrimental to both. He would have agreed with A. J. Vaughan that 'To degrade religion to the position of a mere purveyor of motive to morality is not more dishonourable to the ethics which must ask, than to the religion which must render such assistance.'[2] The prudential, utilitarian ethic of Tillotson, which had found such favour with Addison and a host of other lay and clerical preachers earlier in the century, had been tried and found wanting. Even from the viewpoint of morality it was unsatisfactory. Something more than an appeal to reason was necessary before morals were universally acknowledged and observed.

The Reasonableness, the Dignity, the Beauty of Virtue, are doubtless natural, and ought to be strong Recommendations of it. But how faint Impressions do they make on the Ignorant and Slow of Apprehension, on Minds agitated with Passions, or hardened in Sins! And indeed how soon do such Impressions, if single and unsupported, fade away out of all Minds, or dwindle into mere Speculation, amidst the Temptations of a bad World, the Allurements of Sense, and the Treacheries

[1] *Sermons,* i. 143-4.
[2] Quoted by M. Pattison, *Essays and Reviews,* p. 293.

of *a deceitful Heart*! Again: the temporal Advantages of Virtue and bad Effects of Wickedness, ordinarily speaking, are weighty Arguments. But still, how often doth that Weight fall on the wrong Side; or give little Help, if any, to the right! In short, many Incitements to think and act as we ought, are in general useful: but none is at all Times sufficient, excepting only the Fear of God *taught as the Truth is in Jesus.*[1]

Wesley would have had no quarrel with the sentiments expressed here.

In another respect, too, Secker seems to be one with the evangelicals: he insists upon the prime importance of the Bible as a guide to Christian living. His dissenting parents and training had impressed upon him the centrality of scripture in religious worship and belief.[2] Just as the Church was not merely a human institution but the mystical body of Christ on earth, so the Bible was not just the best of books but the final and unalterable dicta of God. This view of the Bible he based principally on a Pauline passage on which he preached five sermons: '*All Scripture is given by Inspiration of God: and is profitable for Doctrine, for Reproof, for Correction, for Instruction in Righteousness: that the Man of God may be perfect, thoroughly furnished unto all good Works.*'[3] Believing thus, it is little wonder Secker is reluctant to ascribe anything but a literal interpretation to any part of scripture. To doubt the truth of one passage is to vitiate all. And if to preserve the unimpeachable authority of scripture means acknowledging the existence of an anthropomorphic Satan, then so it must be.

When the Days of his miraculous Fasting were completed, the Tempter came to him in a visible Form: a Thing, which we have neither any Reason from hence to fear will ever be our own Case, or to believe is ever the Case of other common Men; nor yet to doubt of

---

[1] *Sermons,* iii. 10–11.

[2] Secker had been intended for the Presbyterian ministry. He was sent to Tewkesbury Academy operated by perhaps the best and best-known dissenting educator of the eighteenth century, Samuel Jones. A classmate there was Joseph Butler and a lifelong friendship was begun.

[3] *Sermons,* vi. 1.

its having been his, from its never being ours or theirs. For the whole Life of *Christ* was so full of Wonders, that the History of his Temptation is perfectly agreeable to the rest: and we must either question all, or no Part.[1]

Such a fundamentalist view of the Bible is entirely consonant with the Calvinism of George Whitefield, John Newton, William Grimshaw, and Augustus Toplady. And if Secker would have been repelled by the idea of identification with such 'fanatical' company, he ought on occasions to have been less 'enthusiastic' himself.

Man is a fallen Creature: *We are dead*, as the Apostle strongly expresses it, *and our Life is hid with Christ in God.* Our hope of future Happiness lies not in ourselves, but is reposited in the Hands of the blessed *Jesus*, who purchased it with his Blood: and *where our Treasure is, there must our Hearts be also.* Without affectionate and habitual Movements of the Soul towards the Father of Mercy, the Author of Salvation, the Inspirer of Holiness; without a deep Sense of past Guilt and present Imperfection, an humble Faith in the Merits of our glorified Redeemer, and a firm Reliance on the Grace of the Divine Comforter, all our Virtue, all our Piety, will avail us nothing. For, when we have done our best, *we are* but *unprofitable Servants.*[2]

This passage invites comparison with evangelical preaching not only because of its latent emotionalism, but by virtue of its scriptural idiom as well. Despite Horace Walpole's statement to the contrary,[3] Secker's sermons abound in Biblical quotations. He almost always concludes with a flourish of texts. His intimate familiarity with the Bible is evident from the way in which he ranges freely from Genesis to Revelation, choosing quotes or making allusions. Fundamentally, though, he is a New Testament preacher, and relies heavily upon the Pauline epistles.

[1] *Sermons*, ii. 113.
[2] Ibid., ii. 139–40.
[3] *Memoirs*, i. 65–6: 'His discourses from the pulpit, which, by a fashion that he introduced, were a kind of moral essays, were as clear from quotations of Scripture, as when he presided in a less Christian society; but what they wanted of Gospel, was made up by a tone of fanaticism that he still retained.'

Perhaps it is Paul's influence which is responsible for Secker's emphasis upon the reality of personal sin. Augustan preaching generally was more concerned with collective evil than private wrong. The concern was for society, and matters of right and wrong tended to be judged on the basis of their benefit or detriment to the social order. It was for this reason that many leading clergy (e.g., Atterbury, Hoadly, Sacheverell, and Swift) felt compelled to take a vigorous part in the politics of the time. Indeed, for some the line dividing theology and politics disappeared altogether, and their efforts were spent in denouncing the evils of Leviathan. Secker, on the other hand, insisted that sin was first of all an offence against God, and its solution lay in seeking his forgiveness.

To expect eternal Life through a Saviour who died for us, is the fundamental Doctrine of the Christian Profession: the Article, that distinguishes our Faith from all others, and with which our Religion stands or falls. The New Testament therefore dwells much on the Importance of this Belief: and especially the Epistles of St. *Paul* inculcate it every where. He *determined*, though a Man of extensive Knowledge, *not to know any Thing among* those whom he instructed, to insist on no Subject, comparatively speaking, *save Christ Jesus, and him crucified.*[1]

As this passage indicates, the Atonement was the central doctrine in his theology.

Despite his obvious theological affinities with Wesley, Secker could never bring himself to countenance the Methodist movement. Something in him responded to its vitality and zeal; something else, more easily articulated because closer to the stream of religious consciousness of the age, rebelled. In a letter to his brother, 1739, he gives some indication of these ambivalent feelings:

Our nephew George has been here two nights from Coventry and went away this morning for Hackney. . . . He met two men on horse-back singing psalms upon the road who I suppose are in the same turn

[1] *Sermons*, i. 145–6.

with your Methodists at Nottingham. They all set out at first I
believe with a very good intention but have run into Indiscretions and
Extravagancies: and some of them, particularly Mr. Whitefield,
seem blown up with Vanity which I fear hath & will lead them into
mighty wrong behaviour.[1]

His references to Methodists in his *Eight Charges* usually
include praise for their vigour and blame for their perfervid
zeal.

But there is still another side of Secker which must be
considered: he is also something of a moralist. Many of his
sermons have a pedagogic tone, as though the author saw
himself in the rôle of teacher as well as priest and evangelist.
Porteus felt that Secker's chief excellence rested in his
exposition of 'the severe Laws of didactic Composition'.[2]
Throughout his ministry he upheld the waning practice of
catechising young and old alike.[3] Also, his method of
introducing a sermon by placing the text in its historical
setting and noting points of interest about prevailing
conditions or ideas would appear as much a didactic as a
homiletic device.

As in the sermons of Swift, Butler, Sterne, and Crabbe,
there is an emphasis in Secker on the necessity of fulfilling
daily tasks and duties. The third volume of the *Sermons*
contains a series of twelve such ethical discourses. They are
directed towards five groups: the young, the aged, and the
poor are each given two sermons in which their duties are
explained, while the rich and the sick are treated to three
each. The detail is infinitesimal, and must have proved
nearly as tedious and soporific to the hearer as it does now
to the reader. Yet it does serve to point up Secker's desire
to instruct his parishioners in the fine art of daily living.[4]

[1] Lambeth Palace Library, Secker MS. 1719, Fragment, f. 15 r–v.

[2] *Sermons*, i. lxxix.

[3] While at St. James's he wrote thirty-nine lectures on the Church Catechism
for his parishioners' guidance. They were published in 2 vols., 1769.

[4] See also *Sermons*, iii, sermons 3 and 4 where, in preaching from the text
'Young Men likewise exhort to be sober-minded', he warns against the moral pit-
falls of youth. In yet another sermon (i, ser. 5), on 'Lovers of Pleasures, more than
Lovers of God', he surveys and denounces most of the social evils of the day.

Although not particularly fond of Secker, Richard Hurd was forced to admit that 'These sermons are remarkable for their soft and gentle insinuation, for a prudent application to different tempers and characters, for the prevention and anticipation of popular prejudices, and for a certain conciliating calmness, propriety, and decency of language.'[1]

In his theology, as in his life, moderation was all. The philosophy by which he lived owed almost as much to the Aristotelian 'golden mean' as to the teachings of Jesus. The most distinguishing feature of his theology is his constant search for the *via media*:

THE Word, *Moderation*, signifies in the Original that Reasonableness of Mind, which curbs the Exorbitancies of all our Passions, Appetites and Imaginations; confining us to proper Degrees of being affected by the Things about us, and of exerting ourselves in Relation to them: from which larger Meaning it is naturally and easily contracted to express more especially the due Restraint of Desire and Anger, Fear and Sorrow.[2]

In his moments of greatest insight, however, Secker acknowledged that moderation might easily become a euphemism for complacency. Nor did he have to look far for proof of this fact:

an open and professed Disregard to Religion is become, through a Variety of unhappy Causes, the distinguishing Character of the present Age; that this Evil is grown to a great Height in the Metropolis of the Nation; is daily spreading through every Part of it; and, bad in itself as any can be, must of Necessity bring in most others after it. Indeed it hath already brought in such Dissoluteness and Contempt of Principle in the higher Part of the World, and such profligate Intemperance, and Fearlessness of committing Crimes, in the lower, as must, if this Torrent of Impiety stop not, become absolutely fatal. And God knows, far from stopping, it receives, through the ill Designs of some Persons, and the Inconsiderateness of others, a continual Increase. Christianity

---

[1] F. Kilvert, *Memoirs of the Life and Writings of the Rev. Richard Hurd, D.D.* (1860), p. 272.

[2] *Sermons*, vii. 375.

is now ridiculed and railed at, with very little Reserve: and the Teachers of it, without any at all.[1]

Much of this blatant disregard for religion, Secker was forced to concede, was attributable to the somnolent moderation of contemporary preaching. It is therefore because of this that he counsels his clergy at Oxford to be cognizant of the need for 'instructive and affecting Sermons delivered with discreet warmth'.[2]

Smooth Discourses, composed partly in fine Words which they do not understand, partly in flowing Sentences which they cannot follow to the End; containing little that awakens their drowsy Attention, little that inforces on them plainly and home what they must do to be saved; leave them as ignorant and unreformed as ever, and only lull them into a fatal Security.[3]

'We have in Fact', Secker says in another place, 'lost many People to the Sectaries by not preaching in a manner sufficiently evangelical.'[4] Dr. Johnson, with characteristic conviction, expressed a similar opinion while explaining the success of Methodist preaching: 'To insist against drunkenness as a crime, because it debases Reason, the noblest faculty of man, would be of no service to the common people: but to tell them that they may die in a fit of drunkenness, and shew them how dreadful that would be, cannot fail to make a deep impression.'[5] Neither Johnson nor Secker can be said genuinely to have entered into sympathy with Methodist teaching and practice, but both were forced to admit that its preaching provided greater incentives for moral behaviour.

Secker's views on preaching are set forth in his third charge after assuming the primacy. They are of particular interest and importance because they represent one of the

[1] *Eight Charges delivered to the Clergy of the Dioceses of Oxford and Canterbury* (1769), pp. 4–5.
[2] Ibid., p. 252.
[3] Ibid., p. 275.
[4] Ibid., p. 299.
[5] *Boswell's Life*, i. 459–60.

few attempts by eighteenth-century divines to articulate a system of homiletics.[1] The previous century, of course, had produced a surfeit of sermon handbooks, or *artes concionandi*. In his study of seventeenth-century preaching W. F. Mitchell devotes a chapter to an evaluation of these works.[2] Of greatest significance is Keckermann's Latin treatise, *Rhetoricae Ecclesiasticae*, first published in 1606. This work influenced every major treatise on preaching in the seventeenth century. And even when it was forgotten—as seems to have been the case in the eighteenth century—its influence upon homiletic theory and practice is still apparent. Secker, no less than others, was indebted to this excellent study.

Keckermann, whose interest is more homiletic than rhetorical, suggests a fivefold division for the sermon. The preacher should begin with his text: announce it and place it in historical perspective. This, Keckermann calls *praecognitio textus*. The second step is to announce the several major headings under which the subject is to be treated, thus allowing the audience a glimpse of the sermon in outline and helping them to follow more easily the logical development of the theme. Keckermann's term for this is *partitio et propositio*. *Explicatio verborum*, the third step, permits the preacher to fill in the historical background and 'open the sense' of the passage he has selected. In *amplificatio*, he is able to bring forward proofs and evidences to support his thesis. He can also refute the arguments of his detractors and thereby confirm the belief of the faithful. The last phase, *applicatio*, in Mitchell's words ,'was more than a mere conclusion, for though the word peroration still conveys the idea of a final stirring appeal, conclusions had come to be often only artistic endings, and the aim of the preacher was not how to conclude his address gracefully, but how to drive home his shafts to the hearts of his hearers'.[3]

---

[1] Swift is another; but his 'Letter to a Young Gentleman' is much more cursory and informal than Secker's third charge.

[2] *English Pulpit Oratory*, pp. 93–130.

[3] Ibid., p. 96.

Like Keckermann, but in less detail, Secker discusses in his third charge every phase of preaching from preparation to delivery. And it is interesting to note how closely the points he makes correspond with those made by Keckermann. Begin with the text, Secker advises; and make sure it is one which lends itself to simple and fruitful analysis. 'Such a Text is most convenient, as will branch out of itself into the main Parts of your Discourse: but at least you should make it appear to be the Ground-Work of your Discourse, and not an After-thought.'[1] Clever hermeneutics must never be attempted. With the text introduced and the relevant historical and scriptural data given, the preacher should proceed to introduce his main headings. 'It is usually best to propose your general Heads together, before you proceed upon them separately, and to give Notice when you come to each.'[2] These two steps (*praecognitio textus* and *partitio et propositio*) Secker calls 'the explanatory Part'. He then summarizes the other steps in his method of address: 'After the explanatory Part, Proofs from Reason and Scripture take the next place: then Inferences, if any useful ones follow peculiarly from what hath preceded; and lastly Exhortations to suitable Practice, which can hardly ever be omitted, and ought to be such as may leave a durable Impression.'[3] Secker accepts almost exactly as Keckermann had laid it down a century and a half before the fivefold division; there is no suggestion of another homiletic approach.

Next, Secker considers the problems involved in sermon delivery. The word 'oratory' has unpleasant connotations for him. It conjures up images of misdirected or unscrupulous preachers preying upon the emotions of the ignorant and innocent. For him, as for many people in the twentieth century, oratory had assumed an aura of odium because of its association with what is now called 'herd-psychology'.

[1] *Eight Charges*, p. 293.
[2] Ibid.
[3] Ibid., p. 294.

But even the best qualified to exhort must keep within due Bounds; convince the Judgement before they attempt to warm the Passions . . . And our Nation is more disposed, than most others, to approve a temperate Manner of Speaking. Every Thing, which can be called Oratory, is apt to be deemed Affectation: and if it goes a great Length, raises Contempt and Ridicule. . . . whereas Warmth of Affection, excited to a proper Degree by the rational Enforcement of solid Arguments, promises to be durable, and will never do Harm.[1]

But to be bereft of all oratorical devices might well cost the preacher his audience's attention. Once more Secker searches to find the middle way. Somewhere between the theatrical and statuesque lies the golden mean of sermon delivery.

Yet somewhat of Gesture, appearing to be artless, and regulated by Propriety, may be very useful, especially in the warmer Parts, of Exhortation, Reproof, or even Argument. For to be altogether motionless, when the Subject is animating, and our Language perhaps vehement, seems an Inconsistency; and may raise a Doubt, whether we are in earnest. But still Defect in Action is better than Excess.[2]

Generally speaking, there are four ways in which a sermon may be delivered. (1) It may be read, *verbatim*, from a prepared manuscript. (2) It may be given *extempore*, with the preacher relying on a skeleton outline or trusting entirely to memory. (3) It may be first written out, then committed to memory, and delivered *memoriter*. (4) It may be prepared in manuscript, condensed to outline, and delivered from notes. Secker, without explicitly describing these methods, in fact considers all four, weighs briefly their merits, and finally chooses the last as best. For a preacher to read his sermon, he contends, is for him to risk losing his hearers' attention through his inability to 'enforce his Words by significant Looks: to perceive from the Countenances of his Hearers, what they comprehend, and by what they are moved'.[3] The *memoriter* address requires powers of reten-

---

[1] *Eight Charges*, pp. 306–7.
[2] Ibid., p. 312.
[3] Ibid., p. 313.

tion uncommon to most preachers, and even for those of exceptional memories there is a danger that the sermon will sound rehearsed and stilted. Extemporaneous preachers often fall victim to impertinence and incoherence. They tend to 'utter off Hand such Crudities, as they could not bear to write down; and think the meanest of extempore Effusions good enough for the Populace'.[1] Predictably, Secker prefers the *via media*: 'There is a middle Way, used by our Predecessors, of setting down, in short Notes, the Method and principal Heads, and enlarging on them in such Words as present themselves at the Time. Perhaps, duly managed, this would be the best.'[2] The best, but by no means the easiest. Much study and a constant use of the file are the key to successful sermon preparation:

Now on the contrary, previously studying and writing Sermons tends to fill them with well digested and well adapted Matter, disposed in right Order: especially, if you will carefully revise them every Time you preach them; supply Deficiencies, blot out Repetitions, correct Improprieties, guard against Misapprehensions, enlighten what is obscure, familiarize what is too high, transpose what is wrongly placed, strengthen the weak Parts, animate the languid ones. Your Composition needs not be at all the stiffer, but may be the freer, for the Pains thus employed upon it.[3]

In this respect Secker is surprisingly modern. W. E. Sangster, in one of the best known twentieth-century books on preaching,[4] expresses similar views concerning preparation and delivery. Secker's modernity is evidenced too by his consideration of how a preacher should ingratiate himself with his congregation. The Augustan age, like the present, was not amenable to authoritative or vituperative oratory. A more natural, conversational style was called for.

Every Man's Voice and Utterance, as well as his Face, belongs to himself alone; and it is vain to think either of looking or talking like such or such a one. Therefore preserve what is native in you: free it

---

[1] *Eight Charges*, p. 314.
[2] Ibid., p. 315.
[3] Ibid., pp. 314–15.
[4] *The Craft of the Sermon* (1954). See especially ch. 7: 'Methods of Preparation'.

from adventitious Faults: improve it, if you can: but remember, that you may deprave it by the Endeavour; and certainly will, if you change it essentially. Speak to your People, as you would in Conversation, when you undertake to inform or persuade a Friend, in a Concern of great Moment; only with more Deliberateness, more Strength and Energy, in Proportion to the Numbers: and vary both your Stile and your Elocution, as in Conversation you always do, suitably to your Matter.[1]

Beilby Porteus claimed for Secker that naturalness and ease of expression he sought to encourage in others. But there were respects in which Secker himself felt he had not been true to his homiletic ideal: 'I am very sensible, that in all Particulars before-mentioned I have been far from observing sufficiently myself the Rules which I have now recommended to you: but hope I shall make some Amends, though late, to the Church of Christ, by exhorting and directing others.'[2] It remains now to consider how closely his preaching practice conforms to his theory.

Secker's sermons follow the structural design adumbrated in his third charge. The emphasis will naturally vary from sermon to sermon; in one there may be a long textual exegesis ('the explanatory Part') and a short peroration ('Exhortation to suitable Practice'), while another may stress proofs from reason rather than from scripture. Neither is it uncommon for him to omit announcing his articulated divisions at the beginning, choosing instead to introduce each aspect of his argument as he is ready to develop it. Nevertheless, his basic approach is the same for all.

A sermon on 'the unpardonable sin'[3] will serve to elucidate his method. The text is long, and allows ample scope for exposition:

Wherefore I say unto you: All Manner of Sin and Blasphemy shall be forgiven unto Men: but the Blasphemy against the Holy Ghost shall not be forgiven unto Men.

[1] *Eight Charges*, p. 310.
[2] Ibid., p. 322.
[3] *Sermons*, i. 191–217.

And whosoever speaketh a Word against the Son of Man, it shall be forgiven him: but whosoever speaketh against the Holy Ghost, it shall not be forgiven him, neither in this World, neither in the World to come.

(Matt. xii: 31, 32)

It is, of course, a theological spinosity, and Secker is aware of that fact. He sets to work at once to explode some of the fallacious theories about the identity of this sin. He mentions sins which hitherto had been interpreted as blasphemy against the Holy Ghost, but concludes that none of them is unpardonable.

Next, he announces the four principal divisions he has made in his subject, and proceeds to draw 'inferences' from each in turn. 'I. What the Blasphemy against the Holy Ghost, mentioned by our Saviour is.' His task here is one of definition. Though he enjoyed a considerable reputation as a classical and Hebraic scholar, Secker makes no parade of scholarship in tracing the word blasphemy back to its Greek origin. Turning to scripture, he considers New Testament examples of this kind of blasphemy and concludes: 'On the Whole therefore, the only Persons, whom we have Ground to think guilty of *the Blasphemy against the Holy Ghost*, meant in the Text, are they, who from bad Motives, and, as we say, in cold Blood, revile and rail against such Operations of the divine Spirit, as are performed in their own Presence.'[1]

'II. What is intended by his Declaration that *it shall not be forgiven, neither in this World, nor that to come.*' He mentions only to reject those interpretations which would moderate the severity of Christ's pronouncement. He is convinced that Christ meant exactly what he said, and that only a literal interpretation is valid. 'It would indeed be presumptuous to restrain the Mercies of God: but it is equally and perhaps more dangerous to extend them farther, than he permits us.'[2]

'III. Why he passes so heavy a Sentence on this one

[1] *Sermons*, i. 200.
[2] Ibid., i. 203.

Sin.' The answer is apparent: such a sin, by its very nature, precludes repentance and, consequently, forgiveness.

'IV. What things do, or do not, approach towards it.' He considers those sins which may give rise to blasphemy against the Holy Ghost, and in so doing brings the sermon down to the plane of moral practice. His concluding exhortation is shorter than usual and not quite typical of the evangelical flourish with which he normally finishes. Perhaps he felt the expository bent of the sermon demanded an unimpassioned conclusion.

Secker is a deliberative preacher and a conscious prose stylist. He leaves nothing to propitious inspiration; all is carefully planned. Above all he desires clarity of expression.

Let your Sentences, and the Parts of them, be short, where you can. And place your Words so, especially in the longer, that your Meaning may be evident all the Way. For if they take it not immediately, they have no Time to consider of it, as they might in reading a Book: and if they are perplexed in the Beginning of a Period, they will never attempt going on with you to the End: but give up the Whole, as out of their Reach. Avoid Rusticity and Grossness in your Stile: yet be not too fond of smooth and soft and flowing Language; but study to be nervous and expressive; and bear the Censure of being unpolished, rather than uninfluencing.[1]

In this passage he demonstrates his awareness of some of the finer points of style. He himself made effective use of the rapier thrust of the short sentence and the slaying stroke of the period. He knew also how important it was to the potency and cadence of a sentence to have proper words in proper places.

His sermons are punctuated with aphorisms, many of which represent considerable projections of thought. Unlike Butler, he is not concerned merely to pack as much meaning as possible into a sentence. He strives also to achieve balance and fluidity. Nor does he disdain to use such an obvious device as alliteration when he deems it necessary:

[1] *Eight Charges*, pp. 296–7.

We may drown the Voice of Conscience in turbulent Passions and vehement Pursuits of Profit or Pleasure; we may coolly and deliberately refuse to obey it: but it will speak, and from Time to Time will be heard.[1]

Human Happiness is a tender Plant, which every rude Breath is sufficient to blast.[2]

Some, by their psychological tone, remind one of Butler:

Knowledge and Prudence require Industry and Experience to attain them: Worth and Probity require thoughtful Self-inspection.[3]

Therefore it is not the Warmth of Temper, with which we are born, and against which we strive, but the wilful or heedless Indulgence of it, that unfits us for the Duties of Life.[4]

Others have the idiomatic ring of the Book of Proverbs:

Idle Reading indeed completes the Destruction of the Time, that idle Conversation spares us. But judicious Writings on the Subject of Conduct, religious, moral, and prudent, are at once the Medicine and the Nourishment of the Mind.[5]

For Discipline without Instruction is mere Tyranny: and Instruction without Discipline, little better than useless Talk.[6]

Mistake not the Beginning of Life for the Whole. Providence in great Wisdom hath furnished every Period of it with proper Satisfactions of its own, and proper Employments for the Service of the next. Youth is to prepare us for the comfortable Enjoyment of Manhood: Manhood for that of old Age: each Part of our Existence on Earth for the Blessedness of Heaven.[7]

The measured cadence so apparent in these examples is typical of Secker's prose generally. He is fond of the resonant phrase and the well-rounded period. Even his rhetorical questions have a rhythmic motion:

[1] *Sermons,* i. 87.
[2] Ibid., ii. 274.
[3] Ibid., i. 101.
[4] Ibid., vii. 377.
[5] Ibid., i. 102.
[6] *Fourteen Sermons,* p. 10.
[7] *Sermons,* iii. 58.

Is not every Man capable of seeing, let him be ever so little acquainted with Nature, that the Heavens and the Earth, the Order of the Seasons, the Returns of Day and Night, the whole Frame of Things in general, is full of Use and Beauty; and must be the Work of amazing Power, Wisdom and Goodness? ... Doth not every Man perceive, that he is *fearfully and wonderfully made*; that the several Parts of his Composition are exactly fitted to the several Purposes of Life; the Eye for seeing, the Ear for hearing, each Member for its respective End? And his inward Inclinations and Affections no less so, than his outward Limbs? Must not every Man be sensible, that the Supports and Conveniences, which he enjoys, are not supplied him merely by his own Care; but chiefly by the Providence of another, *who maketh his Sun to rise, his Wind to blow, his Rain to descend*, his Earth to be fruitful? Hath not every Man heard it owned, that the more diligently any one Part of Nature is examined, the fuller Proofs it affords, that an almighty, allwise and gracious Being, must be the Author of the Whole?[1]

Secker's is not a highly coloured prose. Apart from scriptural images there is hardly any figure at all. Where metaphor and simile occur they are so commonplace as to go almost unnoticed.

But the Conversation of most Persons is full of unobserved Faults and bad Tendencies: which, like a Multitude of small Expenses, make us Debtors beyond what we could imagine: and by continual, though slighter Impressions on our Morals and Piety, gradually undermine what the most violent open Assault could not have overturned.[2]

But, as they, who look at the Sun too intently, dazzle their Eyes, till all around them, and even the Light itself appears dark: so Men have strained their Thoughts, in comparing and measuring the Weakness of their own Faith and Resolution against the Strength of *Abraham's*, till they have been quite confounded with it.[3]

It must be confessed that Secker is too fond of the 'smooth and flowing' language he warned others against. His constant striving to achieve balance makes his prose

---

[1] *Sermons*, i. 83-4.
[2] Ibid., i. 225-6.
[3] Ibid., iv. 343-4.

heavy on occasions and too obviously rhetorical. Spates of antitheses and parallelisms[1] inevitably prove cloying and divert the reader's attention from the message to the style of the sermon.

Given this proclivity, however, Secker's prose is generally pellucid, fluent, and carefully modulated. James Sutherland's statement that 'The eighteenth-century author succeeded to a remarkable degree in writing personally without thrusting his personality upon the reader'[2] could well be applied to Secker. He indulges no private anecdotes, no confessional asides. Neither are there any glaring idiosyncrasies in his style of writing. In these respects he looks backward rather than forward, for evangelical prose and preaching, springing as they did from an intensely personal religious experience, are markedly individual.

The virtues of Secker's style are those of his person: dignified, formal, authoritative. In these and other respects he resembles Isaac Barrow. Like Barrow he exhausted the possible interpretations and implications of a text.[3] Both employed an elaborate, though seldom complex, sentence structure and diction, and each was capable, when the occasion demanded, of rising to a rare grace and beauty. Both wielded with ease the aphoristic sentence and the Ciceronian period. And each was exact and judicious in his choice of language. It must be acknowledged, however, that Barrow was the greater intellect and scholar.

Ultimately, it is difficult to determine Secker's place of importance among eighteenth-century preachers. His influence upon subsequent Anglican preaching both by virtue of his own popular style and his instructions in homiletics was considerable. His 'Instructions given to Candidates for Orders', in which he reiterates some of his views on preaching set forth in more detail in his third charge, passed through fifty editions in half a century.[4] Yet for all his

---

[1] See *Sermons*, i. 124; and iv. 17–18.

[2] *On English Prose*, p. 75.

[3] For an exposition of Barrow's oratory, see Mitchell, pp. 321–30.

[4] Rowden, *Primates*, p. 309.

authority, popularity, and influence, he has not been remembered. A critic in the *Monthly Review* came close to explaining both the reason for the fame he achieved in his lifetime and the oblivion he has been relegated to ever since, when he wrote of the sermons:

Most of them are, indeed, very useful and judicious discourses, containing many excellent observations on human life, and the manners and principles of the age we live in. The preacher always expresses himself with plainness and perspicuity; often with great force, sometimes with elegance; and there are several passages in his sermons, which clearly show the truth of an observation made in the *review of his life and character, viz.* that he might easily have acquired the reputation of a fine writer, had he not sacrificed it to the much nobler ambition of being an useful one.[1]

Janus-like, Secker looks in both directions. In many ways he is a transitional figure, prescient enough to feel the pull of the future but too orthodox to break with the past. In both his theology and his preaching he focuses the century-long struggle between the mind and the heart for religious supremacy.

[1] *Monthly Review,* xliii (1770), 192.

LAURENCE STERNE
From a portrait in the National Portrait Gallery, London.

LAURENCE STERNE
(1713–1768)

'*A Theological Flap upon the Heart*'

THERE IS no better illustration of the difference in moral temperament between the nineteenth and twentieth centuries than that found in a comparison of their attitudes to Laurence Sterne. As though pricked with shame at their ancestors' bludgeoning of him, twentieth-century critics have tried to make restitution by adopting an altogether more sympathetic view of Sterne's life and character. And it was his character—not his work—which stood badly in need of sympathy. For even while they aspersed his person, the Victorians acknowledged his literary genius. They could only explain him as 'the most conspicuous example that could be quoted in favour of the dangerous thesis that literary and moral excellence belong to different spheres'.[1] By this separation of Sterne's character and work, thus making it possible to damn the one while praising the other, nineteenth-century critics assuaged both their moral and literary sensibilities.

Had Sterne not been a clergyman criticism would have been less severe. The brazen innuendo of certain passages in *Tristram Shandy* would have been put down to bad taste and left at that. Nor would he have been so severely censured for

[1] Stephen, *English Thought*, ii. 375.

the apparent indiscretion of his private life. But Englishmen —and this was particularly true of nineteenth-century Englishmen—have always tended to hold to the idea that religion and pleasure are somehow mutually exclusive. For this reason the proposition that a genuine religious devotion and a salacious wit could coexist in a man of the cloth hardly bore thinking about, much less serious discussion. So it was that the same uninhibited genius which brought Sterne acclaim as a writer earned him the image of a ribald and hypocritical cleric.

Thackeray led the charge for the Victorians. In a lecture in *English Humourists of the Eighteenth Century* he attacks Sterne's character, decrying him in a manner more revealing of Thackeray himself than of Sterne. D. W. Jefferson has called this essay 'one of the disgraces of English criticism'.[1] Among the barbed epithets Thackeray hurls at Sterne are 'delicious divine', 'coward', 'wretched worn-out old scamp', 'vain, wicked, witty and false', 'feeble wretch', 'this actor, this quack'. Then he sums up with vitriolic relish:

There is not a page in Sterne's writing but has something that were better away, a latent corruption—a hint, as of an impure presence. Some of that dreary *double entendre* may be attributed to freer times and manners than ours, but not all. The foul Satyr's eyes leer out of the leaves constantly: the last words the famous author wrote were bad and wicked—the last lines the poor stricken wretch penned were for pity and pardon.[2]

Herbert Read did adequate justice to this piece of criticism when he wrote: 'Thackeray's lecture is positively splenetic in tone, and seems to possess a violence and a baselessness more worthy of psychological than critical attention.'[3]

Hardly less splenetic in his assessment of Sterne was Leslie Stephen: 'No man of equal literary eminence excites less respect or even less genuine sympathy. He showed, as we cannot deny, a corrupt heart and a prurient

---

[1] *Laurence Sterne*, 'Writers and their Work', no. 52 (1954), p. 8.
[2] *English Humourists* (1853), pp. 291-2.
[3] *The Sense of Glory* (1929), p. 127.

imagination. He is a literary prostitute. He cultivates his fineness of feeling with a direct view to the market; and when we most admire his books, we most despise the man.'[1] Stephen and Thackeray, of course, represent the extremest form this reaction against Sterne took. There were others, however, who, though less emotional, were scarcely less emphatic. 'Sterne', said Bagehot, 'was a pagan. He went into the Church; but Mr. Thackeray, no bad judge, said most justly that his sermons "have not a single Christian sentiment".'[2] Even H. D. Traill, though largely sympathetic to Sterne, felt it his duty to reproach him for impropriety:

There can be no denying . . . that Sterne is of all writers the most permeated and penetrated with impurity of thought and suggestion; that in no other writer is its latent presence more constantly felt, even if there be any in whom it is more often openly obtruded. The unclean spirit pursues him everywhere, disfiguring his scenes of humour, demoralizing his passages of serious reflection, debasing even his sentimental interludes.[3]

Convinced that Sterne was at best a man of doubtful morals, it is not surprising that the Victorians took little notice of *The Sermons of Mr. Yorick*. What spiritual enlightenment could there be in the discourses of a man who was an inveterate rake, to whom the ministry meant nothing more than sufficient income and leisure to indulge his philandering? Moreover, it was obvious that these sermons had been published for purely mercenary ends and to meet a demand cleverly created by the author himself in *Tristram Shandy*.

Stamped upon the sermons was a further stigma which proved a deterrent even to those who wished to consider them from a literary point of view. Sterne was a known plagiarist. His sermons were no sooner off the press— especially those published after his death, in 1769—than readers and reviewers were discovering passages in them

[1] *English Thought*, ii. 374–5.
[2] *Literary Studies* (1879), ii. 110.
[3] *Sterne*, 'English Men of Letters' (1882), pp. 147–8.

which had been cribbed directly from Tillotson, Hall, Clarke, Foster, Blair and others. Certain it was that more plagiarisms would come to light as time passed. Few therefore were willing to risk quoting *The Sermons*, either to illustrate the tenor of Sterne's thought or the texture of his prose, for fear of discovering later that they had indeed been quoting someone else.

There was one nineteenth-century writer, however, who refused to be intimidated by either this risk or the *ex cathedra* pronouncements of Thackeray, Stephen, and Bagehot. He was Paul Stapfer, a Frenchman. His book, *Laurence Sterne: Sa Personne et Ses Ouvrages* (1870), though frequently ignored or accorded a perfunctory nod of acquaintance by commentators on Sterne, is one of the most important landmarks in Sternian criticism. Stapfer did not set out to exonerate Sterne; he simply felt that a re-examination of this much maligned man and his works might prove an 'enterprise avec plus d'humeur'. 'J'ai commencé cette étude sur Sterne', he says, 'avec une indifférence parfaite pour sa personne, et plus d'antipathie que d'admiration pour ses œuvres.'[1] All that was to change.

A mesure que j'ai avancé dans mon étude, je me suis senti plus d'intérêt pour l'homme et plus de goût pour l'écrivain. J'ai compris peu à peu que la grande réputation littéraire de Sterne n'avait rien d'injuste ni d'outré, et que le monde avait en ceci raison comme toujours. J'ai bientôt vu aussi que la mauvaise réputation morale de Sterne n'était pas toute méritée, et qu'en cela le monde se montrait, comme toujours, plus ami de la médisance que de la vérité.[2]

Sterne emerges from Stapfer's study as a sensitive and sincere artist and a man of great charm and endearment.

Mais l'homme Sterne était, entre autres choses, un artiste et un philosophe, un bel esprit et un cœur sensible, un ennemi des charlatans et des pédants, un ennemi des vieilles méthodes et des idées banales, un ennemi de la gravité parce qu'elle est neuf fois sur dix une affectation,

---

[1] Stapfer, p. 300.
[2] Ibid.

un calcul et un mensonge, un ami de la plaisanterie à tout propos et hors de propos. *L'homme Sterne* était encore un caractère inégal, sujet à de brusques changements d'humeur, gai et tout à coup sérieux ou même triste, optimiste et soudain misanthrope, le plus capricieux des auteurs et des hommes dans sa manière de penser, de sentir et d'écrire.[1]

Almost alone among nineteenth-century critics of Sterne to have done so, Stapfer studied carefully *The Sermons of Mr. Yorick*.[2] He explores in some detail Sterne's homiletic technique and thinks it both original and effective. More important still, he declares his faith in the preacher's motives: 'L'hypocrisie n'entra jamais dans sa nature, et quelque étrange que fût ce ministre de la religion, rien ne serait plus faux que de se le représenter comme un Tartuffe. —Il est à peine plus juste de se le représenter simplement comme un farceur.'[3]

Stapfer's study heralded a new and infinitely more sympathetic era of Sternian criticism. With one notable exception, the twentieth century has acknowledged Sterne as a profoundly gifted writer and has warmed to his charm and wit.[4] It was of course W. L. Cross's superb biography of Sterne which, by uncovering new materials and exploding several malicious traditions which still clung to his subject's character,[5] was most instrumental in repairing his reputation. Since Cross, and largely because of him, a number of important attempts have been made to delineate and explain certain

---

[1] Stapfer, pp. 106–7.

[2] Although such critics as H. D. Traill and George Saintsbury assumed a posture of authority when commenting on the *Sermons*, there is reason to believe that neither had read them with much care, and perhaps most of them not at all. See L. H. Hammond, *Laurence Sterne's Sermons of Mr Yorick* (1948), p. 6.

[3] Stapfer, p. 105.

[4] The exception is Arie Defroe's *Laurence Sterne and his Novels Studied in the Light of Modern Psychology* (1925). Though it offers an interesting analysis of Sterne and his works, this study contains a number of dogmatic value judgements and unproved conclusions. W. B. C. Watkins said of the author that 'the superficialities of which he is guilty and the inconsistencies into which he falls at times in trying to ride Behaviorism and Freudianism simultaneously make his thesis dangerously like Uncle Toby's hobby-horse'. (*Perilous Balance*, p. 100.)

[5] *The Life and Times of Laurence Sterne*, 2 vols. (1925). See especially Cross's account of Sterne's relationship with his mother: i. 91–101.

aspects of Sterne's life and character in an effort to show
their influence upon his work. Herbert Read,[1] W. B. C.
Watkins,[2] and, more recently, Henri Fluchère[3] are perhaps
the most notable contributors to this sympathetic re-
appraisal. The time then has passed when it was necessary
to assume an apologetic posture in writing about Sterne. By
virtue of an eloquent defence he has been acquitted of the
morals charge preferred against him by the nineteenth
century. Not that all in his life was sweetness and light.
No one among his votaries has claimed he was better than
most men; just that he was no worse.

It was not, however, until mid-way through this present
century that a serious scholarly attempt was made to plead
extenuating circumstances to the charge that Sterne in his
sermons was a flagrant plagiarist. The attempt to mitigate
his culpability in this matter was made by an American scholar,
Lancing Van der Heyden Hammond, in his important
work, *Laurence Sterne's Sermons of Mr. Yorick*. Since an
appreciation of Hammond's thesis depends upon a knowledge
of how *The Sermons of Mr. Yorick* originated, it will prove
helpful to look briefly at the history of their publication.

In *Tristram Shandy* Sterne had partly anticipated, partly
created a market for his sermons by having Corporal Trim
read a sample discourse on the text: 'For we trust we have
a good conscience.'[4] The author gave two reasons for including this sermon which Walter Shandy recognized at
once to have come from the pen of Parson Yorick.

The first is, That in doing justice, I may give rest to *Yorick*'s ghost;—
which, as the country-people,—and some others, believe,—*still walks*.

---

[1] 'Introduction' to Scholartis Press edition of *A Sentimental Journey* (1929); and
'Sterne', *The Sense of Glory* (1929), pp. 123–52.

[2] 'Yorick Revisited', *Perilous Balance: The Tragic Genius of Swift, Johnson, and
Sterne* (1939), pp. 99–156.

[3] *Laurence Sterne: de l'homme à l'œuvre* (1961); now translated into English,
Laurence Sterne: From Tristram to Yorick (1965).

[4] This sermon was first preached by Sterne at the summer assizes in York, 29
July 1750, and published the same year. It would later be republished in vol. iv of
Yorick's *Sermons* under the title: 'The Abuses of Conscience Considered.'

The second reason is, That, by laying open this story to the world, I gain an opportunity of informing it,—That in case the character of parson *Yorick*, and this sample of his sermons is liked,—that there are now in the possession of the *Shandy* family as many as will make a handsome volume, at the world's service,—and much good may they do it.[1]

Needless to say, the Shandy family was prevailed upon in this matter, and in 1760 were published the first two volumes of *The Sermons of Mr. Yorick* in the same form and type as *Tristram Shandy* and with an engraving of the author from a portrait by Sir Joshua Reynolds. In a short, apologetic preface Sterne indicates the kind of sermons he has chosen for publication—those which 'turn chiefly upon philanthropy, and those kindred virtues to it, upon which hang all the law and the prophets'.[2] He assures his readers that these are genuine sermons and that 'not one of them was composed with any thoughts of being printed'.[3] He hopes they will not be unkindly received 'for the evidence they bear, of proceeding more from the heart than the head'.[4] Chiefly, however, he wishes to obviate charges of plagiarism.

I have nothing to add, but that the reader, upon old and beaten subjects, must not look for many new thoughts,—'tis well if he has new language; in three or four passages, where he has neither the one nor the other, I have quoted the author I made free with—there are some other passages, where I suspect I may have taken the same liberty, —but 'tis only suspicion, for I do not remember it is so, otherwise I should have restored them to their proper owners, so that I put it in here more as a general saving, than from a consciousness of having much to answer for upon that score.[5]

To facilitate popular and financial success for the sermons, they were published replete with a list of 661 subscribers

[1] *Tristram Shandy*, vol. II, chap. 17, *Works*, Shakespeare Head ed. (1926–7), i. 161.

[2] *The Sermons of Mr. Yorick*, Shakespeare Head ed. (1927), i, vii, hereafter referred to as *Sermons*.

[3] Ibid., i. vii.

[4] Ibid., i. viii.

[5] Ibid.

drawn principally from the ranks of the most celebrated social, political, and literary figures of the age.[1] The combination of advance publicity in *Tristram Shandy*, an impressive subscribers' list, and the Shandean charm of the discourses themselves, was enough: *The Sermons* were generally well-received and widely read.

A feverish round of social activity, an extended visit to France, and a preoccupation with further instalments of *Tristram Shandy* prevented Sterne from exploiting the sermon market for another five years. It was not until the spring of 1765 that he decided to publish two more volumes of Yorick's Sunday best. In a letter to Mr. Foley, his banker in Paris, he reveals both his intention to publish and, inadvertently, his method of enlisting subscribers.

I have made a good campaign of it this year in the field of the literati— my two volumes of Tristram, and two of sermons, which I shall print very soon, will bring me a considerable sum.—Almost all the nobility in England honour me with their names, and 'tis thought it will be the largest, and most splendid list which ever pranced before a book, since subscriptions came into fashion.—Pray present my most sincere compliments to lady H—— whose name I hope to insert with many others.—As so many men of genius favour me with their names also, I will quarrel with Mr. Hume, and call him deist, and what not, unless I have his name too.—My love to Lord W——. Your name, Foley I have put in as a free-will offering of my labours—your list of subscribers you will send—'tis but a crown for sixteen sermons—Dog cheap! but I am in quest of honour, not money.—Adieu, adieu,— believe me, dear Foley.[2]

The two volumes (III and IV in the series) finally appeared in January 1766, but containing only twelve sermons in all, and not sixteen as advertised. The subscription list this time boasted 693 names, and of it Cross remarked: 'To count the stars in the list would be but to enumerate all the

---

[1] The illustrious list included, among others, 6 dukes, 3 duchesses, 28 lords, 20 ladies, 16 earls, 36 sirs, 5 countesses, 20 honourables, 6 bishops, 21 doctors, 3 deans, and 26 reverends.

[2] *Letters of Laurence Sterne*, Shakespeare Head ed. (1927), p. 107, hereafter referred to as *Letters*.

great families of the kingdom; while France contributed to the roll of honor the names of Diderot, d'Holbach, Crébillon, and Voltaire.'[1] In a brief advertisement inserted almost at the end of the second volume, Sterne explains that these sermons are his last to be published 'except the sweepings of the Author's study after his death'.[2]

In 1769—exactly a year after Sterne's death—his wife and daughter Lydia, mindful of the enormous financial success the earlier volumes of sermons had enjoyed, arranged to have 'the sweepings' published. They were issued in three volumes (containing eighteen sermons in all) under the title: *Sermons by the late Rev. Mr. Sterne.*

In all Sterne's sermons, as in *Tristram Shandy*, there is evidence of borrowing, though in the first four volumes the borrowed materials have been reworked and generally improved. The posthumously published sermons, however, are rife with passages of verbatim copying without the necessary acknowledgements. Most reviewers and commentators noted this fact, but no one seemed anxious to point an accusing finger at Sterne, nor did anyone attempt to compile a list of sources to show the nature and extent of his indebtedness. This is perhaps best explained by the permissive attitude to sermonic plagiarizing which prevailed in the eighteenth century.[3] In this regard, Dr. John Ferriar, who took great care to establish *Tristram Shandy*'s indebtedness to Burton, Rabelais, and others, was typical of his time in his less censorious attitude to sermons: 'Charges of Plagiarism in his Sermons have been brought against Sterne, which I have not been anxious to investigate, as in that species of composition, the principal matter must consist of repetitions.'[4]

In 1864 Percy Fitzgerald, in his biography of Sterne, attempted to explore some of the sources of the sermons. By

---

[1] *Life*, ii. 55.
[2] *Sermons*, ii. 66.
[3] See *ante*, pp. 5–9.
[4] *Illustrations of Sterne*, 2nd ed. (1812), i. 123.

then concepts of literary (as of social) morality had undergone considerable change, and Fitzgerald took a stricter
view of unacknowledged borrowing than Ferriar had done.
His investigations led him to conclude that 'while the
originality of "Tristram Shandy" is in the main secure, I am
afraid, in the case of the Sermons, he seems to have cast away
all notions of literary morality'.[1] Fitzgerald left the matter
there, making no attempt at a critical analysis of the borrowed
materials nor yet to assess Sterne's debt to writers other than
Norris and Bentley. In fairness to him it should be said that
the biographical nature of his work made an exhaustive
study of sermon sources virtually impossible.[2]

It remained for Hammond to undertake a systematic
investigation into the nature and extent of Sterne's plagiarisms. His research and analysis suggested two hypotheses:
'first, that the sermons remaining in manuscript at the time
of Sterne's death (subsequently published in Volumes V–
VII) were written earlier than the others and that Volumes
I–IV contain his later and most finished compositions for
the pulpit; secondly, that all but one of the forty-five
sermons had been committed to paper, at least in rudiment-
ary form, prior to 1751.'[3] To support his claim that there
is an artistic development in the sermons which is coincident
with a diminution in borrowing, and which foreshadows the
flowering of Sterne's genius in *Tristram Shandy* and *A
Sentimental Journey*, he compares two sermons whose dates
of composition are known: 'The Charity Sermon' (i.e.
'Elijah and the Widow of Zarephath') and 'The Abuses of
Conscience Considered', preached and printed in York in
1747 and 1750 respectively.[4] The superiority and greater
originality of the later sermon are indisputable.

---

[1] *The Life of Laurence Sterne*, Appendix B, ii. 214.

[2] The same plea could be entered for W. L. Cross. It should be noted, however,
that in his *Life* Cross made a praiseworthy attempt to assess the extent of Sterne's
borrowings from his greatest debtors—Tillotson, Young, Hall, Clarke, Wollaston,
and Leightonhouse.

[3] *Sterne's Sermons*, p. vii.

[4] Ibid., pp. 50–64.

From this and other evidence, Hammond argues that by the time Sterne was writing such sermons as 'The Abuses of Conscience Considered', 'The Prodigal Son', and 'The Levite and His Concubine' he was already conscious of the literary powers stirring within him, and so found it less necessary to crib from others. When he came to publish his sermons he selected those which had greatest claim to originality. Hammond concludes:

As has been shown in the earlier chapters of this study, Yorick's borrowings were many and, at times, brazen; but practically without exception the glaring instances are to be met with only in the three posthumous volumes, which were not prepared for publication by the author. In other words, the last group of eighteen sermons, as Yorick left them, were nothing more than ordinary homilies, composed for immediate parish use and without design for future publication; they may, therefore, be considered in the light of oral discourses. These are the sermons in which nearly all the verbatim copying is to be found; and it was upon quotations from these that most of the earlier critics based their charges of plagiarism. So that however the reader may feel disposed to regard the sincerity and pertinency of Sterne's general apology, if extended so as to include all the sermons, there should be little objection to accepting, quite literally, the assurance that no offence was intended, when that assurance is restricted to the first four volumes. What Yorick published he made his own and, despite the suggestions he took from others, no one but him could have written the first twenty-seven discourses. It was solely to these that his Preface had reference; and here he may be absolved completely from having attempted conscious literary deception.[1]

The cardinal implication of this thesis is clear: the case against Sterne as a homiletic charlatan (like the charge that he was a lecherous and unprincipled priest) must be dismissed. Had he wished to deceive, he would hardly have borrowed so liberally from such popular preachers as Tillotson, Clarke, Foster, and James Blair. In rifling the works of others, Sterne was doing no more than engaging in a practice that was commonly accepted in his day even

[1] *Sterne's Sermons*, p. 89.

if it were never explicitly condoned.[1] And, as Hammond suggests, there is upon those twenty-seven discourses Sterne himself prepared for the press that stamp of Shandean charm which leaves no doubt about their authorship.

All this granted; there still remains unanswered a crucial question: what evidence is there that Sterne was sincere in his profession of faith and that he took seriously the responsibilities of his holy calling? It is one thing to exonerate him from charges of lechery and duplicity, it is quite another to show that he cared faithfully for the souls of his parishioners. And yet there is evidence, albeit inconclusive in itself, to suggest that he did so care.

For almost thirty years Sterne was a country parson in Yorkshire, responsible for the spiritual enlightenment and comfort of congregations in Sutton-on-the-Forest, Stillington, and, after 1760, Coxwold. In addition, for twenty years he was a prebendary of York cathedral, a position which enabled him to preach in the great Minster twice a year. Until the publication of *Tristram Shandy* (1759–60), when he achieved instant fame and was lionized by the London *beau monde*, Sterne had known a quite unremarkable life, performing his clerical duties, it would seem, as best he knew how. A questionnaire sent out by Archbishop Herring to his clergy in 1743 brought this reply from Sterne:

VIII   Public Service is duely perform'd twice every Lord's Day.

IX   I Catechise every Sunday in my Church during Lent, But explain our Religion to the Children and Servants of my Parishioners in my own House every Sunday Night during Lent, from six o'clock till nine. I mention the Length of Time as my Reason for not doing it in Church.

---

[1] Nor was it only the preacher who borrowed in this manner. Poets, too, took similar liberties. In his *Preface to Eighteenth Century Poetry*, p. 134, J. R. Sutherland says: 'The eighteenth-century reader was well aware that some second-rate writers were mere plagiaries; but there was no widespread feeling against imitation, no tendency to point scornfully at some passage and say, "This is simply lifted from Dryden", or "He got that from the *Rape of the Lock*". On the contrary, so long as the poet passed Pope's test and repaid with something of his own, his imitations were counted as poetical assets.'

X The Sacrament is administered five Times every Year in my Church. There are about 250 Communicants above one Half of wch communicated last Easter.[1]

Canon S. L. Ollard, who along with P. C. Walker edited these visitation returns, says of Sterne's reply: 'In all the hundreds of returns which Mr. Walker and I have examined this is unique and stands alone. It shows that in 1743, whatever was the case later, Sterne took his work as a parish priest very seriously.'[2] This opinion is confirmed by Cross, who apparently knew nothing of Ollard's discovery, but who knew Sterne perhaps more intimately than any other scholar: 'Sterne could always be relied upon to perform with fidelity all ecclesiastical offices with which he was charged by his archbishop or by his dean and chapter. When absent from Sutton or Coxwold, he was careful to place over them capable curates, and to see to it that his surrogates made annual visitations to those other parishes lying within the jurisdiction of his commissaryships.'[3]

Ultimately, however, it is his sermons which furnish the best evidence of Sterne's faith and devotion; though this is hardly apparent at first sight. These laconic addresses appear to have little to recommend them as sermons; none of the usual laudatory epithets seem to apply; they have none of Butler's profundity of thought; none of Wesley's

[1] *Archbishop Herring's Visitation Returns* (1929), iii. 93.

[2] *TLS*, 18 March 1926, p. 217. Perhaps the truth about Sterne as priest lies somewhere between the picture of a diligent and dedicated pastor suggested by Archbishop Herring's returns and the 'crazy', 'crackbrained', and wholly indolent vicar described by John Croft in his 'Anecdotes of Sterne vulgarly Tristram Shandy', *The Whitefoord Papers*, ed. W. A. S. Hewins (1898), pp. 225–35. Croft's account can be challenged on the grounds that his evidence is largely based on gossip and his attitude to Sterne is hostile. Neither of these charges can be laid against Richard Greenwood, an old servant of Sterne's who told Joseph Hunter, a Yorkshire antiquarian and literary historian, in the early 1800s that Sterne 'did not attend well to the duties of his situation' where parish matters were concerned. See *PMLA*, lxxx (Dec. 1965), 549–53. Hunter's notes on Sterne were discovered in the British Museum by James M. Kuist of the University of Western Ontario, and published by him in *PMLA*. They are the most important Sterne find since the visitation returns of Archbishop Herring were published in 1929.

[3] *Life*, ii. 219.

fire; none of Swift's rapier thrust; none of Berkeley's
conviction. They are in fact what the critic of the *Monthly
Review* called them in his review article of May 1760—
'moral essays'.[1] Shorn of their texts there is little to distinguish
any of them from a *Spectator* essay. Yet they are more
than the moralistic mouthings of an apathetic parson who
had to fill up half an hour each week with a homily. To read
them all with an open mind is to conclude with Paul Stapfer
that

Sterne était bref et substantiel; mais il avait un mérite plus rare encore:
j'entends la *sincérité* de sa prédication. Il comprenait tout ce qu'il
prêchait, et il le croyait. Je ne dis point qu'il le pratiquât: ceci est une
tout autre affaire; mais il le croyait, et il le comprenait. Ce qu'on
appelle en anglais le *cant* et en français le *patois de Chanaan*, cet
inintelligible jargon composé de métaphores bibliques obscures et mal
traduites, ne vint jamais offusquer ni sa pensée ni sa diction.[2]

It was not Sterne's *métier* to expatiate on the profundities
of life, death, and salvation. Neither does he elect to defend
the honour of the Church from the salvoes of her detractors.
He is neither a philosopher nor a polemicist. The theme of
his preaching is played in a lower key. He speaks of trust,
the importance of keeping it, the tragedy of betrayal; he
speaks of conscience, its source of authority, the wisdom of
obedience to it; he speaks of love, not *agape*, but *philia* and
sometimes *eros*; he speaks of temptation, its subtle ploys and
how to guard against them:

In the lesser evils of life we seem to stand unguarded—and our peace
and contentment are overthrown, and our happiness broke in upon by a
little impatience of spirit, under the cross and untoward accidents we
meet with.—These stand unprovided for, and we neglect them as we
do the slighter indispositions of the body—which we think not worth
treating seriously—and so leave them to nature.[3]

[1] P. 425: 'If we consider them as moral Essays, they are, indeed, highly com-
mendable, and equally calculated for the entertainment and instruction of the
attentive Reader.'
[2] Op. cit., p. 104.
[3] *Sermons*, i. 177-8.

Above all, Sterne stresses the need for compassion in all human relationships. His postscript allusion to *A Sentimental Journey* in a letter to Mrs. James, 12 November 1767, could as aptly have been made to his sermons: 'I told you my design in it was to teach us to love the world and our fellow creatures better than we do—so it runs most upon those gentler passions and affections, which aid so much to it.'[1]

In theology, *per se*, Sterne had only a peripheral interest. There is almost a complete absence of doctrinal exposition in the *Sermons*; he is untroubled by the mystery and paradox which surround Christianity. He accepts the authority and teaching of the Church because it is the Church and because it has never occurred to him seriously to question it. The same is true of the Bible. At many points his interpretation of religion betrays the influence of Archbishop Tillotson, from whom he had borrowed so freely in his sermons. Nowhere is that influence better discerned than in Sterne's definition of the purpose of religion: 'the great end of all religion ... is to purify our hearts—and conquer our passions—and in a word, to make us wiser and better men—better neighbours—better citizens—and better servants to God.'[2]

In keeping with his Latitudinarian sentiments, Sterne rarely mentions the last two Persons of the Godhead. By contrast, God the Father looms large as 'a powerful, a wise and good being, who first made the world and continues to govern it;—by whose goodness all things are designed—and by whose providence all things are conducted to bring about the greatest and best ends'.[3] Though he is not unmindful of the fact that God is committed ultimately to mete out justice, he prefers to dwell on his divine love and mercy.

Sterne stresses the social and communal aspects of religion. Where the evangelicals exhorted men to get right

---

[1] *Letters*, p. 174.
[2] *Sermons*, i. 80.
[3] Ibid., i. 176.

with God, Yorick counselled them to get right with each other. Man, he believed, was a gregarious creature whose life and religion became meaningful as he found his place in society. God had placed in man such 'appetites and inclinations' as only 'society and friendship' can satisfy.

No one therefore who lives in society, can be said to live to himself,—he lives to his GOD,—to his king, and his country.—He lives to his family, to his friends, to all under his trust, and in a word he lives to the whole race of mankind: whatsoever has the character of man, and wears the same image of GOD that he does, is truly his brother, and has a just claim to his kindness.[1]

The theme 'it is not good for man to be alone' recurs time and again in the *Sermons*. In one of his best-known homilies, 'The Levite and His Concubine', Sterne mobilizes this sentiment to justify the fornicatory relationship which exists between the two principal characters: 'Nature will have her yearnings for society and friendship;—a good heart wants some object to be kind to—and the best parts of our blood, and the purest of our spirits suffer most under the destitution.'[2] Then follows one of the most lyrical passages in the whole of Sterne's writings:

Let the torpid Monk seek heaven comfortless and alone—GOD speed him! for my own part, I fear, I should never so find the way: let me be wise and religious—but let me be MAN: wherever thy Providence places me, or whatever be the road I take to get to thee—give me some companion in my journey, be it only to remark to, How our shadows lengthen as the sun goes down;—to whom I may say, How fresh is the face of nature! How sweet the flowers of the field! How delicious are these fruits![3]

---

[1] *Sermons*, i. 84.

[2] Ibid., i. 207.

[3] Ibid., i, 207–8. As W. B. C. Watkins and others have shown, Sterne dreaded loneliness and ennui. To guard against them he sought the company of men and women wherever he happened to be, from the Demoniac Society in Yorkshire to the drawing rooms of London and the salons of Paris. Perhaps even his much publicized flirtations can be best seen as his antidote against loneliness. Such an explanation would seem to find support in a very revealing letter sent by Sterne to John Woodhouse in May 1765: 'I am glad that you are in love—'twill cure you

To Sterne, the greatest enemies of a happy and harmonious society were prudery and intolerance. He hits out hard and often against those who, though ignorant of the facts, sit in judgement upon their fellow men. Perhaps it is because he himself has suffered at the hands of gossip-mongers that he condemns them so unequivocally: 'give but the outlines of a story,—let *spleen* and *prudery* snatch the pencil, and they will finish it with so many hard strokes, and with so dirty a colouring, that *candour* and *courtesy* will sit in torture as they look at it.'[1] And fiendishly subtle are the agents of spleen and prudery: 'How frequently is the honesty and integrity of a man, disposed of, by a smile or a shrug?—How many good and generous actions, have been sunk into oblivion, by a distrustful look,—or stampt with the imputation of proceeding from bad motives, by a mysterious and seasonable whisper?'[2] There is nothing either abstruse or impractical in Sterne's philosophy. He holds that whatever increases human happiness is right and whatever militates against it is wrong. 'If there is an evil in this world, 'tis sorrow and heaviness of heart.'[3] This explains Yorick's dislike of gravity in *Tristram Shandy*[4] and his faith in the efficacy of laughter:

If 'tis wrote against any thing,—'tis wrote, an' please your worships, against the spleen; in order, by a more frequent and a more convulsive elevation and depression of the diaphragm, and the succussations of the intercostal and abdominal muscles in laughter, to drive the *gall* and other *bitter juices* from the gall bladder, liver and sweetbread of his majesty's subjects, with all the inimicitious passions which belong to them, down into their duodenums.[5]

(at least) of the spleen, which has a bad effect on both man and woman—I myself must ever have some Dulcinea in my head—it harmonises the soul—and in those cases I first endeavour to make the lady believe so, or rather I begin first to make myself believe that I am in love—but I carry on my affairs quite in the French way, sentimentally—"l'amour" (say they) "*n'est rien sans sentiment*".' *Letters*, p. 108.

[1] *Sermons*, i. 205.
[2] Ibid., i. 132.
[3] Ibid., ii. 13.
[4] See vol. I, chap. 11.
[5] *Tristram Shandy*, vol. IV, chap. 22.

Sterne's desire to promote happiness stems from his faith in the fundamental goodness of men. His sermon, 'Vindication of Human Nature', is exactly what its title suggests. The preacher argues that since man is made in the image of God he has therefore partaken of the nature of the Divine and must be essentially good. Thus it is 'false' and 'pernicious' to conclude from the evil machinations of a few that the whole world is wicked:

I cannot help observing by the way, that there is scarce any thing which has done more disservice to social virtue, than the frequent representations of human nature, under this hideous picture of deformity, which by leaving out all that is generous and friendly in the heart of man, has sunk him below the level of a brute, as if he was a composition of all that was mean-spirited and selfish. Surely, 'tis one step towards acting well, to think worthily of our nature; and, as in common life, the way to make a man honest, is, to suppose him so, and treat him as such.[1]

'Sterne', Arthur H. Cash has justly observed, 'had no neurotic fear of sin. He was free of the Puritan's over-confident condemnation of others, and of the anguished self-doubt which drives the Puritan frantically through life. He was trustful of man's moral capacity and secure in an orderly universe ruled by a just God of reason. Consequently, Sterne glossed no faults, crusaded for no reforms.'[2]

His willingness to believe in the honesty and integrity of men injected into Sterne's sermons an optimism rarely found in a preacher. Again, it was Stapfer who was foremost among the few who noticed: 'L'idée qui est au fond de toute la prédication de Sterne, c'est un optimisme modéré, en vertu duquel il croit surtout au bien dans la nature humaine et dans le gouvernement du monde, sans nier pour cela le mal et le désordre.'[3] Sterne found nothing in Christian teaching which forbad pleasure and enjoyment. On the

[1] *Sermons*, i. 82.
[2] 'The Sermon in Tristram Shandy', *ELH*, vol. 31, no. 4 (4 December 1964), p. 417.
[3] Op. cit., p. 126.

contrary: 'When the affections so kindly break loose, Joy, is another name for Religion.'[1] Such a message was all the more salutary for coming at a time when a powerful evangelical movement was denouncing nearly all worldly pleasure as sinful.

Though it could hardly have differed more in its expression, Yorick's was as much a religion of the heart as was Wesley's. Certainly the founder of Methodism could not have faulted this sentiment in *Tristram Shandy*:

I have undergone such unspeakable torments, in bringing forth this sermon, quoth *Yorick*, upon this occasion—that I declare, *Didius*, I would suffer martyrdom—and if it was possible, my horse with me, a thousand times over, before I would sit down and make such another: I was delivered of it at the wrong end of me—it came from my head, instead of my heart—and it is for the pain it gave me, both in the writing and the preaching of it, that I revenge myself of it, in this manner.—To preach, to shew the extent of our reading, or the subtilties of our wit—to parade in the eyes of the vulgar, with the beggarly accounts of a little learning, tinselled over with a few words which glitter, but convey little light and less warmth—is a dishonest use of the poor single half hour in a week which is put into our hands—'Tis not preaching the gospel—but ourselves—For my own part, continued *Yorick*, I had rather direct five words point-blank to the heart.—[2]

It is not that Sterne is devoid of intellectual content in the *Sermons*, or that he pooh-poohs learning. He had read Locke with some discernment,[3] and though not aware of all the implications of Lockean thought, had assimilated enough to provide a respectable intellectual basis for his preaching. But in reality he was no more a philosopher than he was a theologian; at least, not in any academic sense. His appeal was to a sense of decency and fair play, not so much because it could be reasoned to be prudent (as Tillotson would have it), but because it could be felt to be true. He once described

---

[1] *Sermons*, i. 233.
[2] Vol. IV, chap. 26.
[3] See K. MacLean, *John Locke and English Literature of the Eighteenth Century* (1936).

his preaching as a 'theological flap upon the heart'.[1] No one has yet found a more apt image. His sermons are a gentle reminder that we are 'to love the world and our fellow-creatures better than we do'.

In his orthodoxy and his preoccupation with conduct Sterne as a preacher resembles Swift. But here the similarity ends. Swift's pessimism about, and indictment of, man and society contrast sharply with Sterne's 'optimisme modéré'. One has but to compare a sermon like 'Upon Sleeping in Church' with any of Sterne's discourses to observe the difference in the outlook of the two men. Even Swift's attempts at humour could have evoked little more than a nervous, intimidated smile from his congregation:

And there sat in a Window a certain young Man named Eutychus, *being fallen into a deep Sleep; and while* Paul *was long preaching, he sunk down with Sleep, and fell down from the third Loft, and was taken up dead.*

I HAVE chosen these Words with Design, if possible, to disturb some Part of this Audience of half an Hour's Sleep, for the Convenience and Exercise whereof this Place, at this Season of the Day, is very much celebrated.[2]

Sterne had little flair for satire, and still less inclination to indulge the kind of swingeing criticism which the Dean of St. Patrick's used so effectively. In 'The Levite and His Concubine' Sterne made clear his feelings on this score:

certainly there is a difference between *Bitterness* and *Saltness*,—that is, —between the malignity and the festivity of wit,—the one is a mere quickness of apprehension, void of humanity,—and is a talent of the devil; the other comes down from the Father of Spirits, so pure and abstracted from persons, that willingly it hurts no man; or if it touches upon an indecorum, 'tis with that dexterity of true genius, which enables him rather to give a new colour to the absurdity, and let it pass. —He may smile at the shape of the obelisk raised to another's fame,— but the malignant wit will level it at once with the ground, and build his own upon the ruins of it.—[3]

---

[1] *Letters*, ed. L. P. Curtis (1935), p. 134.
[2] *Irish Tracts and Sermons*, p. 210.
[3] *Sermons*, i. 214.

Thus where Swift vociferates, Sterne smiles benignly at the shortcomings of men. To condemn him for failing to undertake reformations is, as R. D. S. Putney suggests,[1] to miss the point. Sterne believed that man was not so much depraved as deprived, and that it was festivity of wit, not malignity, which was needed to spur humanity to nobler motives and service. Putney's words are as true of *The Sermons of Mr. Yorick* as of *Tristram Shandy*: 'The greatness of the novel and its abiding charm reside in Sterne's humor, that mixture of pathos and wit that sheds its warm glow over the representation of the frailties and foibles as well as the strength of man's nature, matters upon which Sterne was far better informed than most of his critics.'[2]

A century ago Paul Stapfer thought it necessary to issue a warning to those who set about examining Sterne's sermons: 'Quand on cite les sermons d'un original tel que Sterne, il est difficile de ne pas céder à la tentation de courir d'abord à ce qui est excentrique. Il serait beau et sage d'y résister.'[3] It would seem now, however, that the pendulum has swung slightly too far in the opposite direction, and what needs to be borne in mind is that any study of Sterne as preacher which ignores his eccentricity will prove truncated. For even in his demeanour and dress there was something which drew attention to him: 'he never could enter a village, but he caught the attention of both old and young.—Labour stood still as he pass'd,—the bucket hung suspended in the middle of the well,—the spinning-wheel forgot its round,—even chuck-farthing and shuffle-cap themselves stood gaping till he had got out of sight.'[4]

Apart from that delightful vignette, no more eloquent description of Sterne survives than the portrait of him by Sir Joshua Reynolds. In the portrait Sterne is seated, his

[1] 'Laurence Sterne, Apostle of Laughter', *Eighteenth Century English Literature*, ed. J. L. Clifford (1959), p. 280.
[2] Ibid.
[3] Op. cit., p. 114.
[4] *Tristram Shandy*, vol. I, chap. 10. There can be little doubt that the autobiographical content is high in that bizarre description of Parson Yorick.

elbow resting on a table, and his head propped up by his hand. His clerical dress is typical of the time—gown, bands, black knee-breeches, and powdered wig. The wig, slightly tilted to one side,[1] lends to the picture an air of sportive irony which seems perfectly in keeping with the character of its subject. The black, clerical robes hang about him in casual disarray. A wasted, consumptive look is evidence of his protracted fight with pulmonary tuberculosis. He has high cheek-bones, an expansive forehead, a gently protruding lower lip, and a nose that presides with unchallenged authority over the rest of his face. His mouth betrays a bemused smile, while dark, enigmatic eyes seem to dare the viewer to guess what Shandean intrigue the mind behind them is machinating.

Yet 'With all this sail, poor *Yorick* carried not one ounce of ballast'.[2] And as he mounted the pulpit on a Sunday morning his painfully gaunt figure (with 'two spider legs'), rebellious robes, and satyr-like face ('pale as a dishclout') must surely have prepared his congregation for the unusual sermon it was about to hear.[3]

On at least one count, however, the congregation could rest assured: the 'theological flap upon the heart' would be brief. Only Samuel Ogden among popular preachers of the age delivered shorter sermons.[4] The consumptive state of his lungs would hardly have permitted Sterne to preach out the hour glass as some of his colleagues were doing. But in

---

[1] According to Richard Greenwood, Sterne 'when [composing] would often pull down his [wig] over one eye, & remove it from side to side'. *PMLA*, lxxx, 550.

[2] *Tristram Shandy*, vol. I, chap. 11.

[3] It is worth noting that a later, more celebrated Sterne took greater pains with his dress. 'Five years of London and Paris made out of him a Chesterfield. He grew scrupulous, though not extravagant, in dress; and no man of the age was more at ease in society—more courteous and more urbane. On his first coming to London, Reynolds painted him most fittingly in the clerical gown which he wore as Vicar of Sutton. In Carmontelle and Gainsborough he appeared in the costume of an aristocrat. And yet Yorick, possessing good taste, never assumed the fashionable colors of the period, but chose instead the equally fashionable complete black, with conspicuous white lace ruffles, neat and dignified, becoming a man of his age and profession as well as a man of the world.' Cross, *Life*, ii. 65–6.

[4] See Hammond, pp. 100–1.

any case he had not the slightest desire to overwhelm his hearers with a torrent of words or a cascade of sound. While promising George Whateley that he would preach at the Foundling Hospital, he let drop some incidental remarks on his approach to homiletics:

On April the 5th, 1761, and sure as the day comes, and as sure as the Foundling Hospital stands, will I—(that is, in case I stand myself) discharge my conscience of my promise in giving you, not a half hour (not a poor half hour), for I never could preach so long without fatiguing both myself and my flock to death—but I will give you a short sermon, and *flap* you in my turn:—preaching (you must know) is a theological flap upon the heart, as the dunning for a promise is a political flap upon the memory:—both the one and the other is useless where men have *wit enough* to be honest.[1]

It is clear from this that for Sterne the pulpit is no longer the Mount Olympus it was for men like Donne and Taylor a century before. The preacher no longer stands six feet above contradiction; he is but a man speaking to men, cognizant of the limitations to both his person and his office. But however deficient in sublimity and mystery it may be, Sterne's preaching has a grace and humility worthy of its purpose. His short theological flap may lack oracular authority, but it is none the less sincere and effective.

With Sterne the sermon comes closer to passing over entirely into the field of literature than with any other preacher of the eighteenth century. He dispenses with practically all homiletic appurtenances; there is nothing to indicate an outline—no major headings, subdivisions, or Roman numerals; no repetitions, recapitulations, and nothing which even faintly resembles a peroration. Only the presence of a Biblical text distinguishes one of Sterne's sermons from a vigorous moral essay.

Sterne appears deliberately to disregard the conventions of sermon construction. His endings, for example, are so abrupt that the reader is left suspended. Examples are rife: here is one from 'Felix's Behaviour towards Paul':

[1] *Letters*, ed. Curtis, p. 134.

Religion which lays so many restraints upon us, is a troublesome companion to those who will lay no restraints upon themselves;—and for this reason there is nothing more common to be observed, than that the little arguments and cavils, which such men have gathered up against it, in the early part of their lives,—how considerable soever they may have appeared, when viewed through their passions and prejudices, which give an unnatural turn to all objects,—yet, when the edge of appetite has been worn down, and the heat of the pursuit pretty well over,—and reason and judgement have got possession of their empire—

—They seldom fail of bringing the lost sheep back to his fold.

May GOD bring us all there. Amen.[1]

Occasionally, Sterne feels the traditional homiletic conclusion is vapid and so he introduces a quasi-relevant digression to which he can give practical application. The sermon on the Prodigal Son affords the best example. Having got the Prodigal safely back home, the preacher abandons the traditional application of the story, feeling he has nothing to add to what has already been said and written: 'These uses have been so ably set forth, in so many good sermons upon the prodigal son, that I shall turn aside from them at present, and content myself with some reflections upon that fatal passion which led him,—and so many thousands after the example, *to gather all he had together, and take his journey into a far country*.'[2] Then, relying heavily upon Locke's *Essay Upon Education*, he is off on a consideration of the advantages of travel, and the necessity for parents to ensure that their sons make the Grand Tour with a competent escort, 'one who knows the world, not merely from books— but from his own experience:—a man who has been employed on such services, and thrice made the *tour of Europe, with success*'.[3] It may well be that it was in sermons such as this that Sterne first became aware of the possibilities latent in the technique of digression, a technique he uses so effectively in *Tristram Shandy*.

[1] *Sermons*, i. 225–6. See also ibid., i. 36; ii. 123; and ii. 166.
[2] Ibid., i. 234.
[3] Ibid., i. 236.

'I like the sermon well, replied my father,—'tis dramatic, —and there is something in that way of writing, when skilfully managed, which catches the attention.'[1] So Sterne, having placed himself ingeniously in the position of objective commentator on his own sermon, is able to suggest to his readers how they should regard his discourses. In presenting this sermon in *Tristram Shandy*, he took care to give it a dramatic setting. Chapter 17 of volume II is wholly taken up with a description of Trim's stance and posture for reading the sermon. In delivering it Trim is so caught up in the pathos of the scenes he describes that he is quite overcome by emotion and has to stop for a time. Walter Shandy's analytical mind cuts through to the crux of the matter and identifies the reason for the sermon's effectiveness: ''tis dramatic.' And Doctor Slop, whom one might suppose an expert on homiletic as well as obstetric matters, agrees: 'We preach much in that way with us.'[2]

Trim's performance is one indication of Sterne's interest in the relationship between preaching and acting. Another is found in a letter written by Sterne to his wife from Paris in March 1762. Throughout Lent of that year he had heard the sermons of one of Europe's most dynamic pulpit orators, Père Clement, preacher to the King of Poland. In his letter Sterne tries to express the secret of Clement's magnetic appeal:

I have been three mornings together to hear a celebrated pulpit orator near me, one Père Clement, who delights me much; the parish pays him 600 livres for a dozen sermons this Lent; he is K. Stanislas's preacher—most excellent indeed! his matter solid, and to the purpose; his manner, more than theatrical, and greater, both in his action and delivery, than Madame Clairon, who, you must know, is the Garrick of the stage here; he has infinite variety, and keeps up the attention by it wonderfully; his pulpit, oblong, with three seats in it, into which he occasionally casts himself; goes on, then rises, by a gradation of four steps, each of which he profits by, as his discourse inclines him: in

[1] *Tristram Shandy*, vol. II, chap. 17.
[2] Ibid.

short, 'tis a stage, and the variety of his tones would make you imagine there were no less than five or six actors on it together.[1]

Sterne was able to identify Clement's technique because he himself had attempted to employ it in his own sermons. 'His best sermons', said Cross, 'are embryonic dramas, in which an effort is made to visualize scene and character, as though he were writing for the stage.'[2] In one of his best, 'The Levite and His Concubine', he effects a gripping beginning by creating an imaginary figure, solely by pro- sopopoeia, and then engaging him in dialogue. A master of the art of contrast, Sterne exploits the difference in moral outlook between his two speakers to maximum effect:

And it came to pass in those days, when there was no king in Israel, that there was a certain Levite sojourning on the side of mount Ephraim, who took unto him a concubine.

Enter the moralist:
    A CONCUBINE!
Yorick is quick to the defence; he pleads extenuating circumstance:

—but the text accounts for it, *for in those days there was no king in Israel*, and the Levite, you will say, like every other man in it, did what was right in his own eyes,—and so, you may add, did his concu- bine too—*for she played the whore against him, and went away.*—

The moralist will not be placated by this sort of casuistry. In measured, falsetto tones he pronounces his sentence:

—Then shame and grief go with her, and wherever she seeks a shelter, may the hand of justice shut the door against her.—

But it is mercy, not justice, which greets her on her return to Bethlehem. Yorick rejoices over her good fortune. Once again the prosopopoeia is successful:

Not so; for she went unto her father's house in Bethlehem-judah, and was with him four whole months.—Blessed interval for meditation

---

[1] *Letters*, ed. Curtis, pp. 154–5.
[2] *Life*, i. 226.

upon the fickleness and vanity of this world and it's pleasures! I see the holy man upon his knees,—with hands compressed to his bosom, and with uplifted eyes, thanking heaven, that the object which had so long shared his affections, was fled.—[1]

This is a typical beginning. The preacher grips his congregation by stating a proposition which appears to conflict with some accepted social convention or scriptural truth. All is reconciled in the end. But by the time the congregation realizes that it has been taken in by a clever rhetorical trick, and the preacher is not really at odds with scripture, Sterne has achieved what he set out to do.

'*It is better to go to the house of mourning, than to the house of feasting.*' Thus speaks the lugubrious author of Ecclesiastes. An incensed Yorick will hear nothing of it: 'THAT I deny— but let us hear the wise man's reasoning upon it—*for that* is *the end of all men, and the living* will *lay it to* his *heart: sorrow is better than laughter*—for a crack'd-brain'd order of Carthusian monks, I grant, but not for men of the world.' A shocked audience waits for the preacher to recant this heresy, but he goes on with irresistible logic:

For what purpose, do you imagine, has GOD made us? for the social sweets of the well-watered vallies where he has planted us, or for the dry and dismal deserts of a *Sierra Morena*? are the sad accidents of life, and the uncheery hours which perpetually overtake us, are they not enough, but we must sally forth in quest of them,—belye our own hearts, and say, as your text would have us, that they are better than those of joy? did the Best of Beings send us into the world for this end —to go weeping through it,—to vex and shorten a life short and vexatious enough already?[2]

Of course the recantation comes; Sterne would no more challenge the final authority of the Bible than would Wesley. But it is a subtle and clever recantation, and the audience is scarcely aware it has happened. The houses of mourning and feasting, and the scenes they conjure up, are juxtaposed. In the end the congregation is persuaded to choose the house

[1] *Sermons*, i. 204.
[2] Ibid., i. 14.

of mourning, not because sorrow, *per se*, is better than
jollity, but because the lessons it teaches are more valuable.

This same technique of thesis, antithesis, and synthesis is
employed in 'Vindication of Human Nature'. Here is the
arresting beginning:

For none of us liveth to himself.
. . . No man liveth to himself! Why?—Does any man live to any thing
else?—In the whole compass of human life can a prudent man steer
to a safer point?—Not live to himself!—To whom then?—Can any
interests or concerns which are foreign to a man's self have such a
claim over him, that he must serve under them,—suspend his own
pursuits,—step out of his right course, till others have passed by him,
and attained the several ends and purposes of living before him?[1]

And again in Yorick's favourite sermon, 'The Abuses of
Conscience Considered': '*For we trust we have a good
Conscience.* TRUST!—Trust we have a good Conscience!—
Surely, you will say, if there is any thing in this life which a
man may depend upon, and to the knowledge of which he
is capable of arriving upon the most indisputable evidence,
it must be this very thing,—Whether he has a good Conscience, or no.'[2] Having engaged his listeners' interest,
Sterne has no intention of allowing it to flag, even if it
means omitting or altering part of the Biblical narrative. In
'The Levite and His Concubine', for example, he ignores
the horrible catastrophe which befell the Concubine (Judges,
xix, 22–30). With the Levite, his Concubine, and her father
reconciled, the preacher takes his leave of the story: 'It
serves no purpose to pursue the story further; the catastrophe is horrid; and would lead us beyond the particular
purpose for which I have enlarged upon thus much of it,—
and that is, to discredit rash judgement, and illustrate from
the manner of conducting this drama, the courtesy which
the *dramatis personae* of every other piece, may have a right
to.'[3]

[1] *Sermons*, i. 81.
[2] Ibid., ii. 67.
[3] Ibid., i. 211.

With the story of Shimei ('The Character of Shimei') Sterne takes a much greater liberty, ascribing to Shimei motives for his dissimulatory behaviour towards David which the scriptural account will not support. When David had fled in danger of his life before his rebellious son, Absalom, Shimei heaped derision on the old king. Later, when a triumphant David returned to claim his throne, Shimei rushed out to greet and acclaim him. A long-standing blood-feud between Shimei's people, the Benjamites, and the House of Israel explains why he taunted and insulted David, while a natural fear for his life would seem responsible for his volte-face. Sensing that blood-feuds and their ramifications might lack interest and relevance for a sophisticated eighteenth-century audience, Sterne modified the story to make Shimei appear an unprincipled fortune-hunter.

O Shimei! would to heaven when thou wast slain, that all thy family had been slain with thee; and not one of thy resemblance left! but ye have multiplied exceedingly and replenished the earth; and if I prophesy rightly—Ye will in the end *subdue* it.

There is not a character in the world which has so bad an influence upon the affairs of it, as this of Shimei: whilst power meets with honest checks, and the evils of life with honest refuge, the world will never be undone: but thou, Shimei, hast sapp'd it at both extremes; for thou corruptest prosperity—and 'tis thou who has broken the heart of poverty: and so long as worthless spirits can be ambitious ones, 'tis a character we shall never want. O! it infests the court—the camp—the cabinet—it infests the church—go where you will—in every quarter, in every profession, you see a Shimei following the wheels of the fortunate through thick mire and clay.—[1]

The exegete might protest against this deliberate misconstruction of scripture. But, as H. D. Traill suggests, 'it makes a more piquant and dramatic picture to represent Shimei as a type of the wretch of insolence and servility compact, with a tongue ever ready to be loosed against the unfortunate, and a knee ever ready to be bent to the strong'.[2]

[1] *Sermons*, i. 186–7.
[2] *Sterne*, p. 98.

As a creator of 'piquant and dramatic' pictures Sterne has few rivals in either literature or homiletics. During those long years as a country parson, cut off from many of the cultural and intellectual enjoyments of his age, and as yet unaware of the great talent lying dormant within him, Sterne had found much satisfaction in painting. His familiarity with the technical terminology of this art is exhibited in *Tristram Shandy*.[1] In *The Sermons* he calls upon his knowledge of the technique of picture composition to construct vivid and poignant scenes. His treatment of the Prodigal Son's departure affords a good illustration:

I see the picture of his departure:—the camels and asses loaden with his substance, detached on one side of the piece, and already on their way:—the prodigal son standing on the foreground, with a forced sedateness, struggling against the fluttering movement of joy, upon his deliverance from restraint:—the elder brother holding his hand, as if unwilling to let it go:—the father,—sad moment! with a firm look, covering a prophetic sentiment, 'that all would not go well with his child,'—approaching to embrace him, and bid him adieu.[2]

Once again it is an exploitation of contrast which gives the picture its dramatic impact. Equally arresting is a scene in 'Elijah and the Widow of Zarephath'. To show his own gratitude, as well as the power of God, to the widow who has befriended him, Elijah miraculously restores her dead child to life.

It would be a pleasure to a good mind to stop here a moment, and figure to itself the picture of so joyful an event.—To behold on one hand the raptures of the parent, overcome with surprise and gratitude, and imagine how a sudden stroke of such impetuous joy must operate on a despairing countenance, long accustomed to sadness.—To conceive on the other side of the *piece*, the holy man approaching with the child in his arms—full of honest triumph in his looks, but sweetened with all the kind sympathy which a gentle nature could overflow with upon so happy an event. It is a subject one might recommend to the pencil of a great genius.[3]

[1] See Cross, *Life*, i. 105 ff.
[2] *Sermons*, i. 228.
[3] Ibid., i. 59–60.

Sterne's genius for inventing and delineating character has never been in serious doubt. English literature can boast few characters more real or endearing than Uncle Toby, Walter Shandy, and Corporal Trim. For his sermons, however, the *dramatis personae* are provided by scripture, and even Sterne could not alter radically their patterns of behaviour. What he can do, and does, is to speculate on the psychological motivation of some course of action. While retelling the parable of the Good Samaritan, for example, he gives the central character a third dimension by imputing to him a stream of consciousness as he beholds the helpless wretch lying in a ditch:

Good GOD! what a spectacle of misery do I behold—a man stripped of his raiment—wounded—lying languishing before me upon the ground just ready to expire,—without the comfort of a friend to support him in his last agonies, or the prospect of a hand to close his eyes when his pains are over. But perhaps my concerns should lessen when I reflect on the relations in which we stand to each other—that he is a Jew and I a Samaritan.—But are we not still both men; partakers of the same nature—and subject to the same evils?—let me change conditions with him for a moment and consider, had his lot befallen me as I journeyed in the way, what measure I should have expected at his hand.—Should I wish when he beheld me wounded and half-dead, that he should shut up his bowels of compassion from me, and double the weight of my miseries by passing by and leaving them unpitied?—But I am a stranger to the man;—be it so,—but I am no stranger to his condition—misfortunes are of no particular tribe or nation, but belong to us all, and have a general claim upon us, without distinction of climate, country or religion. Besides, though I am a stranger—'tis no fault of his that I do not know him, and therefore unequitable he should suffer by it:—Had I known him, possibly I should have had cause to love and pity him the more—for aught I know, he is some one of uncommon merit, whose life is rendered still more precious, as the lives and happiness of others may be involved in it: perhaps at this instant that he lies here forsaken, in all this misery, a whole virtuous family is joyfully looking for his return, and affectionately counting the hours of his delay. Oh! did they know what evil hath befallen him—how would they fly to succour him.— Let me then hasten to supply those tender offices of binding up his wounds, and carrying him to a place of safety—or if that assistance comes too late, I shall comfort him at least in his last hour—and, if I can do nothing else,—I shall soften his misfortunes by dropping a tear of pity over them.[1]

Thus it is that a new window of interest is opened on a parable whose very familiarity is often the greatest impediment to its purpose.

Sterne shows similar ingenuity in attempting to resuscitate interest in a rather unattractive Biblical figure, Herod. In depicting Herod's character, Sterne is first of all forced to abandon scripture, since 'in general it furnishes us with few materials for such descriptions',[2] and to draw heavily on the ancient Jewish historian, Josephus. Then, to explain the contradictions of Herod's personality, he employs an over-simplified version of a Lockean psychological concept, that of the ruling passion. His conclusion is that 'the character of Herod, as complicated as it is given us in history—when thus analysed, is summed up in three words —*That he was a man of unbounded ambition, who stuck at nothing to gratify it*'.[3] It may be, as Kenneth MacLean observes of Sterne, 'unworthy of his fine philosophical training and close acquaintance with Locke's *Essay*' to say that 'Herod would have been a good man were he not an almost innocent victim of his ruling passion for power',[4] since 'Locke asserts man's freedom to suspend his actions until his desires are elevated'.[5] But such criticism is largely beside the point. What mattered most to Sterne was not whether his sermons were consistent in their thesis with this or that school of philosophical thought, but whether they, and the scenes and characters they figured forth, gripped the interest and touched the hearts of his audience. Once more Stapfer must be allowed the final word: 'il

[1] *Sermons*, i. 33–4.
[2] Ibid., i. 105.
[3] Ibid., i. 110.
[4] *John Locke*, p. 48.
[5] Ibid., p. 47.

possédait à un haut degré . . . la finesse psychologique; le pouvoir de créer des caractères, de combiner des situations; le talent de peindre et de faire parler des personnages, des sentiments nobles, touchants ou ridicules; le pathétique, la couleur, le naturel, la vérité, le style.'[1]

John Traugott argues that Sterne, in the tradition of Erasmus, Rabelais, and Swift, is a facetious rhetorician, indulging his ingenious fancy and manipulating dialectical devices to ensnare the reader and force him to examine his motives for behaviour. This technique, Traugott contends, though it is perfected in *Tristram Shandy*, has its 'holy beginnings' in the sermons.[2] It was as a preacher that Sterne became aware of the power of rhetoric to delight or disturb an audience. Nor is Traugott the first to make such an observation. Here is what the poet Gray had to say about Sterne's discourses in a letter to Thomas Wharton, dated June 1760: 'have you read his sermons (with his own comic figure at the head of them)? they are in the style I think most proper for the Pulpit, & shew a very strong imagination & a sensible heart: but you see him often tottering on the verge of laughter & ready to throw his perriwig in the face of his audience.'[3] Gray's opinion, though perhaps slightly overstated, is perceptive enough. Sterne, as has already been shown, was constantly exploiting his hearers' emotions, first offending their moral sensibilities by a seemingly blasphemous statement, then, by means of some adroit dialectical footwork, eluding blame himself while leaving his congregation to puzzle the reason for its outrage.[4]

---

[1] Op. cit., pp. 103–4.

[2] *Tristram Shandy's World* (1954), p. 98.

[3] *Correspondence of Thomas Gray*, eds. P. Toynbee and L. Whibley (1935), ii. 681.

[4] If this device needs further illustration, it is furnished by an article first published in *The Gentleman's Magazine*, lxiv. 406–7, and signed 'Eboracensis'. Having noted Sterne's habit of beginning a sermon with 'some jest . . . which, at first sight, should seem blasphemy, impiety, or madness' but which was followed invariably by 'an explanation which terminated in a miserable insipidity', the author illustrates his point by reference to a sermon which has not survived. 'Preaching one day on the mystery of the Trinity, he began with the period, "*I deny that there is in God, Unity of Essence, and Trinity of Persons*"; and there he

Nor is it just in their unusual beginnings that Sterne exploits rhetoric in the sermons. He can, when he desires, run the gamut of rhetorical devices in a single sermon, and all the while, one feels, he is studying their effects upon his audience. A relatively short passage from a little-known sermon, 'Hezekiah and His Messengers', will serve to demonstrate this point. The preacher is harping on a favourite theme—the duplicity and hypocrisy of which men are guilty by refusing to own to the world the real motives for their actions. Suddenly, sensing perhaps that interest is beginning to lag, he pulls out all the rhetorical stops.

VANITY bids all her sons to be generous and brave,—and her daughters to be chaste and courteous.—But why do we want her instructions?— Ask the comedian who is taught a part he feels not—

Is it that the principles of religion want strength, or that the real passion for what is good and worthy will not carry us high enough?— GOD! thou knowest they carry us too high—we want not *to be*—but *to seem*—

Look out of your door,—take notice of that man: see what disquieting, intriguing and shifting, he is content to go through, merely to be thought a man of plain dealing:—three grains of honesty would save him all this trouble:—alas! he has them not.—

Behold a second, under a shew of piety hiding the impurities of a debauched life:—he is just entering the house of GOD:—would he was more pure—or less pious:—but then he could not gain his point.

Observe a third going on almost in the same track,—with what an inflexible sanctity of deportment, he sustains himself as he advances:— every line in his face writes abstinence;—every stride looks like a check upon his desires: see, I beseech you, how he is cloak'd up with sermons, prayers and sacraments; and so bemuffled with the externals

stopped. The hearers began to look at one another as if scandalized, or at least suspended, waiting for the issue of that blasphemous heresy; and, when our preacher thought that he had caught them, he proceeded with the poorness of adding "Thus says the Arian, the Manichean, the Socinian; but I shall prove it against them by Scripture, by Councils, by Fathers." ' While no other evidence of this sermon survives, it is sufficiently like some other of Sterne's sermons to have the ring of authenticity.

of religion, that he has not a hand to spare for a worldly purpose;—he has armour at least—Why does he put it on? Is there no serving GOD without all this? Must the garb of religion be extended so wide to the danger of it's rending?—Yes truly, or it will not hide the secret—and, What is that?

—That the saint has no religion at all.

—But here comes GENEROSITY; giving—not to a decayed artist—but to the arts and sciences themselves.—See,—he *builds not a chamber in the wall apart for the prophet*; but whole schools and colleges for those who come after. LORD! how they will magnify his name!—'tis in capitals already; the first—the highest, in the guilded rent-roll of every hospital and asylum—

—One honest tear shed in private over the unfortunate, is worth it all.

What a problematic set of creatures does simulation make us! Who would divine that all that anxiety and concern so visible in the airs of one half of the great assembly should arise from nothing else, but that the other half of it may think them to be men of consequence, penetration, parts and conduct?—What a noise amongst the claimants about it? Behold *Humility*, out of mere pride,—and honesty almost out of knavery:—*Chastity*, never once in harm's way,—and courage, like a Spanish soldier upon an Italian stage—a bladder full of wind.—

—Hark! that, the sound of that trumpet,—let not my soldier run,—'tis some good Christian giving alms. O, PITY, thou gentlest of human passions! soft and tender are thy notes, and ill accord they with so loud an instrument.[1]

Personification, interrogation, aposiopesis, erotesis, apostrophe, antithesis, asyndeton, irony, humour: they are all here. Climax is reached by a clever alternation between command, exclamation, statement, and appeal. Throughout, the Shandean dash assists timing and emphasis, and, where necessary, creates a staccato effect to indicate the preacher's emotional strain.

Biographers of Sterne, while recognizing the wealth of dramatic potential in his sermons, have hesitated to make

[1] *Sermons*, i. 198–200.

claims for him as an orator, and in fact have generally assumed that his talent was solely literary. This, one suspects, is due mainly to the tendentious, but difficult to disprove, remark by John Croft that 'When it was Sterne's turn to preach at the Minster half of the Congregation usually went out of Church as soon as he mounted the Pulpit, as his Delivery and Voice were so very disagreeable.'[1] Other facts about Sterne's preaching, however, known all along, have not squared with Croft's account. For example, could a man so unaffecting in the pulpit as Croft suggests have made such a stirring appeal on behalf of the charity schools of York in 1747 as to bring in a collection of sixty-four pounds?[2] Or could a man whose voice and delivery were altogether disagreeable delight a highly literate, not to say sceptical, audience with a sermon at the British embassy in Paris in 1764?[3] With the publication in 1965 of Joseph Hunter's notes on Sterne, new and more explicit evidence came to light which contradicts Croft and confirms what many scholars have long believed, that Sterne was an affecting and effective preacher. Richard Greenwood told Hunter that,

when he preached, the audience were quite delighted with him, & he never preached at Sutton but half the [congregation] were in tears— The Minster was crowded whenever it was known that he was to preach—he used often to preach nearly extempore. He had engaged to preach at [Farlington] a few miles from Sutton, & when there found he had forgot his sermon—he only [asked] for a bible, & composed a most excellent sermon which he delivered from a scrap of paper no bigger than his hand.[4]

Nor did he restrict his oratorical talents to the pulpit. 'Sterne', Greenwood goes on, 'was a Justice of peace & would often espouse a cause which he was [sure] of bringing thro' at the Quarter Sessions, he could talk down the Lawyer

[1] *Whitefoord Papers*, p. 231.
[2] See Cross's *Life*, i. 82.
[3] See ibid., ii. 32–3.
[4] *PMLA*, lxxx. 549–50.

so—this he delighted in.'[1] Admittedly, Greenwood was seventy-nine years old when Hunter interviewed him, and he was speaking of events which had taken place a half century or more before. Nevertheless, his account is lucid and based on first-hand knowledge of Sterne and his congregations. It seems all the more authentic because it corroborates the internal evidence of the sermons themselves.

There is a danger, however, in seeking to explain Sterne's art in terms of rhetoric, the danger that the subtle genius— that 'impalpable energy which defies analysis'[2]—of his style will be missed. And there is a unity of style in Sterne's writings which makes this danger equally as real to the *Sermons* as to his two great works of fiction. Perhaps his own views on eloquence, set forth in a sermon,[3] provide as fine a clue as any to a better appreciation of his unique prose style.

There are two sorts of eloquence, the one indeed scarce deserves the name of it, which consists chiefly in laboured and polished periods, an over-curious and artificial arrangement of figures, tinsel'd over with a gaudy embellishment of words, which glitter, but convey little or no light to the understanding. This kind of writing is for the most part much affected and admired by people of weak judgement and vitious taste, but is a piece of affectation and formality the sacred writers are utter strangers to.—It is a vain and boyish eloquence; and as it has always been esteemed below the great geniuses of all ages, so much more so, with respect to those writers who were acted by the spirit of infinite wisdom, and therefore wrote with that force and majesty with which never man writ.—The other sort of eloquence is quite the reverse to this, and which may be said to be the true characteristic of the holy Scriptures; where the excellence does not arise from a laboured and far-fetched elocution, but from a surprising mixture of simplicity and majesty, which is a double character, so difficult to be united, that it is seldom to be met with in compositions merely human.[4]

[1] *PMLA*, lxxx. 550.
[2] Read, *Sense of Glory*, p. 147.
[3] *Sermons*, ii. 226 ff., 'Search the Scriptures'. Newman paid this sermon the compliment of quoting from it at length in section 2 of the lecture 'Literature' in *Lectures and Essays on University Subjects*.
[4] Ibid., ii. 229.

'A surprising mixture of simplicity and majesty' is an apt description of Sterne's own style. For while it can boast simplicity of vocabulary and design, it has an elegance and grace of movement which can well be described as majestic.

In *The Sermons*, as elsewhere, Sterne is personal in pitch and informal. He takes the reader into his confidence and offers him counsel. This intimate author-reader (or parson-parishioner, as it initially was) relationship suited Sterne's temperament well, for among other things he was one of literature's greatest gossips. 'Writing', he says, 'when properly managed, (as you may be sure I think mine is), is but a different name for conversation.'[1]

Like all preachers, Sterne aimed at persuasion. Only rarely, however, does he attempt to overpower his audiences with the cumulative force of rhetoric. He tries rather to engage their passions with the subtlety and beauty of language. And there is in his language an enchantment which is irresistible. His prose moves with perfect poise and ease, relying not on ornament but on the intrinsic music the words create in concert with each other.

No writing seems to flow more exactly into the very folds and creases of the individual mind, to express its changing moods, to answer its lightest whims and impulse, and yet the result is perfectly precise and composed. The utmost fluidity exists with the utmost permanence. It is as if the tide raced over the beach hither and thither and left every ripple and eddy cut on the sand in marble.[2]

Only occasionally does he succumb to the temptation to luxuriate in his descriptions. One such passage, however, is worth citing since Sterne alone among eighteenth-century preachers has the ability and daring to include it in a sermon.

It was the case of the prodigal—he arose to go unto his father.—

—Alas! How shall he tell his story? Ye who have trod this round, tell me in what words he shall give in to his father, the sad *Items* of his extravagance and folly?

[1] *Tristram Shandy*, vol. II, chap. 11.
[2] Virginia Woolf, Introduction to *Sentimental Journey* (1928), p. viii.

—The feasts, and banquets which he gave to whole cities in the east, —the costs of the Asiatick rarities,—and of Asiatick cooks to dress them—the expenses of singing men and singing women,—the flute, the harp, the sackbut, and of all kinds of musick—the dress of the Persian courts, how magnificent! their slaves how numerous!—their chariots, their horses, their palaces, their furniture, what immense sums they had devoured!—what expectations from strangers of condition! what exactions!

How shall the youth make his father comprehend, that he was cheated at Damascus by one of the best men in the world;—that he had lent a part of his substance to a friend at Nineveh, who had fled off with it to the Ganges;—that a whore of Babylon had swallowed his best pearl, and anointed the whole city with his balm of Gilead;—that he had been sold by a man of honour for twenty shekels of silver, to a worker in graven images;—that the images he had purchased had profited him nothing;—that they could not be transported across the wilderness, and had been burnt with fire at Shusan;—that the apes and peacocks, which he had sent for from Tharsis, lay dead upon his hands; and that the mummies had not been dead along [*sic*] enough, which had been brought him out of Egypt:—that all had gone wrong since the day he forsook his father's house.

—Leave the story—it will be told more concisely.—*When he was yet afar off, his father saw him,*—Compassion told it in three words—*he fell upon his neck and kissed him.*[1]

Though this is not altogether typical of Sterne, it is indicative of the imaginative daring with which he approached homiletics, and of his refusal to be hamstrung by the conventions of religious prose. Perhaps there exists no more revealing statement of his approach to preaching than that found at the beginning of 'The Prodigal Son'.

I KNOW not whether the remark is to our honour or otherwise, that lessons of wisdom have never such power over us, as when they are wrought into the heart, through the groundwork of a story which engages the passions: Is it that we are like iron, and must first be heated before we can be wrought upon? or, Is the heart so in love with

[1] *Sermons*, i. 230–1.

deceit, that where a true report will not reach it, we must cheat it with a fable, in order to come at truth?[1]

The sermons themselves provide an affirmative answer to these questions. Yorick is forever engaging men's passions by imagining dialogue, depicting character, painting verbal portraits, dramatizing scenes, employing rhetoric, manipulating words, and telling stories. 'When the heart flies out before the understanding, it saves the judgement a world of pains.'[2] The transition from sacred to secular literature necessitated little change in Sterne's technique.

Strictly speaking, Sterne is typical of nothing except genius. Yet in his refusal to be fettered by the religious and literary conventions of the past, he embodies a spirit that gained in strength as the eighteenth century progressed. This was the age in which the traditional hierarchy of literary *genres* was finally overthrown, and the epic poem was superseded by the novel. In homiletics this spirit was manifested in an attempt to rid the form of the sermon of the last vestigial influence of classical oratory. This effort, begun with Archbishop Tillotson and supported by most eighteenth-century preachers, found its extremest expression in Sterne's theological flap.

[1] *Sermons*, i. 227.
[2] *Sentimental Journey*, Shakespeare Head ed. (1927), p. 17.

GEORGE WHITEFIELD
From a portrait by J. Wollaston in the National Portrait Gallery, London.

VI

GEORGE WHITEFIELD
(1714–1770)

Enthusiasm Resurgent

GEORGE WHITEFIELD was the most controversial preacher
of the eighteenth century, and perhaps the greatest extemporaneous orator in the history of the English church. He
was variously regarded by his contemporaries as saint or
demon; as an apostle sent from God to arouse men from the
somnolence of Augustan religion, or as an embarrassment
to the true and temperate spirit of Christianity; as a man of
faith and altruism, or as a grandiose impostor who revelled
in his personal fame and grew rich by his 'humanitarian'
enterprises. Passionately loved, passionately hated, Whitefield was never ignored. The man he was, like the gospel he
preached, forced men to make a decision.

Unlike his fellow Methodist, John Wesley, Whitefield
did not organize his converts into societies; his own people,
he was forced finally to admit, were 'a rope of sand'.[1] Yet
it would be difficult to exaggerate the importance of his
preaching and personality upon the church and society of
his day. His meteoric rise to fame[2] has hardly any precedent
in the history of English pulpit oratory. His influence

[1] Quoted by W. B. Brash, *Methodism* (1928), p. 54.
[2] See J. Gillies, *Memoirs of the Life of the Reverend George Whitefield* (1772), pp.
14–16.

extended into every part of the British Isles and across the sea to America. Thousands flocked to hear him wherever he preached, and few came away from his services unaffected. With absolute faith in the primacy of preaching, he never missed an opportunity to give a sermon.[1] He preached from pulpits, balconies, windows, staircases, mountebank stands, coffins of executed criminals, on street corners, in church yards, and in open fields. And always there was an urgency in what he had to say; an urgency none the less sincere for being dramatically expressed.

He placed all store by a religion of the heart, a religion that could be felt. His emergence as a popular preacher signified the end of an era of reasoned restraint in religious experience. His impassioned oratory, and the paroxysms it engendered, seemed to many to mark a revival of that bugbear of Augustan England—enthusiasm.

Whitefield's success as a preacher and his contribution to English oratorical prose can only be understood in the light of his religious belief. Since he made no attempt to formulate a systematic theology, his sermons provide the most explicit statement of what he actually believed.

Like many other great preachers, he was not noted for his theological acumen. His strenuous preaching schedule left little time for study of any kind. Not that he believed there was much profit to be gained from study. He held learning suspect and frequently denounced those ministers who were more concerned to become scholars than saints. His own theological concepts were few and remarkably ingenuous. At times, too, he was inconsistent, being influenced more by the exigencies of the moment than by a hard and fast theology.

Because he gave so little time to study and preparation,

[1] Of the 18,000 sermons Whitefield is estimated to have preached during his 35-year ministry, only 78 were published. By 1772, the date of Gillies's *Works of Whitefield*, 28 collected editions of his sermons had been published, 23 in the U.K. and 5 in America. Collected editions continued to appear to the end of the eighteenth century and beyond. The first complete collection of his sermons was published in 1812, and by 1864 had gone through nine editions.

there is an inevitable sameness about his sermons. Almost any discourse embodies his fundamental beliefs about Christianity. The theme of his preaching is that of evangelicals in every age: in his natural state man is estranged from God; Jesus Christ, by his death and Atonement, has paid the price of that estrangement and made reconciliation with God possible; to achieve salvation man, with the guidance and the grace of the Holy Ghost, must repudiate sin and openly identify himself with Christ. To Whitefield religion, when properly understood, meant 'a thorough, real, inward change of nature, wrought in us by the powerful operations of the Holy Ghost, conveyed to and nourished in our hearts, by a constant use of all the means of grace, evidenced by a good life, and bringing forth the fruits of the spirit'.[1] There was, of course, nothing new in this belief. Its special appeal for eighteenth-century audiences lay partly in the fact that it answered an emotional need the established Church had for too long tried to ignore, and partly in the charismatic personality of the man who revived it.

Both in his own time and since, Whitefield has been regarded as a Calvinist. Yet, though he professed to believe in the doctrine of 'election', he once confessed to John Wesley: 'I never read any thing that *Calvin* wrote; my doctrines I had from CHRIST and his apostles; I was taught them of GOD.'[2] And if he was not conversant with the tenets of Calvinistic theology, neither can he be said to have shared Calvin's propensity for a systematic presentation of thought.

But, whatever its origins, the doctrine of election looms large in Whitefield's preaching. As mankind's 'federal head', Adam, by his disobedience and subsequent expulsion from the garden of delights, had brought all succeeding generations of humanity under the law of sin and death. For Whitefield the evidence of original sin, 'that original

[1] *Works*, ed. J. Gillies (1771–2), v. 161.
[2] Ibid., i. 205.

corruption each of us brings into the world', was all too apparent. The disobedience of little children; the moral dereliction of society; the widespread neglect of religion were all manifestations of this same innate corruption. Even in nature its ramifications could be seen: 'An unhappy mutiny and disorder then fell upon this world; those briars and thorns which now spring up and overspread the earth, were but poor emblems, lifeless representations of that confusion and rebellion which sprung up in, and over-whelmed, the soul of man, immediately after the fall. He now sunk into the temper of a beast and devil.'[1]

God, however, is merciful as well as just, and though he might have damned all Adam's posterity to hell, he elected to save some. Those he chose arbitrarily and without their having done anything to deserve so great a preferment. 'I frankly acknowledge, I believe the doctrine of reprobation, in this view, that GOD intends to give saving grace, through JESUS CHRIST, only to a certain number, and that the rest of mankind, after the fall of *Adam*, being justly left to GOD to continue in sin, will at last suffer that eternal death, which is its proper wages.'[2] To Whitefield it was imperative for a man to recognize that he could do nothing to save himself, that no amount of pleading or good works could avail. All was dependent upon God: 'and remember, you have not chosen CHRIST, but CHRIST hath chosen you.'[3]

Yet, if he was opposed in principle to free grace, it was not always apparent from his practice. His sermons invariably concluded with a protracted invitation to sinners to come to Christ for salvation, an invitation that is entirely democratic and unqualified. Moreover, he acknowledges that there is something left for man to do, that he is not altogether passive in the process of salvation.

O my dear brethren, be found in the ways of GOD; let us not disturb our dear Redeemer by any irregular proceedings; and let me beseech

---

[1] *Works*, vi. 292.
[2] Ibid., iv. 58.
[3] Ibid., vi. 502.

you to strive to love, fear, honour and obey him, more than ever you have done yet; let not the devil engross your time, and that dear Saviour who came into the world on your accounts, have so little. O be not so ungrateful to him who has been so kind to you: What could the LORD JESUS CHRIST have done for you more than he has? Then do not abuse his mercy, but let your time be spent in thinking and talking of the love of JESUS, who was incarnate for us, who was born of a woman, and made under the law, to redeem us from the wrath to come.[1]

Though, in theory, Whitefield considered Arminianism 'the back way to popery', his preaching seems predicated upon a belief in universal salvation.

The basis of all belief and the source of all true wisdom, for Whitefield, was the Bible. It was God's definitive and unalterable statement to man, divinely inspired and eternally relevant. Every part was of equal significance; all could admit of literal interpretation. 'If we once get above our Bibles, and cease making the written word of GOD our sole rule, both as to faith and practice, we shall soon lie open to all manner of delusion, and be in great danger of making shipwreck of faith and a good conscience.'[2] In the Bible he found the answers to his own questions and doubts, and with it he attempted to answer the questions and doubts of others. He always felt it sufficient proof of any point to be able to conclude 'the Bible says so'. In a sermon on 'The Indwelling of the Spirit' he inveighs against an imaginary cynic:

if thou canst prove, thou unbeliever, that the book, which we call *The Bible*, does not contain the lively oracles of GOD; if thou canst shew, that holy men of old, did not write this book, as they were inwardly moved by the Holy Ghost, then will we give up the doctrine of original sin; but unless thou canst do this, we must insist upon it, that we are all conceived and born in sin; if for no other, yet for this one reason, because that GOD, who cannot lye, has told us so.[3]

---

[1] *Works*, v. 260–1.
[2] Ibid., v. 27.
[3] Ibid., vi. 96.

Because he was so entirely persuaded of the infallibility of scripture, he committed much of it to memory, and his sermons are rife with Biblical allusions, quotations, and idiom.

The extent to which he held to a literal interpretation of the Bible is apparent from the sermon, 'The Seed of Woman and the Seed of the Serpent'. This is an attempt to explain and apply the Genesis story of the Fall. It is obvious that Whitefield not only regarded Adam and Eve as historical characters, but the Fall as having an hour-by-hour time sequence.

How soon man fell after he was created, is not told us; and therefore, to fix any time, is to be wise above what is written. And, I think, they who suppose that man fell the same day in which he was made, have no sufficient ground for their opinion. The many things which are crouded together in the former chapter, such as the formation of *Adam's* wife, his giving names to the beasts, and his being put into the garden which GOD had planted, I think require a longer space of time than a day to be transacted in. However, all agree in this, 'man stood not long'. How long, or how short a while, I will not take upon me to determine.[1]

The concern with detail in his description of these events is understood only when one is aware of the vital position the Fall occupied in Whitefield's theology. Here, in Adam's disobedience, was the emanation of all sin and death. Here was the awful origin of all illness and disorder, all poverty and shame. The human plight was a most unenviable one: 'Our whole head is sick, our whole heart is faint; from the crown of the head to the sole of the foot, we are full of wounds, bruises, and putrefying sores. In our flesh there dwelleth no good thing.'[2]

---

[1] *Works*, v. 4–5.

[2] D. Macfarlane, *Revivals of the Eighteenth Century* (n.d.), p. 14. Three sermons by Whitefield, preached in the 'High Church-Yard', Glasgow, are appended to this account of eighteenth-century revivals. These sermons are not included either in the *Works* or the *Eighteen Sermons*, and Macfarlane has paginated them independently of the rest of the book.

But the more repugnant the moral morass into which the first Adam plunged humanity, the more dramatic was the rescue effected by the second Adam, Christ. In the Atonement Whitefield saw a just but merciful God satisfying both sides of his nature. The poignant and vivid picture he painted for his audience time and again was that of a 'bleeding, panting, dying Saviour' giving his life to propitiate the sins of the world.

As in much evangelical preaching before and since, the concepts of heaven and hell loom large in Whitefield. They were God's ultimate sanctions, and their reality was never doubted by the revivalist. Without them life had no discernible purpose. In the very nature of things it seemed essential that there should be a place where the righteous were rewarded and the ungodly punished. Again the Bible was the basis for belief and the source of detail.

Just as Dante's pen stopped short of describing the beatific vision, so the otherwise intrepid tongue of Whitefield was silenced by the contemplation of heaven.

But I must stop: the glories of the upper world croud in so fast upon my soul, that I am lost in the contemplation of them. Brethren, the redemption spoken of is unutterable; we cannot here find it out; eye hath not seen, nor ear heard, nor has it entered into the hearts of the most holy men living, to conceive how great it is. Was I to entertain you whole ages with an account of it, when you come to heaven, you must say, with the Queen of *Sheba*, 'Not half, no, not one thousandth part was told us'.[1]

But if heaven were veiled by a curtain of resplendency, there was nothing to obstruct his view of hell. On occasions he spoke of hell as a spiritual estrangement from God. 'What is hell,' he once asked, 'but to be absent from Christ?'[2] Generally, however, he saw it as a place with physical dimensions and designed for physical torments: 'I see hell opened for me, I see the damned tormented, I see such a one in hell that I debauched; in the midst of his agony he

---

[1] *Works*, vi. 199–200.
[2] Macfarlane, *Revivals*, p. 32.

said, I am coming to thee, I am coming, I must be damned, God will damn my soul, and died. Take care of jesting with God; there is room enough in hell.'[1] And again: 'Can you live, think you, in everlasting burnings? Is your flesh brass, and your bones iron? what if they are? hell-fire, that fire prepared for the devil and his angels, will heat them through and through.'[2] It is little wonder that, projecting such graphic descriptions of hell, he sent many away from his services distraught with fear. But Whitefield made no apology for this. He believed that it was 'better to have some soul-trouble here, than to be sent to hell by Jesus Christ here-after'.[3]

Whitefield saw it as the duty of every minister of the gospel to employ every homiletic and oratorical device at his disposal to save men from hell. He had little time for preachers who entertained their congregations with moral bromides. 'Besides, my dear friends, it is not the business of the ministers of the gospel merely to entertain people with harangues of dry morality, and leave out Jesus Christ. It is not our business to entertain our people, as Cicero, Seneca, and other heathen moralists did; but we are to preach Christ, not ourselves; we are to preach the hidden mysteries of the kingdom of God.'[4] Moral virtue and good works, he felt, would inevitably issue in a life that was in right relationship with God. It was essential to realize, however, that these were not the means but the manifestations of salvation. Upon this point he was so insistent that eventually the charge of antinomianism was levelled against him. He once exclaimed during a sermon: 'Every minister should be a *Boanerges*, a son of thunder, as well as a *Barnabas*, a son of consolation.'[5] Whitefield's vociferation left little doubt about which spiritual ancestor he favoured.

[1] *Eighteen Sermons Preached by the late Rev. George Whitefield*, ed. J. Gurney (1771), p. 76.
[2] *Works*, v. 231.
[3] *Revivals*, p. 32.
[4] Ibid., p. 5.
[5] *Works*, v. 13.

Much of his thundering was directed at the clergy of his day, whom he considered 'blind, unregenerate, carnal, lukewarm, and unskilful guides'.[1] Many of them, he was convinced, knew no more of true Christianity than a 'blind man does of colours';[2] they had not, as he had, been born again.[3] He was contemptuous also of those 'letter-learned' clergy who tried to prove from books that Jesus Christ was the Son of God.[4] Perhaps here there is something slightly envious in Whitefield's attitude. Not a scholar himself, he viewed with mistrust all intellectual and academic enterprise which did not appear to him to be directed towards the glory of God. He regarded 'plays, Spectators, Pope's Homers, and such like' as 'trifling books'.[5] Then, too, many clergy had refused him the use of their pulpits and for this he could scarcely commend them. It would be wrong to suggest, however, that it was chiefly out of personal enmity that Whitefield was critical of so many of those in holy orders. It is certainly true that for a majority of eighteenth-century clergymen the ministry was a less sacred calling and preaching a less engaging task than they were for Whitefield.

Though his theology was pedestrian, his expression verbose, and his argument sometimes inconsistent, yet there

---

[1] *Revivals*, p. 18.

[2] *Works*, v. 135.

[3] Whitefield's conversion took place while he was still at Oxford. Later he described what had happened: 'About the End of the seven Weeks, and after I had been groaning under an unspeakable Pressure both of Body and Mind for above a Twelvemonth; GOD was pleased to set me free in the following Manner.—One Day, perceiving an uncommon Drought, and a disagreeable Clamminess in my Mouth, and using Things to allay my Thirst, but in vain, it was suggested to me, that when *Jesus Christ* cried out, "I thirst," his Sufferings were near at an End. Upon which, I cast myself down on the Bed, crying out, I thirst! I thirst!—Soon after this, I found and felt in myself that I was delivered from the Burden that had so heavily oppressed me! The Spirit of Mourning was taken from me, and I knew what it was truly to rejoice in GOD my Saviour, and, for some Time, could not avoid singing Psalms wherever I was.' *A Short Account of God's Dealings with the Reverend Mr. George Whitefield* (1740), pp. 48–9.

[4] *Works*, vi. 156.

[5] *Sketches of the Life and Labours of the Rev. George Whitefield* (1849), p. 36.

12—E.C.P.

was an importunity about Whitefield's message which his audiences could not ignore. He believed that every man should be given the opportunity to accept salvation. Through preaching, whose efficacy he never doubted, he would proffer that opportunity to as many as would listen. 'My dear friends, I would preach with all my heart till midnight, to do you good, till I could preach no more. O that this body might hold out to speak more for my dear Redeemer! Had I a thousand lives, had I a thousand tongues, they should be employed in inviting sinners to come to Jesus Christ!'[1] Such were the demands the gospel made upon him; such were the ardour and enthusiasm he brought to his calling.

To trace the tradition of Whitefield's manner of preaching it is necessary to go back to the medieval friar. The methods and practices of the friar, as G. R. Owst has described them,[2] provide a clear precedent. Like that of the friar, Whitefield's mission was essentially an evangelizing one. Both itinerated; both drew their congregations from the poorer social classes; both preached mainly in the open air. The friar eyed with suspicion the more scholarly monk, and was in turn frequently regarded with contempt. Whitefield's relations with the orthodox clergy of his time were, as has been indicated, not dissimilar to this. Like the friar, also, he extemporized in his preaching, and interlarded his sermons with *exempla* and, at times, pungent vernacular expressions.

Although during the Reformation the friar's style of preaching generally went out of fashion, there was one dynamic figure who did more than anyone else to preserve the tradition. He was Hugh Latimer (1490–1555). Whitefield's affinities with him are striking. Latimer was an awakener of men; he spoke directly to their condition and in language that often shocked the more refined. 'In Latimer's sermons', says Canon Smyth, 'we can see the traditional use of the *exempla*, and especially of personal *exempla*, in undiminished vigour. His racy anecdotes, his use

---

[1] *Revivals*, p. 48.
[2] *Literature and Pulpit in Medieval England*, pp. 5–6.

of popular proverbs, his outspokenness, and his directness and homeliness of speech, come straight out of the very heart of medieval homiletics.'[1] Garrulous, fearless, sometimes tactless, possessed by the message he preached, Latimer probed and prodded until the sinner could hold out no longer:

Here you may perceive, that all those persons that will not be corrected for their faults, that cannot bear godly admonitions, they talk never with God to his pleasure; they be not ruled by God's spirit, and so not meet for him. All rebellious persons, all covetous persons, all lecherous persons, all liars, drunkards, and such like, be not in the case to talk with God. God will not hear them; he cannot abide them; they stink before his face, as long as they come before him with such abominable sins, not intending to leave them.[2]

Whitefield too had learned—perhaps from Calvinism—that it was necessary to deal bluntly with his hearers. Like Latimer, therefore, he fumed and fulminated, believing it necessary to berate his hearers in order to convict them of their spiritual negligence. Nor did his vituperation prevent his audiences from experiencing an intense affection for him. Benjamin Franklin expressed surprise at the 'strange respect felt by the people for a man who, to their faces, called them "half beasts and half devils" '.[3] Equally surprising to him was 'the change soon made in the manner of our inhabitants. From being thoughtless or indifferent about religion, it seemed as if all the world were growing religious, so that one could not walk through the town in an evening without hearing psalms sung in different families of every street.'[4]

Whitefield's relationship with his audience was unusually intimate. To establish this rapport he punctuated his sermons with personal reminiscences, anecdotes, and, at times, confessions. Neither did he feel the need to apologize for

[1] *Art of Preaching*, p. 108.
[2] *Sermons by Hugh Latimer*, Everyman's Library ed. (1906), p. 287.
[3] J. Parton, *Life and Times of Benjamin Franklin* (1892), i. 250.
[4] Ibid., i. 250.

constantly drawing attention to himself; in fact, his homiletic strategy demanded it. Before he could win men's hearts he had to win their trust; before he could win their trust he had to convince them that even his most vehement outbursts were motivated by love:

Therefore, my brethren, I beseech you, in the bowels of love and compassion, that you would come unto JESUS. Do not go away scoffing, offended, or blaspheming. Indeed, all I say is in love to your souls; and if I could be but an instrument of bringing you to JESUS CHRIST, if you were to be never so much exalted, I should not envy, but rejoice in your happiness: If I was to make up the last of the train of the companions of the blessed JESUS, it would rejoice me to see you above me in glory. I do not speak out of a false humility, a pretended sanctity; no, GOD is my judge, I speak the truth in CHRIST, I lie not, I would willingly go to prison, or to death for you, so I could but bring one soul from the devil's strong holds, into the salvation which is by CHRIST JESUS.[1]

The preacher's urgency springs from his own experience of sin and of the release from it through grace:

O ye servants of the most high God, if any of you are here to-night, though I am the chief of sinners, and the least of all saints, suffer the word of exhortation. I am sure I preach feelingly now; God knows I seldom sleep after three in the morning; I pray every morning, Lord, convert me, and make me more a new creature to-day. I know I want to be converted from a thousand things, and from ten thousand more: Lord God, confirm me; Lord God, revive his work.[2]

As these passages indicate, Whitefield's was a candid and confessional mode of preaching. The catharsis his sermons so often effected was due in no small measure to the preacher's ability to get close to his audience in this manner.

Whitefield was effusive and volatile. Consequently, his prose is fluid and undisciplined. Only by reading him aloud and with animation can one become aware of the effectiveness of such language.

[1] *Works*, vi. 298.
[2] *Eighteen Sermons*, p. 132.

It is an observation no less true than common, that kindled coals, if placed asunder, soon go out, but if heaped together, quicken and enliven each other, and afford a lasting heat. The same will hold good in the case now before us. If christians kindled by the grace of GOD, unite, they will quicken and enliven each other; but if they separate and keep asunder, no marvel if they soon grow cold or tepid. If two or three meet together in CHRIST's name, they will have heat: but how can one be warm alone?

Observe, 'How can one be warm alone?' The wise man's expressing himself by way of question, implies an impossibility, at least a very great difficulty, to be warm in religion without company, where it may be had. Behold here, then, another excellent benefit flowing from religious society; it will keep us zealous, as well as steady, in the ways of godliness.[1]

There is a nervous, energetic quality about his prose. Short, pointed phrases follow hard upon each other. The effect is cumulative; the audience is subdued more by the welter of points scored and appeals made than by the force of the argument.

It must be acknowledged, however, that while Whitefield's sermons, reinforced by his oratorical powers, made for excellent listening, they are now rather disappointing reading. They lack variety and polish. Many of the best qualities of his preaching have been lost between pulpit and press. The repetition which proved so effective on the lips of the speaker becomes tedious when read. As a prose stylist, he suffers in comparison with more literate contemporaries such as Berkeley, Sterne, and Wesley. But as an orator he excelled them all.

Much of his pulpit power and popular success he owed to his extraordinary voice. No open-air speaker[2] ever possessed a more valuable gift. Capable of immense projection, it enabled Whitefield to make himself heard at great distances and by vast numbers of people. Were there only the word of an enthusiastic follower that he preached to

[1] *Works*, v. 112–13.
[2] Whitefield was first among the Methodists to adopt field-preaching. Wesley, encouraged by Whitefield's success, reluctantly followed.

congregations of more than twenty thousand in the open
air one would be justified in treating the report *cum grano
salis*. But there can scarcely be a charge of exaggeration
brought against Benjamin Franklin's description of an
experiment he carried out in Philadelphia on Whitefield's
first visit to that city.

I had the curiosity . . . to learn how far he could be heard, by retiring
backward down the street towards the river, and I found his voice
distinct till I came near Front Street, when some noise in that street
obscured it. Imagining then a semicircle, of which my distance should
be the radius, and that it was filled with auditors, to each of whom I
allowed two square feet, I computed that he might well be heard by
more than thirty thousand. This reconciled me to the newspaper
accounts of his having preached to 25,000 people in the fields, and to
the history of generals haranguing whole armies, of which I had
sometimes doubted.[1]

But the field-preacher's voice was possessed of another
quality quite as remarkable as its power of projection.
Loudness is usually associated with dissonance. Not so, it
would appear, in Whitefield's case. His voice had an orphic
tone, a rare timbre and sonority, and a range which enabled
him to give expression to almost every human emotion.
Garrick marvelled at its richness and malleability, and observed that Whitefield could melt an auditory from euphoric
joy to tears merely by varying his pronunciation of the
word 'Mesopotamia'. The greatest actor of his time went
on to say that he would willingly part with a hundred guineas
if he could say 'oh' with the same pathos and effect as
Whitefield.[2] Whether playing the part of *Boanerges* or
Barnabas, whether convicting or entreating, the preacher's
voice was equal to the occasion.

Whitefield enjoyed many of the gifts of a great actor. In
addition to his remarkable voice, he had a protean face, a
penchant for the histrionic, and an almost perfect sense of
timing in both word and gesture. Perhaps ultimately, as

[1] Parton, *Life*, i. 250.
[2] Cited by L. Tyerman, *The Life of the Reverend George Whitefield* (1877), ii. 355.

S. C. Henry has suggested, Whitefield's appeal and success may be best explained in terms of the theatre: 'The place at which Whitefield's dramatic ability touched the lives of his audiences was that of the human predicament. He spoke to man's eternal question: What shall I do to be saved? The individual in the pit heard the strange man on the boards speaking of a restlessness that any man knew and of a certainty that every man sought.'[1]

By virtue of his sonorous voice and acting ability, Whitefield could enliven an otherwise indifferent homily or give verisimilitude to a Biblical scene. While recounting an incident from scripture, he would suddenly strike a pose, adopt the dramatic present-tense, and sound a note of pathos by his tremulous voice and tears. Of Christ in Gethsemane:

See, see, O my soul, how he sweats! But what is that which I see! BLOOD—*drops* of blood—*great* drops of blood falling to the ground. Alas! was ever sorrow like unto this sorrow? Hark! what is that I hear? Oh, dolorous complaint! 'Father, if it be possible, let this cup pass from me.' Hark! he speaks again. Amazing! the Creator complains to the creature: 'My soul is exceeding sorrowful, even unto death; tarry ye here, and watch with me.' And now he retires once more. But see how his agony increases—hark! how he prays, and that, too, yet more earnestly: 'Father, if it be possible, let this cup pass from me.'[2]

Of Abraham's intended sacrifice of Isaac:

O what pious, endearing expressions passed now alternately between the father and the son! *Josephus* records a pathetic speech made by each, whether genuine I know not: but methinks I see the tears trickle down the Patriarch *Abraham*'s cheeks; and out of the abundance of the heart, he cries, Adieu, adieu, my son; the LORD gave thee to me, and the LORD calls thee away; blessed be the name of the LORD: adieu, my *Isaac*, my only son, whom I love as my own soul; adieu, adieu. I see *Isaac* at the same time meekly resigning himself into his heavenly Father's hands, and praying to the most High to strengthen his earthly parent to strike the stroke.[3]

---

[1] *George Whitefield, Wayfaring Witness* (1957), pp. 177–8.
[2] Cited in *Sketches*, pp. 263–4.
[3] *Works*, v. 46.

As well as informing scriptural scenes in this manner, Whitefield excelled in impromptu dramatization of all kinds. One of his favourite techniques was to select an appropriate metaphor and sustain it to a climax.

On one occasion, he was preaching before the seamen of New York, when suddenly assuming a certain nautical tone and manner that were irresistible, he thus suddenly broke in with, 'Well, my boys, we have a clear sky, and are making fine head-way over a smooth sea, before a light breeze, and we shall soon lose sight of land. But what means this sudden lowering of the heavens, and that dark cloud arising from beneath the western horizon? Hark! Don't you hear distant thunder? Don't you see those flashes of lighning? There is a storm gathering! Every man to his duty! How the waves rise, and dash against the ship! The air is dark! The tempest rages! Our masts are gone! The ship is on her beam-ends! What next?' This climax of nautical horror was described and uttered in a manner so true to nature, that the sailors started to their feet, and shouted, 'The long boat! take to the long boat!'[1]

This passage demonstrates Whitefield's rhetorical mastery. With a single sentence the mood and scene are set. Tension mounts as three short, ominous questions are followed by seven alarming exclamations, and the piece is climaxed with a shriek of desperation: 'What next?'

It is not difficult to imagine the reaction of Whitefield's hearers to such moving dramatization. Nor was it only the poor and unlettered who felt the orator's power to create for his audience an intense vicarious experience. Even the 'disinterested' philosopher, David Hume, could not but warm to Whitefield's eloquence. Of a particular sermon Hume said: 'it was accompanied with such animated yet natural action, that it surpassed any thing I ever saw or heard in any other preacher.' He then went on to illustrate:

'The attendant angel,' exclaimed Whitefield in the midst of his sermon, after a deep, solemn pause—'the attendant angel is just about to leave the threshold of this sanctuary, and ascend to heaven. And shall he ascend, and not bear with him the news of one sinner, among all this multitude, reclaimed from the error of his ways?' Then stamping with his foot, and throwing his eyes and hands to heaven, he exclaimed, with a loud piercing voice, 'Stop, Gabriel, stop, ere you enter the sacred portals, and yet carry with you the news of one sinner converted to God.'[1]

An amusing anecdote demonstrating the effect of White-field's oratory is told in connection with the fashionable Lord Chesterfield. As a guest at Lady Huntingdon's chapel, he was listening rapt as Whitefield spoke of man's plight in his natural state of sin. The preacher compared man to a blind mendicant who, in the blackest night and on a bleak and treacherous hillside, suddenly loses his dog. Helpless, he staggers near the precipice of a cliff. So graphic was White-field's description and so enthralling his animation that just as the beggar was about to topple into the abyss below, Chesterfield fell forward into the aisle and exclaimed: 'Good God! he is gone!'[2]

'Whitefield', says Horton Davies, 'was a volcano—often brilliantly lurid and coruscating with sparks; occasionally he exuded only ashes.'[3] The figure is a good one. Frequently during a sermon he would 'erupt' and pour down upon sinners the lava of reproof:

Hear this, all ye self-justiciaries, tremble, and behold your doom! a dreadful doom, more dreadful than words can express, or thought conceive! If you refuse to humble yourselves, after hearing this parable, I call heaven and earth to witness against you this day, that GOD shall visit you with all his storms, and pour all the vials of his wrath upon your rebellious heads; you exalted yourselves here, and GOD shall abase you hereafter; you are as proud as the devil, and with devils shall you dwell to all eternity. 'Be not deceived, GOD is not mocked'; he sees your hearts, he knows all things. And, notwithstanding you may come up to the temple to pray, your prayers are turned into sin, and you go down to your houses unjustified, if you are self-justificaries; and do you know what it is to be unjustified? why, if you are unjusti-fied, the wrath of GOD abideth upon you; you are in your blood; all the curses of the law belong to you: cursed are you when you go out,

---

[1] Cited in *Sketches*, pp. 264–5.
[2] Ibid., p. 265.
[3] *Worship and Theology*, p. 146.

cursed are you when you come in; cursed are your thoughts, cursed are your words, cursed are your deeds; every thing you do, say, or think, from morning to night, is only one continued series of sin.[1]

Some felt his language was unduly abrasive; others thought he abused his pulpit privileges. The Duchess of Buckingham was outraged by such churlish exhibitions. In a letter to the Countess of Huntingdon (Whitefield's patroness) she protested that the doctrines of Whitefield and his fellow Methodists were 'most repulsive, and strongly tinctured with impertinence and disrespect towards their superiors . . . It is monstrous to be told, that you have a heart as sinful as the common wretches that crawl on the earth.'[2] But Whitefield prided himself in the fact that his was a 'market-place language'. That some should have been offended by his 'monstrous' approach was further manifestation of spiritual pride, a situation which made his remonstrations only the more necessary.

This disregard for propriety in his choice of diction is nowhere better illustrated than in the sermon, 'The Resurrection of Lazarus'. There, sparing none of the lurid detail, he describes the putrefying body of Lazarus.

Come, ye dead, Christless, unconverted sinners, come and see the place where they laid the body of the deceased *Lazarus*; behold him laid out, bound hand and foot with grave-cloaths, locked up and stinking in a dark cave, with a great stone placed on the top of it! View him again and again; go nearer to him; be not afraid; smell him, ah! how he stinketh. Stop there now, pause a while; and whilst thou art gazing upon the corpse of *Lazarus*, give me leave to tell thee with great plainness, but greater love, that this dead, bound, entombed, stinking carcase, is but a faint representation of thy poor soul in its natural state: for, whether thou believest it or not, thy spirit which thou bearest about with thee, sepulchred in flesh and blood, is as literally dead to GOD, and as truly dead in trespasses and sins, as the body of *Lazarus* was in the cave.[3]

[1] *Works*, vi. 46.
[2] *The Life and Times of Selina Countess of Huntingdon*, ed. A. C. H. Seymour (1840), i. 27.
[3] *Works*, vi. 123.

Whitefield was not above singling out groups and individuals to bear the brunt of his vituperation. On one occasion, when preaching in a small New England town, an elderly gentleman in the congregation fell asleep. Taking note of the man, the preacher suddenly brought down his hand upon the pulpit and his foot upon the floor with such force that the sound reverberated through the building. Then fixing his eyes upon the startled old fellow, he said: 'Ay, ay ... I have waked you up, have I? I meant to do it. I am not come here to preach to stocks and stones; I have come to you in the name of the Lord God of Hosts, and I must, and I will have an audience.'[1]

Whitefield's treatment of the popular comedian Shuter when the latter attended service at the 'Soul-Trap'[2] was equally humiliating. Shuter was at the peak of his career, and especially renowned for his portrayal of Ramble.[3] In the midst of a protracted and impassioned plea to sinners to accept salvation, Whitefield paused, directed his gaze at Shuter and exclaimed: 'And thou, poor Ramble, who hast long rambled from him, come thou also. O, end thy ramblings by coming to Jesus.' Acutely embarrassed, the actor hurried to the preacher after the service and said: 'I thought I should have fainted—how could you serve me so?'[4] But for Whitefield any departure from the norm of pulpit behaviour, or any subsequent discomfiture on the part of those thus singled out, could be justified by reference to the end which all was designed to achieve.

That end was conversion. The preacher's task was to make his hearers aware that in spite of their moral and social respectability they were sinners standing in need of

---

[1] Cited in *Sketches*, p. 273.

[2] The popular name for Whitefield's tabernacle in Moorfields.

[3] Probably the Ramble in Fielding's 'The Coffee-House Politician; or, the Justice caught in his own Trap'. This comedy, first titled 'Rape upon Rape', was a severe indictment of the administration of the civil law of the day and was first acted 23 June 1730 at the Hay-Market Theatre and revived several times in the eighteenth century.

[4] Cited in *Sketches*, p. 266.

salvation. This might call for the most devastating weapons in his rhetorical arsenal. If persuasion failed, he must over-power his hearers and force them into submission.

One very effective device employed for this purpose was a series of short and pointed questions propounded so rapidly that the listener had no time to formulate answers. This might happen several times during a sermon, but most commonly towards the end. With questions such as these, Whitefield wore down the sinner's defences:

You boast of wisdom; so did the philosophers of *Corinth*: but your wisdom is the foolishness of folly in the sight of God. What will your wisdom avail you, if it does not make you wise unto salvation? Can you, with all your wisdom, propose a more consistent scheme to build your hopes of salvation on, than what has been now laid before you? Can you, with all the strength of natural reason, find out a better way of acceptance with God, than by the righteousness of the LORD JESUS CHRIST? Is it right to think your own works can in any measure deserve or procure it? If not, Why will you not believe in him? Why will you not submit to his righteousness? Can you deny that you are fallen creatures? Do not you find that you are full of disorders, and that these disorders make you unhappy? Do not you find that you cannot change your own hearts? Have you not resolved many and many a time, and have not your corruptions yet dominion over you? Are you not bond-slaves to your lusts, and led captive by the devil at his will? Why then will you not come to CHRIST for sanctification?[1]

It is not uncommon in a single sermon by Whitefield to count sixty or more questions, most of which are clustered together in series of six to ten, and frequently more. Some-times the pace is changed, sometimes the tense, but the attack is relentless. It was a strong citadel indeed which could withstand such bombardment.

The rhetorical question excepted, the most frequently recurring figure in Whitefield's prose is antithesis. Because he tried to contrast the life of sin with the life of redemptive goodness, it is to be expected that antithesis in many forms would occur. Whitefield's antithesis, though forceful, is not

---

[1] *Works*, vi. 200.

usually rhythmic or balanced. And it is never elaborate. Occasionally, however, both rhythm and balance are achieved, and it is then perhaps that Whitefield reaches his greatest heights as an extemporaneous preacher. Antithesis like this is worthy of a more deliberative orator:

While they are singing the songs of the drunkard, you are singing psalms and hymns: while they are at a playhouse, you are hearing a sermon: while they are drinking, revelling and mispending their precious time, and hastening on their own destruction, you are reading, praying, meditating, and working out your salvation with fear and trembling. This is matter enough for a world to reproach you; you are not polite and fashionable enough for them. If you will live godly, you must suffer persecution; you must not expect to go through this world without being persecuted and reviled. . . .

The spirit of the world is hatred; that of CHRIST is love: the spirit of the world is vexation; that of CHRIST is pleasure: the spirit of the world is sorrow; that of CHRIST is joy: the spirit of the world is evil, and that of CHRIST is good: the spirit of the world will never satisfy us, but CHRIST's spirit is all satisfaction: the spirit of the world is misery; that of CHRIST is ease. In one word, the spirit of the world has nothing lasting; but the spirit of CHRIST is durable, and will last through an eternity of ages: the spirit of CHRIST will remove every difficulty, satisfy every doubt, and be a means of bringing you to himself, to live with him for ever and ever.[1]

The second paragraph demonstrates Whitefield's preference for the simplest and most emphatic form of antithesis: the juxtaposition of two strong nouns.

A favourite rhetorical device of great preachers in every age, from St. Paul to the present day, has been the repetition of certain key words or phrases. Sometimes a noun, sometimes a verb, its task is to answer some human need of which the preacher has made his hearers aware. Here again Whitefield excels. Having rebuked his hearers for their moral blindness, he then assures them that they can be made to see. In a single paragraph he repeats the word 'see' seventeen times before concluding thus:

[1] *Works*, vi. 288–9.

If you can mix faith with the promise, and look up to Jesus Christ, you shall see. What shall you see? You shall see wonders; you shall see Christ, and you shall be so ravished with his beauty, that you shall be scarcely able to contain yourself. You shall see fulness and righteousness in the Son of God—something in Christ that will satisfy all your wants; you shall see your interest in him; you shall see that you shall be with him for evermore; you shall see him here by faith, and see him as he is in heaven; you shall see wondrous things. May God recover the sight of all you poor blind sinners.[1]

At times, almost like a faith-healer attempting a cure for some psychosomatic disorder, Whitefield will repeat the word 'heal' with a crescendo of emphasis and emotion. On other occasions, he can soothe and reassure by the quiet, insistent repetition of such a word as 'peace'.

It follows, 'peace'. 'The Kingdom of God is righteousness, and peace.' By peace I do not understand that false peace, or rather carnal security, into which so many are fallen. There are thousands who speak peace to themselves, when there is no peace. Thousands have got a peace of the devil's making; the strong man armed has got possession of their hearts, and therefore their goods are all in peace. But the peace here spoken of is a peace that follows after a great deal of soul trouble; it is like that calm which the Lord Jesus Christ spoke to the wind, 'Peace, be still; and immediately there was a great calm'; it is like that peace which Christ spoke to his disciples, when he came and said, 'Peace be unto you'—'My peace I leave with you.' It is a peace of God's making, it is a peace of God's giving, it is a peace that the world cannot give, it is a peace that can be felt, it is a peace that passeth human understanding—it is a peace that results from a sense of having Christ's righteousness brought home to the soul.[2]

In such a way the 'strange man on the boards' spoke to the deepest longing of the human soul—the longing for peace. Who could refuse an invitation which promised so much?

Whitefield, as one might suspect, was a superb raconteur. Like good evangelists in every age, he had what seemed an inexhaustible store of anecdotes and illustrations. And always they are to the point. No words are wasted in the

[1] *Revivals*, p. 14.
[2] Ibid., pp. 44–5.

telling, and his mobile face, resonant voice, and perfect sense
of timing could transform even the most homely illustration:
'I have heard of one who began low; he first wanted a house,
then, says he, I want two, then four, then six; and when he
had them, he said, I think I want nothing else; yes, says his
friend, you will soon want another thing, that is, a hearse and
six to carry you to your grave; and that made him tremble.'[1]
At this forceful reminder of the imminence of death, it
is more than likely that the audience trembled too. But
Whitefield presses home the attack: to procrastinate conversion is to flirt with disaster:

I believe men ought to be converted, but the common saying is, I don't
care to be converted yet; we think it is time enough to be converted. Is
not this acting like the cardinal, when told he was elected pope, and
desired to come that night and have the honour of pope conferred on
him; because it was pretty late said, it is not a work of darkness, I will
put it off till the morning; before which they chose another pope, and
he lost his triple crown. You may think to put it off till the morning,
though before the morning you may be damned.[2]

Not all Whitefield's anecdotes were designed to make
men fear and tremble. He was not devoid of humour, nor
was he unaware that occasionally it was necessary to ease
the tension his prophetic message created. 'I have heard of a
lady that was so fond of gaming, that though she had the
pangs of death upon her, yet when in the midst of her fits,
or just coming out of one, instead of asking after Jesus,
where he was to be found, she asked, what is trumps?'[3]
Sometimes the punch-line is longer in coming, but it is
worth waiting for:

A blessed minister of Christ, in Scotland, told me a story he knew for
truth, of a dreadful answer a poor creature gave on her death-bed . . .
this person when dying was asked by a minister, where do you hope to
go when you die? says she, I don't care where I go; what, says he,
don't you care whether you go to heaven or hell? no, says she, I don't

[1] *Eighteen Sermons*, p. 121.
[2] Ibid., pp. 125–6.
[3] Ibid., pp. 122–3.

care whither I go; but, says he, if you was put to your choice where would you go? says she, to hell; to that he replied, are you mad, will you go to hell? yes, says she, I will; why so? says he; why, says she, all my relations are there.[1]

In Whitefield's humorous relief one is again reminded of Latimer, who himself had a limitless 'stock of merry tales—not the cut-and-dried moralized anecdotes of the *Gesta Romanorum*, but incidents that he had noted in his busy life among the people'.[2]

In addition to his great gifts of oratory Whitefield possessed a homiletic mind—a mind that gleaned parables and illustrations from the commonplace happenings of life. Everything from the bleating of a sheep to the London water supply was fair game for his highly charged imagination:

I have often thought since I went to see the water-works, that it was an emblem of Christ; there is a great reservoir of water from which this great city is supplied; but how is it supplied from that reservoir? why by hundreds and hundreds of pipes: but where does this water go, does it go only to the dissenters or to the church people, only to this or that people? no, the pipes convey the water to all; and I remember when I saw it, it put me in mind of the great reservoir of grace, that living water that is in Christ Jesus, and the pipes are the ordinances by which his grace is conveyed to all believing souls, God grant we may be of that happy number.[3]

His ecumenism, as well as his aptitude for drawing analogies, is apparent here.

Most of his illustrations, however, were taken from the Bible. He drew them from Old and New Testament alike, believing all to be eternally applicable to the human situation. Scriptural images and idiom pervade his language, and even his everyday speech was greatly influenced by the rhetorical form of the Bible.[4]

---

[1] *Eighteen Sermons*, p. 355.
[2] Introduction to *Sermons by Hugh Latimer*, p. xv.
[3] *Eighteen Sermons*, p. 13.
[4] See Henry, *George Whitefield*, p. 98.

Ultimately, it is impossible to avoid a comparison of Whitefield with John Wesley, so inseparably have historical circumstances linked together their names and achievements. It was primarily because of their combined influence that the character of English religion was so radically changed. Together, also, they reshaped the conception of the popular preacher.

The two had much in common: a dynamic religious experience whose culmination was 'conversion'; a passion to spread the good news of the Christian gospel; a disdain for the 'dry husks of morality' which seemed to them the only spiritual food the Church of England was offering its hungry flock; and a desire to alleviate some of the social injustice and duress under which men laboured. But for all their similarities, there were significant differences. Apart from their upbringings, which could hardly have been more unlike,[1] there was the still greater difference of native endowment. Wesley's talents and temperament were those of a scholar; Whitefield's those of an actor. Wesley's triumph as a popular preacher may almost be said to have been in spite of his gifts; Whitefield's precisely because of them. Though Wesley was the more astute thinker, organizer, and teacher, Whitefield was supremely the finer orator.

Their talents, as Davies has noted, were complementary. The candour and boldness of Whitefield counterbalanced Wesley's sense of dignity and propriety. 'In short, the restraint and calmness of Wesley made him the superb organizer that he was; while Whitefield's passionate temperament, bell-like voice, gifts of mimicry, dynamic gestures, and uninhibited speech were to make him the exciting preacher that he was.'[2] It may be going too far to suggest, as Southey did, that if Wesley had never lived Whitefield would have given birth to Methodism.[3] But it is

---

[1] Wesley was a child of a rectory; Whitefield of a public house and inn.
[2] *Worship and Theology*, p. 145.
[3] Quoted by A. D. Belden, *George Whitefield—The Awakener* (1930), p. 4.

true to say that without the flaming torch of his oratory evangelicalism would not have become the conflagration it did in eighteenth-century England.

In an age when reasonable men had agreed to condemn outright all manifestations of enthusiasm, Whitefield was bound to engender criticism. His highly personal and emotional style of preaching indicted him as the apotheosis of enthusiasm. And it was he, not Wesley, who became the target for satirists. For though people might disagree with Wesley's theology, they could scarcely attack the man. Scholarly, conservative in everything but religion, impeccable in dress and manners, Wesley was eminently respectable. Whitefield created quite a different impression. To many he seemed tactless, insensitive, churlish, and, above all, egotistic. Who, for example, but an egotist of the first order would publish his autobiography at the age of twenty-six? Whereas, therefore, attacks on Wesley tended to be against his theology, those on Whitefield were mainly against his person.[1]

To a high churchman like Dr. Johnson, who found reassurance in the staid and solemn reserve of the Church of England, Whitefield was an anomaly and a threat to the *status quo*. Though both had been at Pembroke College, Oxford, Johnson was unimpressed by either the character or talent of his fellow alumnus. Boswell felt that Whitefield's 'eloquence was powerful, his views pious and charitable, his assiduity almost incredible',[2] but Johnson thought he merely 'vociferated, and made an impression'.[3] According to Boswell, 'He would not allow much merit to Whitefield's oratory. "His popularity, Sir, (said he,) is chiefly owing to the peculiarity of his manner. He would be followed by crowds were he to wear a night-cap in the pulpit, or were he to preach from a tree." '[4] Johnson considered Whitefield

---

[1] See A. M. Lyles, *Methodism Mocked* (1960).
[2] *Boswell's Life*, i. 75.
[3] Ibid., v. 36.
[4] Ibid., ii. 79.

much inferior to Wesley, who, he said, thought only of religion and could converse well on almost any subject. Whitefield, he contended, meant well, 'but had a mixture of politicks and ostentation'.[1]

Whitefield never drew as much attention as a mountebank does; he did not draw attention by doing better than others, but by doing what was strange. Were Astley to preach a sermon standing upon his head on a horse's back, he would collect a multitude to hear him; but no wise man would say he had made a better sermon for that. I never treated Whitefield's ministry with contempt; I believe he did good. He had devoted himself to the lower classes of mankind, and among them he was of use. But when familiarity and noise claim the praise due to knowledge, art, and elegance, we must beat down such pretensions.[2]

Thus spoke the most authoritative voice in English literature of the most voluble voice in English religion.

Johnson's exacerbation at Whitefield's popular success was shared by many within and without the Church of England who were willing to join forces with him in beating down such pretensions. Whereas half a century before it might have been necessary to counter such manifestations of enthusiasm with solid argument, now ridicule seemed the most effective riposte. Pope showed the way:

> So swells each wind-pipe; Ass intones to Ass,
> Harmonic twang! of leather, horn, and brass;
> Such as from lab'ring lungs th'Enthusiast blows,
> High Sound, attemp'red to the vocal nose;
> Or such as bellow from the deep Divine;
> There Webster! peal'd thy voice, and Whitfield! thine.[3]

Among those who followed Pope's lead were three of the leading novelists of the period, Fielding, Smollett, and Graves.

Fielding's dislike of Whitefield is apparent from the manner in which he is spoken of in both *Joseph Andrews*

---

[1] *Boswell's Life*, v. 35.

[2] Ibid., iii. 409.

[3] *Dunciad*, ii. 253–8.

(1742) and *Tom Jones* (1749). In the former, Whitefield's name is introduced into a conversation involving the two parsons and a bookseller. Coming from a man so benign and charitable as Parson Adams, this is a severe castigation:

'Sir,' answered Adams, 'if Mr. Whitefield had carried his doctrine no farther than you mention, I should have remained, as I once was, his well-wisher. I am, myself, as great an enemy to the luxury and splendour of the clergy as he can be ... But when he began to call nonsense and enthusiasm to his aid, and set up the detestable doctrine of faith against good works, I was his friend no longer; for surely that doctrine was coined in hell; and one would think that none but the devil himself could have the confidence to preach it.'[1]

In *Tom Jones* Fielding does not miss the opportunity, when his hero visits Whitefield's birthplace, the Bell Inn, Gloucester, to reiterate his disapproval of the evangelist. The Inn, at the time of Tom's visit, was kept by Whitefield's brother and his wife. Of the proprietors and their hostelry the narrator speaks well, explaining that the older Mr. Whitefield is 'absolutely untainted with the pernicious principles of Methodism, or any other heretical sect. He is indeed a very honest plain man, and, in my opinion, not likely to create any disturbance either in church or state.'[2] Some of the 'pernicious principles' of which Fielding speaks are embodied in the character of Thwackum. Thwackum, outwardly pious but lacking in charity, is meant to exhibit a doctrinal affinity with Whitefield and, for the most part, to represent the antithesis of the simple goodness for which Tom stands, unmindful of religion though he may be.

Smollett seems to have regarded Whitefield as something of an itinerating calamity. In his history of England he had railed against Methodism and dismissed Whitefield as a figure of little importance.[3] This same view is expressed, somewhat more interestingly this time, in *Humphry Clinker* (1771). In Clinker, the jejune, ingenuous footman who,

---

[1] *Joseph Andrews*, bk. i, ch. xvii.
[2] *Tom Jones*, bk. viii, ch. viii.
[3] *The History of England* (1790), v. 376.

inebriated with religious enthusiasm, tries his hand at preaching, Methodism is depicted as an aberration more to be regretted than feared. And Whitefield, with whom one is meant to associate Clinker, is pictured as a buffoon rather than as a demon.

Richard Graves attempted a somewhat more sympathetic caricature of Whitefield in *The Spiritual Quixote* (1772). This 'comic romance', subtitled 'The Summer's Ramble of Mr. Geoffrey Wildgoose', relates the adventures of a Methodist proselyte who gives himself over to a summer of preaching. Graves leaves little doubt as to the identity of Wildgoose's model.

But it must be remembered, likewise, that Mr. Wildgoose, notwithstanding the present uncouth appearance of his short hair, had something naturally agreeable in his countenance, and also a very musical tone of voice; and though, in the vehemence of his harangues, he had a wildness in his looks, proceeding from the enthusiastic zeal which possessed his imagination, yet that very circumstance gave a more pathetic force to his eloquence; and he himself appearing so much in earnest and affected with the subject, it had a proportionable effect upon his audience.[1]

His sermons, too, are embellished with direct quotations from Whitefield's works. Wildgoose is certainly naive, but he is by no means a despicable or dissimulatory character. In fact, the reader can scarcely keep from liking him, so amiable is his disposition and so innocently earnest are his intentions.

But there is a further revelation of Whitefield in *The Spiritual Quixote*; he is introduced in person as Wildgoose's inspiration and adviser. In this capacity he is much less endearing. When Wildgoose and his friend arrive at Whitefield's lodgings they are shown to his room by the maid. 'Mr. Whitefield was sitting in an elbow-chair, in a handsome dining room, dressed in a purple night-gown and velvet cap; and, instead of a Bible or prayer-book, as

[1] *The Spiritual Quixote*, bk. iii, ch. iii.

Wildgoose expected, he had a good bason of chocolate, and a plate of muffins well-buttered, before him.'[1] If Wildgoose is surprised by what he sees, what he hears surprises him even more.

Well, brother Wildgoose, says Mr. Whitefield, when and where were you converted? when did you first begin to feel the motions of God's Spirit? in what year, what month, what day, and in what manner, did you receive the secret call of the Spirit, to undertake the work of the ministry? What work of grace has God wrought upon your soul? and what symptoms have you felt of the new birth?[2]

The arrogance of which Whitefield was so frequently accused by his critics is made apparent here. Like many of his contemporaries, Graves seems to have been unsure whether to condemn Whitefield or treat him as a mountebank. In the end he compromised: Whitefield as himself is pompous and hypocritical; Whitefield as Wildgoose is possessed of sufficient candour and charity to win the reader's affection.

It was undoubtedly on the London stage that the most vigorous attack was made upon the belief and character of Whitefield. Some might consider this poetic justice, since 'playhouses' had been the target for some of the evangelist's most emphatic denunciations. There is of course an element of irony in the fact that the man who himself possessed so many natural acting talents should have become the stage's most zealous opponent. But Whitefield's hostility to the theatre was reciprocated with a vengeance. *The Minor* (1760), a comic farce by Samuel Foote,[3] was an indictment of Methodism and, in particular, Whitefield. The latter is caricatured in the person of an unscrupulous preacher, Mr. Squintum, who never actually appears in the play but who is frequently alluded to. (The name, Squintum, is a gibe at

---

[1] *The Spiritual Quixote*, bk. vii, ch. i.

[2] Ibid.

[3] Foote followed *The Minor* with two more satires on Whitefield and Methodism: *The Methodist* (1761) and *The Orators* (1762).

Whitefield's crossed eyes.) In the play Whitefield's character
is aspersed and his theology made to look absurd.

Foote brings the acrimony to a climax in the character of
Mrs. Cole, the keeper of a bawdy-house and a recent convert to Methodism. Regularly throughout the dialogue she
rhapsodizes, sometimes in language reminiscent of Whitefield himself, about her new-found state of grace. Always,
however, she gets back to the business at hand:

Oh, it was a wonderful work. There had I been tossing in the sea of
sin, without rudder or compass. And had not the good gentleman
[Squintum] piloted me into the harbour of grace, I must have struck
against the rocks of reprobation, and have been quite swallowed up
in the whirlpool of despair. He was the precious instrument of my
spiritual sprinkling.—But, however, Sir George, if your mind be set
upon a young country thing, to-morrow night I believe I can furnish
you.[1]

Sir George, a scarcely less reprobate character, takes the
measure of Mrs. Cole's religion: 'How the jade has jumbled
together the carnal and the spiritual; with what ease she
reconciles her new birth to her old calling!—No wonder,
these preachers have plenty of proselytes, whilst they have
the address so comfortably to blend hitherto jarring interests
of the two worlds.'[2] The substance of Foote's criticism is
that in this kind of religion faith alone matters; conduct
counts for very little. Though in fact Whitefield was not
guilty of antinomianism, yet because the emphasis in his
preaching is almost exclusively upon salvation by faith, he
was particularly vulnerable to such a charge.

But if there were those among the literati who wished to
discredit Whitefield, there were also those who stood ready
to defend him. Those characteristics of his preaching which
some interpreted as showmanship or fanaticism seemed to
others the sincere and spontaneous expression of concern by
a man of God for the souls of the fallen.

Nor was it just his converts who were thus favourably

[1] *The Minor*, act I, *Works of Samuel Foote* (1830), vol. ii.
[2] Ibid.

disposed towards Whitefield. Among those who respected him without being much affected by his message of sin and salvation, none was more generous in his praise or loyal in his support than Benjamin Franklin. When others, and some of them in holy orders, questioned Whitefield's probity in connection with monies collected for the Bethesda project,[1] Franklin affirmed his faith in the evangelist's character.

Some of Mr. Whitefield's enemies affected to suppose that he would apply these collections to his own private emolument; but I, who was intimately acquainted with him, never had the least suspicion of his integrity, but am to this day decidedly of opinion that he was in all his conduct a perfectly honest man; and methinks my testimony in his favour ought to have more weight, as we had no religious connection.[2]

For Whitefield the orator, Franklin had still greater respect, and for good reason. He had approved Whitefield's idea of founding an orphanage in the Colonies, but thought that Philadelphia, where supplies and workmen were most easily obtainable, would be the best location. When, against his advice, Whitefield chose Georgia, Franklin decided not to support the project:

'I happened soon after,' says Franklin, 'to attend one of his sermons, in the course of which I perceived he intended to finish with a collection, and I silently resolved he should get nothing from me; I had in my pocket a handful of copper-money, three or four silver dollars, and five pistoles in gold; as he proceeded I began to soften, and concluded to give the copper. Another stroke of his oratory made me ashamed of that, and determined me to give the silver; and he finished so admirably, that I emptied my pocket wholly into the collector's dish, gold and all!'[3]

This account helps to explain how, in an age much less opulent than the present, Whitefield managed to raise in the

---

[1] 'Bethesda' was the name given by Whitefield to an orphanage he founded in Savannah, Georgia, in 1739, and for whose maintenance he assumed responsibility for the rest of his life.

[2] Cited in *Sketches*, p. 259.

[3] Quoted by Parton, *Life*, i. 249-50.

United Kingdom alone some fourteen thousand pounds for his colonial projects.

Another man who respected Whitefield without sharing his religious convictions was the deist, Lord Bolingbroke. In a letter to Lady Huntingdon he lauds Whitefield's talents: 'He is the most extraordinary man in our times. He has the most commanding eloquence I ever heard in any person; his abilities are very considerable; his zeal unquenchable; and his piety and excellence genuine—unquestionable.'[1] Even allowing that some of Bolingbroke's delight with Whitefield springs from the latter's having earned the disfavour of the orthodox clergy, this is still very high praise.

One of the finest tributes to Whitefield came from William Cowper. Like Whitefield, Cowper believed in the doctrine of election. Unlike Whitefield, he could not finally believe that he was one of God's elect. Perhaps it was Whitefield's courage and supreme confidence which appealed most to this timid and sensitive poet:

> He lov'd the world that hated him; the tear
> That dropp'd upon his Bible was sincere:
> Assail'd by scandal and the tongue of strife,
> His only answer was, a blameless life;
> And he that forg'd, and he that threw, the dart,
> Had each a brother's int'rest in his heart!
> Paul's love of Christ, and steadiness unbrib'd,
> Were copied close in him, and well transcrib'd.
> He followed Paul—his zeal a kindred flame,
> His apostolic charity the same.
> Like him, cross'd cheerfully tempestuous seas,
> Forsaking country, kindred, friends, and ease;
> Like him he labour'd, and, like him, content
> To bear it, suffer'd shame where'er he went.
>   Blush, calumny! and write upon his tomb,
> If honest eulogy can spare thee room,
> Thy deep repentance of thy thousand lies,

[1] Cited in *Sketches*, p. 271.

Which, aim'd at him, have pierc'd th'offended skies;
And say, Blot out my sin, confess'd, deplor'd,
Against thine image in thy saint, oh Lord![1]

Throughout his ministry and even after his death the debate about Whitefield's character and preaching was sustained. *Quot homines, tot sententiae*; for every new attacker there was a new defender. On one score, however, nearly all would have agreed: for more than a generation his passionate and dramatic oratory had made him the most sensational preacher on two continents. The English church would have to wait another century—until the emergence of Charles Haddon Spurgeon—before his like would be seen again.

[1] 'Hope', ll. 574–93.

JOHN WESLEY
From a portrait by Nathaniel Hone in the National Portrait Gallery, London.

VII

JOHN WESLEY

(1703–1791)

The Heart's and Mind's Delight

JOHN WESLEY was a man of many talents, all of which he used to great effect in founding Methodism. Author,[1] editor, translator, hymnist, physician, teacher, organizer: all these he was and more. Supremely, however, he was a preacher. And as valuable as were the other parts he played, yet without this one gift—the gift of oratory—it could not now seriously be said of him that he is 'incomparably the most influential English figure in the religious story of the world'.[2] The religious awakening which Wesley represents could not have been effected when it was by any means other than dynamic preaching. Under the spell of his oratory

---

[1] Wesley's literary output is astonishing, especially when it is remembered that it is all the result of his rare hours of leisure. He is easily the most prolific religious writer of his century. In *The Works of John and Charles Wesley: A Bibliography*, (1896) Richard Green summarizes Wesley's production as follows: 233 were original works; 100 were extracted or edited by him; to 8 he wrote a preface or notes only; in 30 he assisted, or was assisted by, his brother Charles. This makes a total of 371 books and tracts. Included among these are numerous editions of hymns, psalms, and sacred poems; a tract containing his 'Thoughts on Marriage and a Single Life'; *Primitive Physic; or an Easy and Natural Method of Curing Most Diseases*; short English, French, Latin, Greek, and Hebrew grammars; *The Complete English Dictionary*; a dissertation on electricity; a 'Compendium of Logick'; concise histories of Rome and England; and a 'Letter to a Friend concerning Tea'.

[2] K. Slack, *The British Churches Today* (1961), p. 63.

thousands received new hope and were persuaded to change
the moral direction of their lives. Thousands more were
stirred to action in behalf of the deprived peoples of England
and the world.

Much of the force and appeal of his preaching was owing
to the extraordinary *charisma* of Wesley the man. Some of it
was the result of the singular interpretation and expression
he gave to the Christian message. Yet the difference between
Wesley's sermons and those of Secker, Sherlock, Berkeley,
or any of the more moderate divines of the period, can hardly
be described as doctrinal. In his acceptance of Original Sin,
the Trinity, the Atonement, Salvation by Faith, and the
Final Judgement, Wesley stands squarely in the classical
Protestant tradition. Where he parts company with Secker
and the others is in the particular emphasis he gives to
certain of these doctrines.

Original Sin, for example, was so much a theological
commonplace with Latitudinarian divines as to require
neither statement nor defence. And it received neither. To
an age which prided itself on its progress and sophistication,
talk of original sin seemed somehow uncouth, certainly
irrelevant. Pelagianism and Socinianism, where they were
thought about at all, were still regarded as heresies, and yet
in retrospect it is clear that both lurked very near the surface
of the received theology of the age. Tillotson, though he
would have denied it, had flirted with both these heresies
by his insistence upon prudent behaviour as the key to
present happiness and eternal reward.

Wesley saw the real danger to Christianity in the neglect
of this doctrine. To ignore or mitigate original sin was to
diminish, perhaps even destroy, the significance of the
Atonement; as he saw it, the two were inseparable. Christ
had suffered the unspeakable agony of crucifixion that man
might have 'dominion over sin', something that no amount
of good works or purity of life could achieve alone.

A denial of original sin contradicts the main design of the gospel, which
is to humble vain man, and to ascribe to God's free grace, not man's

free will, the whole of his salvation. Nor, indeed, can we let this doctrine go without giving up, at the same time, the greatest part, if not all, of the essential articles of the Christian faith. If we give up this, we cannot defend either justification by the merits of Christ, or the renewal of our natures by his Spirit.[1]

'Justification by the merits of Christ' and 'the renewal of our natures by his Spirit' were the essential elements in Wesley's theology: 'If any doctrines within the whole compass of Christianity may be properly termed "fundamental", they are doubtless these two,—the doctrine of justification, and that of the new birth.'[2] Wesley's peculiar interpretation of these two doctrines becomes clearer as his conception of the process of salvation is revealed.

For Saint Paul the protagonists in the unending struggle of life were spirit and flesh; the one striving to attain its eudaemonia in communion with God, the other constantly holding it back. Ultimate victory was possible for spirit because of the merits and sacrifice of Jesus Christ, God's Son. Wesley gave the protagonists new names, grace and nature, but the essence of the conflict remained the same. Man was born into a state of nature ('a state of utter darkness'), but by appropriating the benefits of Christ's Atonement he could progress to the state of grace, with its promise of eternal bliss.

In his Adamic state man is indifferent to the claims of God. He is the sleeper who needs to be roused, the unwitting victim of original sin. Wesley depicts the repugnance of man's plight in a sermon on 'The Circumcision of the Heart':

[Humility] convinces us that we are by nature, 'wretched, and poor, and miserable, and blind, and naked'. It convinces us, that in our best estate we are, of ourselves, all sin and vanity; that confusion, and

---

[1] *Works*, (1872), ix. 429.
[2] *Standard Sermons*, ed. E. H. Sugden, 5th ed. (1961), ii. 226–7. Wesley himself published 133 sermons and 8 (the Fifth Series) were published after his death. The First Series contains 53 sermons, of which 44 make up the Standard Sermons—the doctrinal standard of Methodism.

ignorance, and error reign over our understanding; that unreasonable, earthly, sensual, devilish passions usurp authority over our will; in a word, that there is no whole part in our soul, that all the foundations of our nature are out of course.[1]

Even amid such moral depravity man may, of course, be capable of performing good deeds, and, at times, may render real service to the community or group of which he is a part. But until he has received a dispensation of grace, and until the condemnation of the moral law has been removed from his life, his good deeds are only so many 'splendid sins'.

The preacher's task is to confront such men, apprise them of their estrangement from God, and cause them to feel a sense of guilt for their neglect of salvation. The urgency of the message demands the simplest language and most importune methods of delivery. Congregations must never be allowed to forget the ineluctable fate of the impenitent: 'Be serious. Let the whole stream of thy thoughts, words, and actions flow from the deepest conviction that thou standest on the edge of the great gulf, thou and all the children of men, just ready to drop in, either into everlasting glory or everlasting burnings!'[2] Once awakened, the alarmed conscience gives rise to 'repentance'. The sinner acknowledges his depravity and pleads for God's mercy. This, in Wesleyan terminology, is 'the porch of true religion'. 'Our main doctrines, which include all the rest, are three,—that of repentance, of faith, and of holiness. The first of these we account, as it were, the porch of religion; the next, the door; the third, religion itself.'[3]

Repentance alone then is not enough. It must be accompanied by faith. In Wesley's schema there were two kinds of faith: the spurious and the genuine. He explained the difference in a sermon entitled 'The Discoveries of Faith'. The first kind—the ineffectual—he terms the 'faith of a servant'. This is faith which acknowledges the reality of God, but is

[1] *Standard Sermons*, i. 268.
[2] Ibid., ii. 36.
[3] *Works*, viii. 472.

based upon fear, not love, and even Satan is capable of such faith. It is, however, a beginning, and with proper guidance it can develop into something very much nobler.

Exhort him to press on, by all possible means, till he passes 'from faith to faith', from the faith of a *servant* to the faith of a *son*; from the spirit of bondage unto fear, to the spirit of childlike love: he will then have 'Christ revealed in his heart', enabling him to testify, 'The life that I now live in the flesh, I live by faith in the Son of God, who loved *me*, and gave himself for *me*',—the proper voice of a child of God.[1]

Thus the sinner is born again. Thus he passes from a state of nature to a state of grace.

Wesley's descriptions of the soul's journey from the night of sin to the effulgence of the 'life in Christ' are to some extent autobiographical. On 24 May 1738 he had undergone a memorable emotional and spiritual experience.

In the evening I went very unwillingly to a society in Aldersgate Street, where one was reading Luther's preface to the *Epistle to the Romans*. About a quarter before nine, while he was describing the change which God works in the heart through faith in Christ, I felt my heart strangely warmed. I felt I did trust in Christ, Christ alone for salvation; and an assurance was given me that He had taken away *my* sins, even *mine*, and saved *me* from the law of sin and death.[2]

Writing to his brother Samuel five months later he says: 'I was not a Christian till May the 24th last past.'[3] In later life Wesley would have reservations about the validity of that statement, but that a significant change had taken place in him he would never doubt. A juxtaposition of some sermon titles suggests his conception of what really happened at Aldersgate Street: from being an 'Almost Christian' he became an 'Altogether Christian'; he passed from 'The Righteousness of the Law' to 'The Righteousness of Christ'; whereas before he had been 'Under the Law' now he was

---

[1] *Sermons on Several Occasions* (1838), iii. 225–6.
[2] *Journal*, ed. N. Curnock (1909), i. 475–6.
[3] *Letters*, ed. J. Telford (1931), i. 262.

'Under Grace'; he gave up 'The Faith of a Servant' and received 'The Faith of a Son'.

The conversion experience, effected through genuine faith and repentance, 'justified' the sinner. Justification is a gift of God's grace and, Calvinism notwithstanding, is available not to a predetermined few but to all who truly repent. In the Minutes of 1744 the connection between faith and justification is formally established: 'Q.1. What is it to be justified? A. To be pardoned and received into God's favour; into such a state, that, if we continue therein, we shall be finally saved. Q.2. Is faith the condition of justification? A. Yes; for every one who believeth not is condemned; and every one who believes is justified.'[1]

But Wesley's doctrine of salvation does not conclude with justification. Had it done so his theology would have been vulnerable to a charge of antinomianism, a charge which was already impairing the ministry of George Whitefield. Wesley successfully protected himself by adding another step: '[Justification] is not the being made actually just and righteous. This is *sanctification*; which is, indeed, in some degree, the immediate fruit of justification, but, nevertheless, is a distinct gift of God, and of a totally different nature. The one implies, what God does for us through His Son; the other, what He works in us by His Spirit.'[2] Whereas, then, justification restores men to the 'favour' of God, sanctification, or the new birth, as he sometimes calls it, restores them to his 'image'. 'The one is the taking away the guilt, the other the taking away the power, of sin.'[3] The external evidence of sanctification is good works, and Wesley never misses an opportunity to stress this point. If works without faith were vain, faith without works was impossible.

The distinction between justification and sanctification is more clearly defined still in Wesley's assertion that whereas the former is the province of God the Son, the latter is

---

[1] *Works*, viii. 275.
[2] *Standard Sermons*, i. 119.
[3] Ibid., i. 300.

principally the work of the Holy Spirit. Thus he gives equal importance to Christ's Atonement and the abiding presence of the Holy Ghost. Colin W. Williams believes it is this distinction which gives Wesley's theology its singularity:

In the theology of Luther and Ca[l]vin the emphasis remains on justification. The fact that the believer is *simul justus et peccator* and that Christ is our 'alien righteousness', holds the center of attention in such a way that the transformation of the believer, though real, is secondary. But in Wesley, while justification is the foundation of the Christian life, the center of attention moves to the transforming work of the Spirit in the life of the justified. Here the 'optimism of grace' in Wesley's theology becomes even more apparent.[1]

The claim that the Holy Ghost was the principal agent in conversion was, as Horton Davies points out,[2] anything but a commonplace in eighteenth-century religion. And the assertion by Wesley and Whitefield that it was the 'operations of the Holy Spirit' which were responsible for the paroxysms that accompanied Methodist meetings seemed to many to be heresy or, at best, enthusiasm.[3]

Despite the importance Wesley attaches to the experience engendered by the Third Person of the Trinity, that experience is not for him, as it is for many Free Church Protestants, the ultimate religious authority. Wesley knew human nature too well not to be aware of the vagaries of experience and emotion. Such authority, therefore, he ascribes to the Bible, and in so doing demonstrates again

---

[1] *John Wesley's Theology Today* (1960), pp. 100–1.

[2] *Worship and Theology*, p. 154.

[3] Sterne is typical: 'The last mistake I shall have time to mention, is that which the Methodists have revived, for 'tis no new error—but one which has misled thousands before these days whenever enthusiasm had got footing,—and that is,—the attempting to prove their works, by that very argument which is the greatest proof of their weakness and superstition;—I mean that extraordinary impulse and intercourse with the Spirit of God which they pretend to, and whose operations (if you trust them) are so sensibly felt in their hearts and souls, as to render at once all other proofs of their works needless to themselves.—This, I own, is one of the most summary ways of proceeding in this duty of self-examination; and, as it proves a man's work in the gross, it saves him a world of sober thought and inquiry after many vexatious particulars.' *The Sermons of Mr. Yorick*, i. 166.

that he is squarely fixed in the classical Protestant tradition, a direct descendant of Luther and Calvin. For Wesley the Bible provided the final test of experience; not vice versa: 'The Scriptures are the touchstone whereby Christians examine all, real or supposed, revelations. In all cases they appeal "to the law and the testimony" to try every spirit thereby.'[1] On occasions he could descant on the Bible to the exclusion of all else: 'O give me that book! At any price, give me the book of God! I have it: here is knowledge enough for me. Let me be *homo unius libri.*'[2]

For all this, however, Wesley is not a stringent literalist nor a Bibliolater. He knew the Greek and Hebrew languages too well not to recognize the dangers of literal interpretation. His frequent boast that he was a *homo unius libri* should be taken no more seriously than the unintended irony in his preference for a Latin phrase would suggest.[3] He has little in common with the hard-shell fundamentalists of his own or any other age. His approach to the study and interpretation of scripture is that of a liberal scholar:

I then search after and consider parallel passages of Scripture, 'comparing spiritual things with spiritual'. I meditate thereon with all the attention and earnestness of which my mind is capable. If any doubt still remains, I consult those who are experienced in the things of God; and then the writings whereby, being dead, they yet speak. And what I thus learn, that I teach.[4]

This passage supports G. R. Cragg's conclusion that Wesley 'had built up a carefully balanced doctrine of authority. His appeal was to the Bible, interpreted by reason and confirmed by experience.'[5]

---

[1] *Letters*, ii. 117.

[2] *Standard Sermons*, i. 32.

[3] Sugden notes (ibid., i. 30 n) that in the same paragraph of a *Journal* entry for 14 May 1765, in which he states 'in 1730 I began to be *homo unius libri*, to study (comparatively) no book but the Bible', he acknowledges his debt to Jeremy Taylor's *Holy Living* (from which he had probably got the Latin phrase) and William Law's *Christian Perfection* and *Serious Call*.

[4] *Standard Sermons*, i. 32.

[5] *Reason and Authority in Eighteenth Century England* (1964), p. 161.

Wesley himself, then, read widely and tested his own experience against the recorded experiences of others. Also, he constantly admonished his preachers to read whatever seemed likely to deepen their knowledge of God. This passage from the *Large Minutes* of 1770 is typical:

Read the most useful books, and that regularly and constantly . . . 'But I read only the Bible.' Then you ought to teach others to read only the Bible, and by parity of reason, to hear only the Bible: but if so, you need preach no more. Just so said George Bell. And what is the fruit? Why, now he neither reads the Bible nor anything else. This is rank enthusiasm. If you need no book but the Bible, you are got above St. Paul. He wanted others too. 'Bring the books,' says he, '*but especially the parchments*', those wrote on parchment. 'But I have no *taste* for reading.' Contract a taste for it by use, or return to your trade.[1]

Whitefield, in a mood of fideistic censure, had denounced all secular scholarship: 'our common learning, so much cried up, makes men only so many accomplished fools.'[2] Wesley's scholarly training and sensibilities rendered him incapable of such a statement. Though he accepted the Bible as the highest authority in matters of faith and morals, yet he believed that it is only through an examination of tradition, great writings, and experience itself that the Word of God is made plain.

In view of his attitude to the Bible, it is not surprising to discover that Wesley is careful not to exclude reason from religion. His most explicit statement on the subject is his sermon 'The Case of Reason Considered'. In it he rebukes two groups: those who categorically reject reason, who 'declaim in that wild, loose, ranting manner, against this precious gift of God',[3] and, second, those at the other extreme who 'look upon it as the all-sufficient director of all the children of men; able, by its native light, to guide them into all truth, and lead them into all virtue'.[4] But it is those

[1] Quoted in *Standard Sermons*, i. 30–1 n.
[2] Whitefield, *Works*, vi. 190.
[3] *Sermons on Several Occasions*, ii. 340.
[4] Ibid., ii. 332.

who decry reason that receive the sterner rebuke. In a letter to a friend he expresses succinctly what he hopes will be the Methodist attitude towards reason and religion. 'It is a fundamental principle with us that to renounce reason is to renounce religion, that religion and reason go hand in hand, and that all irrational religion is false religion.'[1]

In 'The Case of Reason Considered' Wesley tries to delineate the part reason should play. 'If you ask, What can reason do in religion? I answer, It can do exceeding much, both with regard to the foundation of it, and the super-structure.'[2] Reason is not another source of revelation but the instrument whereby revelations are tested and interpreted.

Is it not reason (assisted by the Holy Ghost) which enables us to understand what the holy Scriptures declare concerning the being and attributes of God?—concerning his eternity and immensity; his power, wisdom, and holiness? It is by reason that God enables us in some measure to comprehend his method of dealing with the children of men; the nature of his various dispensations, of the old and new covenant, of the law and the Gospel.[3]

Much to Wesley's chagrin, a militant reaction against reason had set in among the more evangelical, many of whom were flocking to Methodism. Furthermore, such popular and eloquent preachers as George Whitefield, John Newton, and Augustus Toplady were proclaiming a brand of Calvinism that seemed inimical to reason. Wesley abhorred such religious enthusiasm. His sermon on 'The Nature of Enthusiasm' is a rebuff to those who permit emotion and imagination to usurp the place of reason in religious experience.[4]

It is essential to recognize, however, that of itself reason 'is utterly incapable of giving either faith, or hope, or love; and consequently, of producing either real virtue, or substantial happiness'.[5] No one knew better than Wesley

[1] *Letters*, v. 364.

[2] *Sermons on Several Occasions*, ii. 334.

[3] Ibid., ii. 335.

[4] *Standard Sermons*, ii. 84–103.

[5] *Sermons on Several Occasions*, ii. 340.

that there is more to religion than merely making the proper moral choices and performing the accepted conventions. 'I made the trial for many years. I collected the finest hymns, prayers, and meditations, which I could find in any language; and I said, sung, or read them over and over, with all possible seriousness and attention. But still I was like the bones in Ezekiel's vision: "the skin covered them above; but there was no breath in them." '[1] Aldersgate Street had changed all that. It was his heart, not his intellect, which had been kindled there. And if that momentous experience did not necessarily contradict reason, neither could it be explained in purely rational terms.

There was a strong element of pragmatism in Wesley's theology. He had little time or patience for the niceties of theological speculation. He once remarked that 'orthodoxy, or right opinions, is, at best, but a very slender part of religion, if it can be allowed to be any part at all'.[2] On those doctrines which he regarded as fundamental to the Christian faith, Wesley, of course, stood firm: 'on the Godhead of Christ . . . I *must* insist as the foundation of all our hope.'[3] But ultimately it was men, and not ideas, which mattered to him. Because of this he insisted on no particular dogma as the right one. In his attitude to belief there is a genuine spirit of ecumenism.

I dare not, therefore, presume to impose my mode of worship on any other. I believe it is truly primitive and apostolical: but my belief is no rule for another. I ask not, therefore, of him with whom I would unite in love, Are you of my church, of my congregation? Do you receive the same form of church government, and allow the same church officers, with me? Do you join in the same form of prayer wherein I worship God? I inquire not, Do you receive the supper of the Lord in the same posture and manner that I do? nor whether, in the administration of baptism, you agree with me in admitting sureties for the baptized; in the manner of administering it; or the age of those

[1] *Sermons on Several Occasions,* ii. 339.
[2] *Works,* viii. 249
[3] *Journal,* v. 254.

to whom it should be administered. Nay, I ask not of you (as clear as I am in my own mind), whether you allow baptism and the Lord's supper at all. Let all these things stand by: we will talk of them, if need be, at a more convenient season; my only question at present is this, 'Is thine heart right, as my heart is with thy heart?'[1]

This concern for what people do, rather than what they profess to believe, helps to explain the strong ethical bent of Wesley's preaching. Thirteen of the forty-four Standard Sermons are based on the Sermon on the Mount. As a homilist he is at his best when preaching a didactic sermon on a moral issue, for it is here that his careful distinctions and persuasive reasoning are shown to best advantage. His desire to be practical and relevant led him to treat such mundane issues as the proper use of money, how to make the most of time, how to dress properly, the education of children, maintaining good health, making a will, manners, temperance, vocation, conversation, leisure, and marriage.[2] His well-known phrase concerning money typifies the kind of practicable advice he gave generally: Gain all you can; Save all you can; Give all you can.[3] Wesley can never be accused of other-worldliness; life here and now was his most pressing concern.

Of supreme value in Wesley's philosophy was the individual soul. He never allowed himself to forget for a minute that the primary purpose of his ministry was to make men aware of their inestimable worth in the sight of God. He held firmly to an Arminian doctrine, with its insistence upon universal salvation, and rejected Calvinism, whose concept of limited redemption and austere view of God he regarded as inimical to the spirit of Christ. And there can be little doubt that it was the optimism of this theology, combined with the lyrical genius of Charles Wesley, which made Methodism so attractive and vital.

These then are the cardinal features of Wesleyan theology

---

[1] *Standard Sermons*, ii. 135–6.
[2] See W. L. Doughty, *John Wesley, Preacher* (1955), ch. ix.
[3] *Standard Sermons*, ii. 309 ff.

as expounded in the *Standard Sermons*. For two hundred years candidates for the Methodist ministry have had to study and approve these sermons. Wesley himself had seen to this. 'In 1763 he prepared a Model Deed for his preaching-houses, in which it was provided that persons appointed by the Conference should "have and enjoy the premises" only on condition "that the said persons preach no other doctrine than is contained in Mr. Wesley's Notes upon the New Testament, and four volumes of sermons".'[1] From this can be seen something of the influence the Standard Sermons have had upon Methodism, and indeed upon Protestantism, for the last two centuries. They are the only eighteenth-century sermons which have been assured an audience in every generation since their publication. And interest has not been confined solely to their content; they have also been held up as models of homiletic and rhetorical art.

It has sometimes been questioned whether Wesley actually preached his sermons as they are written, or whether he had one mode of address for the pulpit and another for the press. Dinsdale T. Young felt that no amount of oratorical panache could have enlivened the published sermons sufficiently to affect congregations in the way Wesley's preaching most assuredly did. He is left, therefore, with only one conclusion, which is, that 'it was not by *those* discourses that Wesley built up his Popular Pulpit. . . . Face to face with the multitude John Wesley preached in a very different style from that which is disclosed in his printed discourses.'[2] W. L. Doughty agrees: 'It is not possible to conceive of any powers of oratory or intensity of zeal for the souls of men that could commend these sermons, as they stand, to the many people whose illiteracy was a disgrace to their age and country, and who probably formed the majority of Wesley's out-of-doors hearers.'[3] But not

[1] *Standard Sermons*, i. 13.
[2] *Popular Preaching* (1929), p. 139.
[3] *John Wesley, Preacher*, p. 84.

everyone shares this view. 'The *Standard Sermons*', says John Lawson, 'are not a collection of dummy sermons. They are not dull theological discourses thinly disguised as spoken addresses. A few of them were indeed written especially for publication, but most of them are sermons that Wesley actually preached. Many of them were preached very frequently, to ordinary congregations, and even in the open air.'[1]

Although he offers no evidence to support his claim, Lawson appears to hold the more plausible view. At least Wesley's introduction to the 1746 edition of the sermons would seem to suggest as much:

Nothing here appears in an elaborate, elegant, or oratorical dress. If it had been my desire or design to write thus, my leisure would not permit. But, in truth, I, at present, designed nothing less; for I now write, as I generally speak, *ad populum*—to the bulk of mankind, to those who neither relish nor understand the art of speaking; but who, notwithstanding, are competent judges of those truths which are necessary to present and future happiness.[2]

Naturally, in preparing his sermons for publication Wesley omitted many of the anecdotes and repetitions that he had used in the pulpit. But this would not affect materially either the homiletic or rhetorical structure of the sermons. And to say there is a dearth of illustration is to ignore the wealth of allusion, picturesque language, proverb, and imagery that were immensely meaningful to the congregations of that day. Couched as they are in a sermon form that is remarkable for its simplicity, and in language that is forceful, flexible, and, in large measure, colloquial, it is not difficult to see how discourses such as 'The Almost Christian', 'The Circumcision of the Heart', and 'The Great Assize' could, even as they now stand, reduce a congregation to contrition and repentance.

What Leslie Stephen says of Wesley's letters could with equal truth be applied to his sermons: 'He goes straight to

---

[1] *Notes on Wesley's Forty-four Sermons* (1929), pp. 1–2.

[2] *Standard Sermons*, i. 29–30.

the mark without one superfluous flourish. He writes as a man confined within the narrowest limits of time and space, whose thoughts are so well in hand that he can say everything needful within those limits. The compression gives emphasis and never causes confusion.'[1] His sermons, too, are celebrated for their economy of statement, logical development, and simplicity of design. His homiletic technique hardly ever varies. The text is introduced, with only as much background given as is relevant to the preacher's present design. Under several (usually three) major headings the arguments are stated and supported. When the sermon is textual (e.g. 'The Scripture Way of Salvation') much time is spent in exegesis. Different translations and nuances of the original Greek or Hebrew are carefully considered. When the sermon is topical (e.g. 'The Great Assize') or thematic (e.g. 'The New Birth') textual and verbal analysis gives way to the construction of forceful analogies. There is never any dallying; points are scored swiftly and effectively. Towards the end there is usually a brief recapitulation (Wesley is ever the teacher), followed by a stirring peroration. The hearer or reader is never left in doubt about what is expected of him. What Wesley has done is taken a method of sermon construction which has already been shorn of elaborate divisions and turgid language and applied it to the needs of evangelism. The result is a sharp, adaptable, and polished homiletic weapon, capable of subduing the most obdurate sinner.

Early in his ministry Wesley, in keeping with his scholarly inclinations, preached from 'an exquisitely neat little MS.'[2] But a dramatic incident in 1735 produced a sudden change in his attitude to sermon delivery. A *Journal* entry for January 1776 tells how it happened: 'I was desired to preach a charity sermon in Allhallows Church, Lombard Street. In the year 1735, above forty years ago, I preached in this church, at the earnest request of the churchwardens,

1 *English Thought*, ii. 348.
2 *Journal*, i. 60.

to a numerous congregation, who came, like me, with an
intent to hear Dr. Heylyn. This was the first time that,
having no notes about me, I preached extempore.'[1] Wesley
liked the freedom of expression, gesture, and emphasis which
extemporaneous preaching allowed, and when, with Whitefield, he took to field-preaching, he found it an inestimable
advantage to be able to address his congregations without
recourse to a manuscript. Extempore delivery did not
eliminate the necessity of sermon preparation for Wesley,
but it did allow him to experiment with a sermon several
times before finally committing it to paper. This may
partially explain why he has such a sureness of touch in the
discourses he chose to publish.

Wesley tried to appeal to the mind and the heart simultaneously. Though not as dramatic as Whitefield, he nonetheless
enjoyed many oratorical gifts. His sermons abound in
passages of strong emotion which, when reinforced by his
personal authority, must surely have achieved their desired
effect. Many such passages concern the end of the world and
the Final Judgement.

How will ye escape? Will ye call to the mountains to fall on you, the
rocks to cover you? Alas, the mountains themselves, the rocks, the
earth, the heavens, are just ready to flee away! Can ye prevent the
sentence? Wherewith? With all the substance of thy house, with
thousands of gold and silver? Blind wretch! Thou camest naked from

---

[1] *Journal*, vi. 96. It was not until 1825, in *The Wesleyan Methodist Magazine*, that
further light was shed on this significant little incident. On Sunday, 28 December
1788, Wesley preached at the Parish church of Allhallows for a third time. 'MR.
LETTS, by virtue of his office as a Steward of the Charity, was appointed to attend
on MR. WESLEY, who, while he was putting on his gown in the vestry, said to him,
"It is above fifty years, Sir, since I first preached in this Church; I remember it
from a particular circumstance that occurred at that time. I came without a Sermon;
and, going up the pulpit-stairs, I hesitated, and returned into the vestry, under
much mental confusion and agitation. A woman, who stood by, noticed my
concern, and said, 'Pray, Sir, what is the matter with you?' I replied, I have not
brought a Sermon with me. She said, putting her hand on my shoulder, 'Is that
all? Cannot you trust GOD for a Sermon?' The question had such an effect upon
me, that I ascended the pulpit, preached extempore, with great freedom to
myself, and acceptance to the people; and have never since taken a written Sermon
into the pulpit" ' (pp. 105–6).

thy mother's womb, and more naked into eternity. Hear the Lord, the
Judge! 'Come, ye blessed of my Father, inherit the kingdom prepared
for you from the foundation of the world.' Joyful sound! How widely
different from that voice which echoes through the expanse of heaven,
'Depart, ye cursed, into everlasting fire, prepared for the devil and
his angels!' And who is he that can prevent or retard the full execution
of either sentence? Vain hope! Lo, hell is moved from beneath to
receive those who are ripe for destruction. And the everlasting doors
lift up their heads, that the heirs of glory may come in!¹

Dr. Johnson believed that the success of Methodist
preachers was owing 'to their expressing themselves in a
plain and familiar manner, which is the only way to do good
to common people'.² It is highly probable that he had
Wesley in mind when he made that statement. The marvel is
how one so refined—even, at times, donnish—as Wesley
could engage in haranguing such as this:

It is to these more especially that our Lord says, 'Why beholdest thou
the mote that is in thy brother's eye'—the infirmities, the mistakes, the
imprudence, the weakness of the children of God—'but considerest
not the beam that is in thine own eye?' Thou considerest not the dam-
nable impenitence, the satanic pride, the accursed self-will, the
idolatrous love of the world, which are in thyself, and which make thy
whole life an abomination to the Lord. Above all, with what supine
carelessness and indifference art thou dancing over the mouth of hell!³

Here he is closer to Latimer than to Tillotson. And no more
than Latimer does he spare his audience. 'What art thou?'
Wesley asks, then answers: 'Know and feel, that thou art a
poor, vile, guilty worm, quivering over the great gulf! What
art thou? A sinner born to die; a leaf driven before the wind;
a vapour ready to vanish away; just appearing, and then
scattered into the air to be no more seen!'⁴

Wesley was a curious blending of the rational and the
emotional, the idealist and the pragmatist, the scholar and

¹ *Standard Sermons*, ii. 418.
² *Boswell's Life*, i. 458–9.
³ *Standard Sermons*, i. 520.
⁴ Ibid., i. 521–2.

the popular orator. As a consequence it is not always easy to square his tactics with his strategy. George Lawton has observed that 'In spite of Wesley's strictures upon the florid and oratorical, he is anything but free from purple patches himself.'[1] He then quotes a passage from one of Wesley's sermons to illustrate his point:

And as if this were not misery enough, see likewise the fell monster war! Hark! the cannon's roar! A pitchy cloud covers the face of the sky! Noise, confusion, terror reigns over all! Dying groans are on every side. The bodies of men are pierced, torn, hewed in pieces: their blood is poured on the earth like water! Their souls take their flight into the eternal world: perhaps into everlasting misery. The ministers of grace turn away from the horrid scene; the ministers of vengeance triumph. Such already has been the face of things in that once happy land, where peace and plenty, even while banished from a great part of Europe, smiled for near a hundred years.[2]

Similarly, it is difficult to reconcile Wesley's idea of the proper length of a sermon with his own practice on occasions. In reply to an Irish lady who had complained to him about the length of services in her part of Ireland he said: 'If any other of the preachers exceed their time (about an hour in the whole service), I hope you will always put them in mind what is the Methodist rule. People imagine the longer the sermon is the more good it will do. This is a grand mistake. The help done on earth God doth it Himself; and He doth not need that we should use many words.'[3] And in a letter to two errant preachers he was even more emphatic: 'Unless you can and will leave off preaching long, I shall think it my duty to prevent your preaching at all among the Methodists.'[4]

Such a warning assumes a touch of comic irony when it is placed alongside several *Journal* entries. The first is for Sunday, 7 October 1739:

[1] *John Wesley's English* (1962), p. 243.
[2] Ibid.
[3] *Letters*, vi. 255.
[4] Ibid., vii. 70.

Between five and six I called on all who were present (about three thousand) at Stanley, on a little green, near the town, to accept of Christ, as their only 'wisdom, righteousness, sanctification, and redemption'. I was strengthened to speak as I never did before, and continued speaking near two hours; the darkness of the night, and a little lightning, not lessening the number, but increasing the seriousness, of the hearers.[1]

On Friday, 19 October 1739, having preached that morning at Newport, Monmouthshire, Wesley went on to Cardiff and preached twice more, at 4 p.m. and at 6 p.m. Overflow crowds came out to hear him expound the last six Beatitudes. Of the latter service he wrote: 'my heart was so enlarged I knew not how to give over, so that we continued three hours.'[2] On Sunday, 13 June 1742, he was in Epworth, preaching in the churchyard from his father's tomb. The service (his fourth of the day) was extended 'for near three hours'.[3] And again at Birstall, 23 April 1745, he was 'constrained to continue [his] discourse there near an hour longer than usual, God pouring out such a blessing that [he] knew not how to leave off'.[4]

Though he obviously knew what it meant to be so filled with the power of the Holy Spirit while preaching as hardly to know when or how to stop, yet there was a kind of evangelical preaching which he refused to condone. 'But of all preaching, what is usually called gospel preaching is the most useless, if not the most mischievous; a dull, yea or lively, harangue on the sufferings of Christ or salvation by faith without strongly inculcating holiness. I see more and more that this naturally tends to drive holiness out of the world.'[5] And as time passed Wesley's abhorrence of 'gospel preaching' increased. 'Let but a pert, self-sufficient animal, that has neither sense nor grace, bawl out something about Christ and His blood or justification by faith, and his

[1] *Journal*, ii. 287–8.
[2] Ibid., ii. 296.
[3] Ibid., iii. 24.
[4] Ibid., iii. 174.
[5] *Letters*, v. 345.

hearers cry out, "What a fine gospel sermon!" "[1] There must be no such madness in his Methodism. On 28 July 1775, Wesley wrote to John King, a Methodist preacher who had achieved outstanding results in Philadelphia and Baltimore. King's technique, it seems, was to rant and thunder at his audience.

Scream no more, at the peril of your soul. God now warns you by me, whom He has set over you. Speak as earnestly as you can, but do not scream. Speak with all your heart, but with a moderate voice. It was said of our Lord, 'He shall not *cry*'; the word properly means, He shall not *scream*. Herein be a follower of me, as I am of Christ. I often speak loud, often vehemently; but I never scream, I never strain myself. I dare not; I know it would be a sin against God and my own soul.[2]

Wesley was aware of the temptation the pulpit presented to men who, as was the case with most of his Methodist lay preachers, were barely literate. To help them he prepared and distributed a pamphlet: *Directions Concerning Pronunciation and Gesture*. After warning preachers against speaking 'too loud', 'too low', 'in a thick, cluttering manner', 'too fast', 'too slow', or 'with an irregular, desultory, and uneven voice, raised or depressed unnaturally or unreasonably', he continued: 'But the greatest and most common fault of all is, the speaking with a tone: Some have a womanish, squeaking tone; some a singing or canting one; some an high, swelling, theatrical tone, laying too much emphasis on every sentence; some have an awful, solemn tone; others an odd, whimsical, whining one, not to be expressed in words.'[3] His advice on how to prevent affectation of this kind is reminiscent of Secker's counsel to the clergy of his diocese.[4] 'To avoid all kinds of unnatural tones, the only rule is this,—Endeavour to speak in public just as you do in common conversation. Attend to your subject, and deliver it

---

[1] *Letters*, vi. 326–7.
[2] Ibid., vi. 167.
[3] *Works*, xiii. 520.
[4] Cf. Secker's *Eight Charges*, p. 310.

in the same manner as if you were talking of it to a friend. This, if carefully observed, will correct both this and almost all the other faults of a bad pronunciation.'[1]

For maximum effect words should be accompanied by appropriate gestures of the hands and body as well as by facial expressions. Wesley's attention to detail in these matters is a fair indication of how closely he had studied the art of oratory. On the use of the hands, for example:

(1) Never clap your hands, nor thump the pulpit. (2) Use the right hand most; and when you use the left, let it be only to accompany the other. (3) The right hand may be gently applied to the breast, when you speak of your own faculties, heart, or conscience. (4) You must begin your action with your speech, and end it when you make an end of speaking. (5) The hands should seldom be lifted higher than the eyes, nor let down lower than the breast. (6) Your eyes should always have your hands in view, so that they you speak to may see your eyes, your mouth, and your hands, all moving in concert with each other, and expressing the same thing. (7) Seldom stretch out your arms side-ways more than half a foot from the trunk of your body. (8) Your hands are not to be in perpetual motion: This the ancients called the babbling of the hands.[2]

This treatise on pronunciation and gesture is also interesting because of the light it throws on Wesley's own method of preaching. For while it is impossible to determine at all precisely the extent to which he observed his own counsel in this matter, yet there can be little doubt that it was fundamentally in the manner of address he outlines for his preachers that he himself achieved his extraordinary success.

In many respects Wesley was the most unlikely popular orator of the eighteenth or any other century. His training and temperament were those of a scholar, and his ability as such was duly acknowledged in 1726 when he was appointed a fellow of Lincoln College, Oxford. In person he was rather short and thin, with very fine, almost feminine,

---

[1] *Works*, xiii. 520.
[2] Ibid., xiii. 527.

features.[1] He was meticulous in his appearance and don-
nishly fastidious in his habits. 'In dress, he was a pattern of
neatness and simplicity. A narrow, plaited stock, a coat with
a small upright collar, no buckles at his knees, no silk or
velvet in any part of his apparel, and a head as white as
snow, gave an idea of something primitive and apostolical:
while an air of neatness and cleanliness was diffused over this
whole person.'[2] And the same impeccable appearance he
exhibited himself he also expected, and sometimes demanded, of others. On 24 April 1769 he wrote to Richard
Steel, one of his preachers in Ireland.

(2) Be cleanly. In this let the Methodists take pattern by the Quakers.
Avoid all nastiness, dirt, slovenliness, both in your person, clothes,
house, and all about you. Do not stink above ground. This is a bad
fruit of laziness; use all diligence to be clean, as one says,

> Let thy mind's sweetness have its operation
> Upon thy person, clothes, and habitation.

(3) Whatever clothes you have, let them be whole; no rents, no
tatters, no rags. These are a scandal to either man or woman, being
another fruit of vile laziness. Mend your clothes, or I shall never expect
you to mend your lives. Let none ever see a ragged Methodist.[3]

Diminutive, donnish, meticulous in dress and manners—
these then are the unlikely attributes of a man who withstood
the elements of nature, the abuse of men, and the criticism
of many of his fellow clergy to proclaim the gospel; who
travelled 250,000 miles and preached 40,000 sermons
during his sixty-year ministry; and who conceived and
executed such a change in the religious life of England as
can only be described as a revolution.

In view of the number of sermons he preached and the
thousands who heard him, it is surprising how few descrip-

---

[1] For a fuller account see L. Tyerman, *The Life and Times of the Rev. John
Wesley*, 4th ed. (1878), iii. 656.

[2] J. Hampson, *Memoirs of John Wesley* (1791), iii. 168.

[3] *Letters*, v. 133. The couplet is from George Herbert's *The Temple*, 'The
Church Porch', stanza 62. Wesley admired Herbert, who was also neat. In 1773 he
edited and published a selected edition of Herbert's sacred poems.

tions of Wesley's style of preaching have come down. Of the few that have, two would seem to have more significance here than the others. The first is by John Nelson, a London stonemason who heard Wesley preach in the Upper Moorfields on 17 June 1739: 'As soon as he got upon the stand he stroked back his hair and turned his face towards where I stood, and I thought fixed his eyes upon me. His countenance struck such an awful dread upon me, before I heard him speak, that it made my heart beat like the pendulum of a clock; and, when he did speak, I thought his whole discourse was aimed at me.'[1] Nelson bears witness to the power, authority, and immediacy of Wesley's preaching. His heart aflame with conviction, his voice urgent and eloquent, Wesley spoke directly and personally to sinners; he held them with his eyes, he addressed himself to their spiritual condition. Little wonder he struck an 'awful dread' into their hearts. But he did not leave them there: he offered them hope and abundant life. 'When he had done,' Nelson continues, 'I said, "This man can tell the secrets of my heart: he hath not left me there; for he hath showed the remedy, even the blood of Jesus." Then was my soul filled with consolation, through hope that God for Christ's sake would save me.'[2]

A more objective observer was Dr. Kennicott. On Friday, 24 August 1744, Wesley preached his last sermon before the University of Oxford. Kennicott, then twenty-four and an undergraduate at Wadham College, was in the congregation. His account of the service is extremely interesting:

On Friday morning . . . he came to St. Mary's at ten o'clock. There were present the vice-chancellor, the proctors, most of the heads of houses, a vast number of gownsmen, and a multitude of private people, with many of Wesley's own people, both brethren and sisters. He is neither tall nor fat; for the latter would ill become a Methodist. His black hair, quite smooth, and parted very exactly, added to a peculiar composure in his countenance, showed him to be an uncommon man. His prayer was soft, short, and conformable to the rules of the university. His text was Acts iv. 31. He spoke it very slowly, and with an agreeable emphasis. . . . When he came to what he called his plain, practical conclusion, he fired his address with so much zeal and unbounded satire as quite spoiled what otherwise might have been turned to great advantage; for, as I liked some, so I disliked other parts of his discourse extremely. I liked some of his freedom, such as calling the generality of young gownsmen 'a generation of triflers,' and many other just invectives. But, considering how many shining lights are here, that are the glory of the Christian cause, his sacred censure was much too flaming and strong, and his charity much too weak in not making large allowances. But, so far from allowances, he concluded, with a lifted up eye, in this most solemn form, 'It is time for Thee, Lord, to lay to Thine hand'; words full of such presumption and seeming imprecation, that they gave an universal shock. This, and the assertion that Oxford was not a Christian city, and this country not a Christian nation, were the most offensive parts of the sermon, except when he accused the whole body (and confessed himself to be one of the number) of the sin of perjury; and for this reason, because, upon becoming members of a college, every person takes an oath to observe the statutes of the university, and no one observes them in all things. Had these things been omitted, and his censures moderated, I think his discourse, as to style, and delivery, would have been uncommonly pleasing to others as well as to myself.[1]

In his ambivalent attitude to Wesley and his preaching, Kennicott is typical of scholars and intellectuals generally of the age. On the one hand, they were shocked by the crudity of his images, the severity of his indictments, and the brazen presumption of his references and approaches to God. On the other hand, they admired, and at times envied, his dedication, his zeal, and his ability to communicate his message to mind and heart alike.

Even his most implacable critics did not question Wesley's sincerity or suggest that he preached only for popular acclaim. And Leslie Stephen, after submitting

---

[1] Quoted by Tyerman, *Life and Times*, i. 449. See B. N. Henderson, 'John Wesley's last University Sermon', *Cornhill Magazine*, lviii (1925), 93–100.

Wesley to a rigorous trial, found him 'absolutely devoid of at least the lower forms of selfish indulgence'.[1] Nor was it the romance of preaching which enchanted him, as it did George Whitefield. Consider, for example, their respective attitudes to field-preaching. For Wesley, as he explains in *A Further Appeal to Men of Reason and Religion* (1743), field-preaching was an expedient, 'a thing submitted to, rather than chosen; and therefore submitted to, because I thought preaching even thus, better than not preaching at all'.[2] His advertisement for field-preaching is hardly likely to win recruits.

Can you sustain them, if you would? Can you bear the summer rain to beat upon your naked head? Can you suffer the wintry rain or wind, from whatever quarter it blows? Are you able to stand in the open air without any covering or defence when God casteth abroad his snow like wool, or scattereth his hoar-frost like ashes? And yet these are some of the smallest inconveniences which accompany field-preaching. Far beyond all these, are the contradiction of sinners, the scoffs both of the great vulgar and the small; contempt and reproach of every kind; often more than verbal affronts, stupid, brutal violence, sometimes to the hazard of health, or limbs, or life. Brethren, do you envy us this honour? What, I pray, would buy you to be a field-preacher? Or what, think you, could induce any man of common sense to continue therein one year, unless he had a full conviction in himself that it was the will of God concerning him?[3]

By contrast, Whitefield's more roseate description is characteristic of his more romantic view of preaching generally. 'The open firmament above me, the prospect of the adjacent fields, with the sight of thousands and thousands, some in coaches, some on horseback, and some in the trees, and at times all affected and drenched in tears together, to which sometimes was added the solemnity of the approaching evening, was almost too much for, and quite overcame me.'[4]

[1] *English Thought*, ii. 348–9.
[2] *Works*, viii. 113.
[3] Ibid., viii. 231.
[4] J. Gillies, *Memoirs*, p. 190.

To preach the word of God was to Wesley an awesome responsibility. As Doughty points out,[1] he hardly ever 'preached'; he 'offered Christ to the people', he 'offered the grace of God', he 'proclaimed the glad tidings', he 'declared the whole counsel of God', he 'opened the scriptures'. Perhaps these periphrases reveal why there is so little humour in Wesley's sermons; a task so solemn, so awful, did not admit of levity in any form. The physical and emotional reaction of Wesley's congregations was frequently more violent than anything produced by Whitefield, and for this reason, that whereas Whitefield was constantly easing the seriousness of his message with humorous anecdotes and asides, Wesley allowed tension to build to an almost unbearable pitch.

Wesley never tired of preaching what for him were the basic issues of Christianity, and it is impossible to discern in his sermons either a shifting of theological position or even an appreciable change in emphasis. He had no reservations about preaching a good sermon many times, believing that it improved with each new preaching. A *Journal* entry for 1 September 1778 is illuminating on this point:

I went to Tiverton. I was musing here on what I heard a good man say long since: 'Once in seven years I burn all my sermons; for it is a shame if I cannot write better sermons now than I could seven years ago.' Whatever others can do, I really cannot. I cannot write a better sermon on the Good Steward than I did seven years ago; I cannot write a better on the Great Assize, than I did twenty years ago; I cannot write a better on the Use of Money than I did nearly thirty years ago; nay, I know not that I can write a better on the Circumcision of the Heart than I did five-and-forty years ago. Perhaps, indeed, I may have read five or six hundred books more than I had then, and may know a little more history, or natural philosophy, than I did; but I am not sensible that this has made any essential addition to my knowledge in divinity. Forty years ago I knew and preached every Christian doctrine which I preach now.[2]

---

[1] *John Wesley, Preacher*, p. 190.
[2] *Journal*, vi. 209.

His published sermons, which represent half a century of preaching, corroborate this statement.

Similarly, it is difficult to trace any significant change or development in Wesley's prose style. And this applies equally to his sermons, his *Journal*, and his more polemical writings. His view as to the proper function of language was formed early and was entirely utilitarian.

Leslie Stephen admitted that Wesley showed 'remarkable literary power', but felt that his writings were 'means to a direct practical end, rather than valuable in themselves, either in form or substance'.[1] Wesley, far from apologizing, would have felt flattered. This was the precise purpose he conceived for language; it was a vehicle of thought, a servant of sentiment. Like a good sword, the greatness of prose lay not in its sheen but in the strength and sharpness of its steel. 'There is no need to hide the fact', says Lawton, 'that almost everything which Wesley wrote was intended to communicate or to vindicate, to convince, to persuade, and to move.'[2]

In the Preface to the First Series of sermons (1746) Wesley tells his readers that his intention in preparing these discourses has been to 'design plain truth for plain people'.

Therefore, of set purpose, I abstain from all nice and philosophical speculations; from all perplexed and intricate reasonings; and, as far as possible, from even the show of learning, unless in sometimes citing the original Scripture. I labour to avoid all words which are not easy to be understood, all which are not used in common life; and, in particular, those kinds of technical terms that so frequently occur in Bodies of Divinity; those modes of speaking which men of reading are intimately acquainted with, but which to common people are an unknown tongue.[3]

Twenty years did little to change Wesley's mind in this matter. Thanks to a contumacious young cleric by the name of Samuel Furly, Wesley was forced to set down more

---

[1] *English Thought*, ii. 348.
[2] *John Wesley's English*, p. 14.
[3] *Sermons on Several Occasions*, i. 1.

explicitly his views on style. Clergymen above all people, he cautions Furly, should '*talk* with the vulgar', and in writing should imitate the 'language of the *common people* throughout, so far as consists with purity and *propriety* of speech'. '*Easiness*', therefore, is the chief virtue; and '*stiffness*, *apparent* exactness, *artificialness* of style the main defect to be avoided, next to solecism and impropriety.'[1] In earlier correspondence Furly had expressed his admiration of Dr. Middleton's style. Wesley will hear nothing of this.

You *point* wrong, Sammy: you aim at a wrong *mark*. If he was a standard for any one (which I cannot possibly allow), yet Dr. Middleton is no standard for a preacher—no, not for a preacher before the University. His action is stiff, formal, affected, unnatural. The art glares, and therefore shocks a man of true taste. Always to talk or write like him would be as absurd as always to walk in a minuet step. O tread natural, tread easy, only not careless. Do not blunder or shamble into impropriety. If you *will* imitate, imitate Mr. Addison or Dr. Swift.[2]

But young Sammy Furly is not easily convinced; nor is he overawed by the reputation and authority of his correspondent. On 15 July 1764 Wesley once more found himself trying to answer Furly's pertinent and persistent question. ' "What is it that constitutes *a good style?*" Perspicuity and purity, propriety, strength, and easiness, joined together.'[3] Once again he attacks the 'stiff' and 'pedantic' style of Dr. Middleton, and reiterates his former advice: 'If you imitate any writer, let it be South, Atterbury, or Swift, in whom *all* the proprieties of a good writer meet.'[4]

Then follows a most revealing passage in which Wesley discusses his own writing practice.

As for me, I never think of my style at all; but just set down the words that come first. Only when I transcribe anything for the press, then I think it my duty to see every phrase be clear, pure, and proper.

[1] *Letters*, iv. 232.
[2] Ibid.
[3] Ibid., iv. 256.
[4] Ibid., iv. 257.

Conciseness (which is now, as it were, natural to me) brings *quantum sufficit* of strength. If, after all, I observe any stiff expression, I throw it out, neck and shoulders.

Clearness in particular is necessary for you and me, because we are to instruct people of the lowest understanding. Therefore we, above all, if we think with the wise, yet must speak with the vulgar. We should constantly use the most common, little, easy words (so they are pure and proper) which our language affords. When I had been a member of the University about ten years, I wrote and talked much as you do now. But when I talked to plain people in the Castle or the town, I observed they gaped and stared. This quickly obliged me to alter my style and adopt the language of those I spoke to. And yet there is a dignity in this simplicity, which is not disagreeable to those of the highest rank.[1]

Despite his counsel, Wesley himself is by no means free of difficult words. He possessed a rich and extensive vocabulary and many of his expressions must have been lost on his largely illiterate congregations. Also, his sermons contain more Hebrew, Greek, and Latin quotations than those of any other popular preacher of the age. But his sentence structure, like Swift's, is loose rather than periodic, thus making his prose generally clear and precise. And it is erroneous to assume that an occasional 'hard' word or Greek quotation will necessarily confuse even an essentially illiterate audience. On the contrary, such devices are sometimes necessary credentials for the preacher who would impress his audience with his superior knowledge and thus give greater authority to his message.[2]

The scholar in Wesley would not be denied. His attempt to camouflage his learning, though sincere enough, was by no means successful. Classical quotations are ubiquitous, given first in the original and then translated. There are innumerable references and allusions to Classical authors: Horace, Virgil, Juvenal, Ovid, Quintilian, Homer, Cicero, Seneca, Terence, Suetonius, and Plato. Nor were his

[1] *Letters*, iv. 257–8.
[2] See Mitchell, *English Pulpit Oratory*, p. 106 and pp. 119–20.

literary interests limited to the Ancients. English authors cited include Shakespeare, Sir John Davies, Milton, Cowley, Prior, Pope, Addison, Edward Young, and James Hervey. But it is to his brother's hymns that he returns most often for a line, a couplet, or a stanza that will sum up the point he is making or evoke a response.

'Blessed are they who' thus 'hunger and thirst after righteousness; for they shall be filled.' They shall be filled with the things which they long for; even with righteousness and true holiness. God shall satisfy them with the blessings of His goodness, with the felicity of His chosen. He shall feed them with the bread of heaven, with the manna of His love. He shall give them to drink of His pleasures as out of the river, which he that drinketh of shall never thirst, only for more and more of the water of life. This thirst shall endure for ever.

> The painful thirst, the fond desire,
>   Thy joyous presence shall remove:
> But my full soul shall still require
>   A whole eternity of love.[1]

Wesley's prose is woven from two principal strands, the Biblical and the colloquial. It is almost impossible to exaggerate the influence of scriptural idiom upon his thought and language. Nor was it an unconscious influence. At the beginning of his ministry, he once told John Newton, he set out to make the Bible his 'standard of *language* as well as sentiment'. He endeavoured 'not only to think but to speak *as the oracles of God*'.[2] He realized his aim. Scriptural reference, allusion, quotation, and expression are the warp and woof of his oratory.

Wesley wrote in the letter and in the spirit of the Bible. His work is 'dramatic' as the Bible is dramatic. The dominating realities of his life and of his writings were persons—persons Divine, celestial, human and diabolical. His concern was with life and being far more than with ideas. Abstractions appealed to him but little; speculation he quite abjured. As far as style goes, Wesley has far greater affinities with the

---

[1] *Standard Sermons*, i. 344.
[2] *Letters*, v. 8.

novelist than with the theologian or the philosopher. There is a personal warmth about his Biblical allusions, figure, phrase and dialogue
which makes his work very lively.[1]

Wesley's use of the colloquial deserves special attention,
for no other work of the eighteenth century offers so complete a catalogue of contemporary evangelical terminology
as the *Standard Sermons*. A vast repository of colourful words
and phrases to describe the Christian experience had of
course existed long before the eighteenth century. Latitudinarian divines, embarrassed by the lurid uncouthness of
much of it, had tried to damn it as 'fanatical' or 'enthusiastic'. Wesley determined to make it legal tender again,
while coining a few vivid phrases of his own. Thus, for him,
the natural man (i.e. man before conversion) is not just a
sinner; he is 'dead in sin', 'dead to God' (i. 118)[2]; 'a
stupid, senseless wretch' (i. 257); 'a stupid, careless sinner'
(i. 258); 'by nature "wretched, and poor, and miserable,
and blind, and naked"' (i. 268); 'a lost, miserable, self-
destroyed, self-condemned, undone, helpless sinner' (i.
285); 'wholly immersed in flesh and blood' (i. 379);
'immersed in the mire of this world, in worldly pleasures,
desires, and cares' (i. 527); 'a rank idolater' (ii. 218).
Collectively, such men are a 'generation of vipers' (i. 484);
'the vulgar herd' (i. 536); 'weak, miserable children of men'
(ii. 11); 'proud, passionate, unmerciful, lovers of the world'
(ii. 17).

But if Wesleyan epithets for man were demeaning,
those for God were in the best and politest Latitudinarian
tradition: 'the Lord of heaven and earth'; 'the great
Lawgiver' (i. 316); 'Being of beings'; 'JEHOVAH, the Self-
existent'; 'the Supreme' (i. 320); 'the righteous Judge' (ii.
42); 'the Judge of the earth' (ii. 416).

This then is the eternal juxtaposition which the evangelist
must figure forth: the apostasy of man and the perfect

[1] Lawton, p. 190.
[2] All references to *Standard Sermons*.

holiness of God. Neither is it enough that a man should
accept, at a purely intellectual level, the fact of his sinfulness.
He must be made 'to feel and weep' for his sin. Hence the
severity of the language the preacher must employ. Wesley's
prose sometimes reeks of the marketplace or the village inn.

How many are the baptized gluttons and drunkards, the baptized liars
and common swearers, the baptized railers and evil-speakers, the
baptized whoremongers, thieves, extortioners? What think you? Are
these now the children of God? Verily, I say unto you, whosoever
you are, unto whom any one of the preceding characters belong, 'Ye
are of your father the devil, and the works of your father ye do.'
Unto you I call, in the name of Him whom you crucify afresh, and
in His words to your circumcised predecessors, 'Ye serpents, ye
generation of vipers, how can ye escape the damnation of hell?'[1]

Wesley's sermons are rife with figure, much of which is
earthy, sensuous, concrete. In more sophisticated company
he could, of course, talk of how 'the arrows of conviction
sink deeper into [the] soul' (i. 257). Or he could give a
nautical aura to his description by referring to Christian
hope as the anchor by which 'a Christian is kept steady in
the midst of the waves of this troublesome world, and
preserved from striking upon either of those fatal rocks,—
presumption or despair' (i. 271). But there were other
audiences upon whom such gentle art was lost. For them
such sins as 'pride, malice, revenge, rage, horror, despair'
became 'the dogs of hell' (ii. 412); the human body became
'this prison of flesh and blood' (ii. 417); indifference in
matters of religion was 'the spawn of hell' (ii. 142); and
to die was to 'sink into the chambers of the grave' (i. 535).

Just as he has metaphors, so he has similes for all occasions. Some are dignified: 'Nay, it will farther appear, that
either all the parts of this discourse are to be applied to men
in general, or no part; seeing they are all connected together,
all joined as the stones in an arch, of which you cannot take
one away, without destroying the whole fabric' (i. 319).

---

[1] *Standard Sermons*, i. 295.

Some are faintly humorous: '[The nominal Christian] can no more feed on this poor, shallow, formal thing, than he can "fill his belly with the east wind"' (i. 344). And some are coarse and lurid, though, albeit, Biblical: 'But how often did He strive to save sinners, and they would not hear; or, when they had followed Him awhile, they turned back as a dog to his vomit!' (i. 395).

To sharpen the contrast between sin and salvation Wesley employed such familiar images as darkness and light, disease and health, slavery and freedom. But there is one figure which recurs more often than any other:

Wesley thought in terms of flame, of fire, heavenly fire, not that of hell, though he always felt that his rescue at the age of six from the blazing Epworth parsonage was symbolic of his being a brand plucked from the burning. Flame and fire were words that came to his lips whenever he wanted to image the inner truth, the divine reality. Had not his heart been 'strangely warmed' at his conversion? 'There are twelve of you,' he told the Methodists of Carlisle, 'and all professing to have hearts on fire with the love of God.' At Woodhouse, when he preached, 'a flame', he said, 'is suddenly broken out'. Fire, the pure devouring element: Christ had said He came 'to throw fire upon the earth', and, ever since Charles had written in a hymn

> Oh that in me the sacred fire
> Might now begin to glow,

Wesley had loved to chant it as he rode about the country on his endless itinerancy; 'Spirit of burning, come!' he would sing; 'Refining fire go through my heart!' And at the end, when very old, he would still recur to the idea of the torch, saying—again the words are his brother's:

> Jesus, confirm my heart's desire
> To work, and speak, and think for Thee,
> Still let me guard the holy fire,
> And still stir up Thy gift in me.[1]

One amendment needs to be made to this otherwise excellent statement. It is not true that Wesley thought of flame and

[1] B. Dobrée, *John Wesley* (1933), pp. 95–6.

fire only as 'heavenly fire, not that of hell'. For every image
of fire as heavenly, purifying, saving, there is one whose
suggestion is hellish, punitive, destroying. Wesley, for all
his liberalism in certain areas of theology, held a very
literalistic view of hell. He spoke of it often as the 'unquenchable fire', and was fond of describing his task as a
minister of the gospel as being 'to pluck [men] as brands
out of the burning'.[1] 'For you will all drop', he once told
his congregation, 'into the nethermost hell! You will all lie
together in the lake of fire; "the lake of fire burning with
brimstone." '[2] His preoccupation with the final conflagration is best illustrated in a passage from one of his best-
known sermons, 'The Great Assize'.

If it be inquired by the scoffers, the minute philosophers, 'How can
these things be? Whence should come such an immense quantity of
fire as would consume the heavens and the whole terraqueous globe?'
... it is easy to answer, even from our slight and superficial acquaintance with natural things, that there are abundant magazines of fire
ready prepared, and treasured up against the day of the Lord. How
soon may a comet, commissioned by Him, travel down from the most
distant parts of the universe! And were it to fix upon the earth in its
return from the sun, when it is some thousand times hotter than a
red-hot cannon ball, who does not see what must be the immediate
consequence? But, not to ascend so high as the ethereal heavens,
might not the same lightnings which 'give shine to the world', if
commanded by the Lord of nature, give ruin and utter destruction?
Or, to go no farther than the globe itself; who knows what huge
reservoirs of liquid fire are from age to age contained in the bowels of
the earth? Aetna, Hecla, Vesuvius, and all the other volcanoes that
belch out flames and coals of fire, what are they, but so many proofs
and mouths of those fiery furnaces; and at the same time so many
evidences that God hath in readiness wherewith to fulfil His word?
Yea, were we to observe no more than the surface of the earth, and the
things that surround us on every side, it is most certain (as a thousand
experiments prove, beyond all possibility of denial) that we ourselves,
our whole bodies, are full of fire, as well as everything round about us.

[1] *Standard Sermons*, i. 527.
[2] Ibid., ii. 236.

Is it not easy to make this ethereal fire visible even to the naked eye, and to produce thereby the very same effects on combustible matter, which are produced by culinary fire? Needs there then any more than for God to unloose that secret chain, whereby this irresistible agent is now bound down, and lies quiescent in every particle of matter? And how soon would it tear the universal frame in pieces, and involve all in one common ruin![1]

On every page of Wesley's prose one finds evidence of a master rhetorician. Despite Leslie Stephen's stricture that in his sermons 'there is little more rhetoric than may be found in a vigorous leading article',[2] Wesley has made a notable contribution to English oratorical prose. It is true his rhetorical devices are not as striking as those of Whitefield, but perhaps therein lies his strength rather than his weakness. His antithesis, for example, never calls attention to itself; but who can doubt its effectiveness?

The Pharisee 'cleansed the outside of the cup and the platter'; the Christian is clean within. The Pharisee laboured to present God with a good life; the Christian with a holy heart. The one shook off the leaves, perhaps the fruits, of sin; the other 'lays the axe to the root'; as not being content with the outward form of godliness, how exact soever it be, unless the life, the Spirit, the power of God unto salvation be felt in the inmost soul.[3]

Similarly, his parallelisms build unobtrusively to a climax. 'But how is a sober Christian to make this inquiry? to know what is the will of God? Not by waiting for supernatural dreams; not by expecting God to reveal it in visions; not by looking for any *particular impressions* or sudden impulses on his mind: no; but by consulting the oracles of God.'[4]

There is one device, however, which Wesley makes no attempt to disguise, and that is the rhetorical question. It is ubiquitous. In one sermon, 'The Catholic Spirit', fifty-eight occur in rapid succession.[5] 'Is thy heart right with God . . .?'

---

[1] *Standard Sermons*, ii. 413–15.
[2] *English Thought*, ii. 359.
[3] *Standard Sermons*, i. 419.
[4] Ibid., ii. 96.
[5] Ibid., ii. 136–8.

'Dost thou believe . . .?' 'Is He revealed in thy soul . . .?' 'Dost thou know . . .?' 'Dost thou seek . . .?' 'And dost thou find . . .?' 'Is God the centre of thy soul . . .?' 'Does the love of God constrain thee . . .?' And on, and on, until the sinner must confess and beg forgiveness. Perhaps, however, his questions are most pungent when he combines them, as he frequently does, with exclamatory answers.

Art thou all sin?—'Behold the Lamb of God, who taketh away the sin of the world!' All unholy?—see thy 'Advocate with the Father, Jesus Christ the righteous!' Art thou unable to atone for the least of thy sins?—'He is the propitiation for' all thy 'sins.' Now believe on the Lord Jesus Christ, and all thy sins are blotted out! Art thou totally unclean in soul and body?—here is the 'fountain for sin and uncleanness!' 'Arise, and wash away thy sins!' Stagger no more at the promise through unbelief! Give glory to God! Dare to believe![1]

Unlike Whitefield, Wesley is not rich in anecdotes and illustrations. He depends upon the rich vein of figure and the compelling immediacy of his language to achieve the results he desired.

Wesley's prose is best described as athletic. It has abundant strength and yet is lithe in its movement and verbally spare; sturdy and yet agile; vigorous and yet relaxed. Such prose is not easily classified. For while it has the vigour and preciseness of Swift and Addison, it has some of the rhetorical power and elegance of Johnson and Burke. In the last analysis, it is, as Lawton said it was, both Ciceronian and Senecan. 'Almost all his literary work was put forth to convince, to persuade, and to change conduct. At the same time, Wesley was more of an artist than he gave himself credit for. . . . He asserted those fundamental principles of literary art which have echoed from Quintilian to Quiller-Couch, namely, that excellence of writing consists of perspicuity, appropriateness, accuracy and persuasiveness.'[2]

'In John Wesley', Bernard Lord Manning once said, 'the

---

[1] *Standard Sermons*, i. 328.
[2] *John Wesley's English*, p. 267.

Methodists had a leader who, by a stroke of divine genius that puts him in the same rank as Hildebrand, St. Dominic, and St. Ignatius Loyola, combined the evangelical passion and experience of Luther with Calvin's ecclesiastical system.'[1] Though not always in such exalting language, Wesley's contribution to church history has always been acknowledged. His contribution to pulpit oratory is no less great. For two hundred years his sermons have been regarded by thousands of preachers as the paradigm of homiletic art. In the theological colleges of one of the world's largest Protestant denominations they are still required reading. No other English sermons, not even those of Donne, Tillotson, or Butler, have enjoyed such widespread attention and influence.

[1] *The Making of Modern English Religion* (1929), pp. 109–10.

CONCLUSION

IT IS DIFFICULT, not to say dangerous, to attempt to generalize about English pulpit oratory in the eighteenth century from a study of six preachers, however representative of the age they may be. Each man's preaching, as has been shown, was as much a product of his temperament and individual experience as of his intellectual and social *milieu*. In broad terms, however, it is possible to indicate the direction preaching took and the emphases it received during the century.

By the beginning of the eighteenth century the 'metaphysical' preaching of Andrewes and Donne had completely disappeared from the English pulpit. Gone too was the Puritan style of preaching, with its elaborate and complicated divisions and its tedious exegesis. The climate of opinion in Augustan England was such as to demand a new approach to homiletics and religion generally. The debate over questions of doctrine, waged with so much vigour by Anglicans and Puritans in the previous century, no longer had much appeal. Mystery and mysticism were purposely neglected, though never openly denied. Morality was the new concern, and its explication and defence became the chief task of the Augustan pulpit.

In speaking of the Augustan age Geoffrey Tillotson has said: 'The poets of the time did not see themselves otherwise than as "men speaking to men"—where "speaking" must be given its full force, and divided off from "chanting" or "singing".[1] This statement would be equally true had it been made about Augustan preachers. The pulpit orator in the first half of the eighteenth century no longer looked down from Olympian heights upon a congregation overawed by his authority. His manner of address was formal (though rarely stiff and never pedantic) and restrained. Archbishop Tillotson—or rather the movement of which he was the most significant figure—by his efforts to rationalize religion and chasten pulpit eloquence, had inadvertently weakened the authority of the preacher. Though public appetite for sermons, both as spoken address or when printed, seemed insatiable, faith in the primacy of preaching had been shaken. '*Here*', says Swift, '*are a bundle of my old sermons; you may have them if you please: they may be of use to you, they have never been of any to me.*'[2] As usual, Swift is more pessimistic than most, but there is little doubt that he expressed the latent fear of many of his contemporaries when he wrote: 'The Preaching of Divines helps to preserve well-inclined Men in the Course of Virtue, but seldom or never reclaims the Vicious'.[3]

From the point of view of homiletics the evangelical revival was an attempt to revitalize pulpit oratory. By rejecting Swift's lugubrious estimate of the value of sermons, Whitefield, Wesley, and the other evangelicals[4] reclaimed for preaching much of its former verve, power, and authority, though not, alas, its literary grace.

It is tempting, and would be easy, to make a list of contrasting elements in eighteenth-century pulpit oratory to show how preaching, like poetry, moved from a point where its content and form were largely dictated by reason and propriety to a point where imagination, spontaneity, and passion prevailed. Such a temptation is to be resisted, since

---

[1] *Augustan Studies* (1961), pp. 69–70.
[2] Quoted by Landa, *Irish Tracts and Sermons*, p. 98.
[3] Quoted by Jackson, *Jonathan Swift, Dean and Pastor*, p. 132.
[4] Notably Grimshaw of Haworth, Romaine of St. Dunstan-in-the-West, Berridge of Everton, Walker of Truro, Venn of Huddersfield, Newton of Olney, Fletcher of Madely, and Scott of Aston Sanford.

it inevitably leads to generalizations about preaching that are no less misleading than those so frequently made in the past about poetry. That said, it is still worth emphasizing that the eighteenth century does reveal a movement away from a style of oratory that is ethical and rational in its content, disciplined and precise in its language, and unimpassioned in its presentation, towards a preaching the content of which is evangelical, the language emotive, and presentation histrionic.

This fact can be illustrated from the preachers represented in this study. At the one extreme is Butler, at the other are Whitefield and Wesley, while Berkeley and Secker may be said to indicate a progression between the two extremes. Sterne, on the other hand, is a needful reminder that even while such a change in emphasis was taking place there were those who either remained impervious to it all or, though aware of what was happening, preferred to give to religion their own peculiar interpretation and expression.

Though Wesley and the evangelicals succeeded in giving back to preaching much of its former authority, they were unable to gain respect, or even approval, within the Church of England for their own effusive style of oratory. The man who finally won a general respect for evangelical preaching was Charles Simeon (1759–1836). He is Wesley's logical successor in the English pulpit tradition. He combined an evangelical fervour with a desire for a systematic presentation of thought. He knew the importance of the sermon to the Protestant tradition and believed that in order to be effective preaching had to be authoritative. During his long incumbency at Cambridge he instructed thousands of young men in the craft of sermon construction and presentation. Canon Smyth has gone so far as to suggest that 'Simeon was almost the first man in the history of the English pulpit since the Middle Ages to appreciate that it is perfectly possible to teach men how to preach, and to discover how to do so'.[1]

Though it does not fall within the scope of this study to

[1] *The Art of Preaching*, p. 175.

examine Simeon's homiletic technique or to assess his contribution to English pulpit oratory, it is proper that this reference should be made to him in conclusion. He best represents the direction preaching was to take after Wesley. He also represents a conscious and successful attempt to unite the finest elements in two connected but distinguishable preaching traditions of the eighteenth century: the clarity, flexibility, and preciseness of the Latitudinarians with the passion, persuasiveness, and authority of the evangelicals.

APPENDIX

The following is a list of most of the major treatises on preaching published in Great Britain in the eighteenth century. It does not purport to be exhaustive; nor has the large number of such works produced in America during the same period been included.[1] (Except where otherwise stated, all books were published in London.)

1701: DELMÉ, JEAN. *The Method of Good Preaching, being the advice of a French Reformed Minister to his son,* tr. from the French by James Owen.

1705–07: EDWARDS, JOHN. *The Preacher: a discourse, shewing what are the particular offices and employments of those of that character in the Church,* in 3 parts.

1712: BLACKWELL, THOMAS. *Methodus Evangelica, or, Discourses concerning the legal method of preaching.*

1713: BARECROFT, J. *Advice to a Son in the University, to which is now added Concionatorum instructio: or, rules for preaching, etc.,* in 2 parts.

1714: BULL, GEORGE. *A Companion for the Candidates of Holy Orders: or, the great importance and principal duties of the priestly office.*

1715: BARECROFT, J. *Ars concionandi: or, an Instruction to Young Students in Divinity,* 4th ed.

[1] For a bibliography which attempts to list homiletic treatises through the ages, including those published in America, see H. Caplan and H. H. King, 'Pulpit Eloquence', *Speech Monographs* xxii, 1955.

1716:   ANONYMOUS. *Some Rules for Speaking and Action;*
         to be observed at the bar, in the pulpit and the senate
         . . . in a letter to a friend, 2nd ed.

1721:   SWIFT, JONATHAN. *A Letter to a young gentleman*
         lately enter'd into Holy Orders.

1722:   FÉNELON, FRANÇOIS DE SALIGNAC DE LA MOTHE.
         Dialogues on Eloquence in general and that of the
         Pulpit in particular, tr. from the French by
         William Stevenson.

1723:   JENNINGS, JOHN. *Two Discourses . . . Of Preach-*
         ing Christ . . . Of Particular and Experimental
         Preaching, with a Preface by Isaac Watts.

1724:   GIBSON, EDMUND. *Directions given by Edmund*
         . . . Bishop of London to the Clergy of his Diocese.
         —— Second edition, 1727.
         —— Third edition, 1738.
         —— [Another edition], 1744.
         —— [Another edition], 1749.

1729:   HENLEY, JOHN. 'Discourse on Action in the
         Pulpit', 2nd ed., in *Oratory Transactions,*
         no. 2.

1731:   BLACKMORE, SIR RICHARD. *The Accomplished*
         Preacher; or, an Essay on Divine Eloquence, ed.
         John White of Nayland (Nayland, Essex).

1734:   ROLLIN, CHARLES. *The Method of Teaching and*
         Studying the Belles Lettres . . . with Reflections on
         Taste; and Instructions with regard to the Eloquence
         of the Pulpit, the Bar, and the Stage, tr. from the
         French.
         —— Fourth edition, 1749.
         —— Sixth edition, 1765.

1744:   ANONYMOUS. *Reading no Preaching; or, a Letter to*
         a young Gentleman . . . concerning the unwarrant-
         able practice of reading the Gospel instead of
         preaching it.

1751:   DODDRIDGE, PHILIP. *Lectures on Preaching and*
         the Several Branches of the Ministerial Office.

*

1752: FORDYCE, DAVID. *Theodorus: A Dialogue Concerning the Art of Preaching, to which is added a Sermon on the Eloquence, and an Essay on the Action of the Pulpit, by James Fordyce.*

1753: WATTS, ISAAC. 'Pattern for a Dissenting Preacher', in *Works.*

1759: GOLDSMITH, OLIVER. 'Of Eloquence', in *The Bee*, no. 7. Many subsequent editions.

1763: [SANDEMAN, ROBERT]. *An Essay on Preaching, lately wrote in Answer to the Request of a young Minister* (Edinburgh).

1765: ANONYMOUS. *An Essay towards pointing out in a short and plain Method the Eloquence and Action proper for the Pulpit*, by Philagoretes.

1765: GOLDSMITH, OLIVER. 'On the English Clergy and Popular Preachers', in *Essays*, iv.
LANGHORNE, JOHN. *Letters on the Eloquence of the Pulpit.*

1766: OWEN, HENRY. *Directions for Young Students in Divinity, with regard to those Attainments which are necessary to qualify them for Holy Orders.*
—— Second edition, 1773.
—— Third edition, 1782.
—— Fourth edition, 1800.

1767: ANONYMOUS. *A Dialogue between the Pulpit and the Reading Desk*, by a Member of the Church of England.
—— [Another edition], 1786.
—— [An abridgement], 1795 (York).

1769: SECKER, THOMAS. 'A Charge delivered to the Clergy of the Diocese of Canterbury in the year 1766', in *Eight Charges delivered to the Clergy of the Dioceses of Oxford and Canterbury.*

1771–4: WESLEY, JOHN. 'Directions concerning Pronunciation and Gesture', in *Works* (Bristol).

1783: BLAIR, HUGH. 'Lecture 19, Eloquence of the Pulpit', in *Lectures on Rhetoric and Belles Lettres.*

1783:   BLAIR, HUGH. Ibid. Sixth edition, 1796.
1787:   GREGORY, GEORGE. *Sermons . . . to which are prefixed, Thoughts on the Composition and Delivery of a Sermon.*
1789:   —— Second edition, corrected.
1790:   PALEY, WILLIAM. *Advice addressed to the young Clergy of the Diocese of Carlisle.*
1796:   GARDINER, JOHN. *Brief Reflections on the Eloquence of the Pulpit.*
1800:   WILLIAMS, EDWARD. *The Christian Preacher; or, discourses on preaching by several eminent divines,* revised and abridged (Halifax).

BIBLIOGRAPHY

Except where otherwise stated, all books were published in London.

I. PRIMARY SOURCES

I *Preachers discussed in detail*

(Only editions of works quoted from, or otherwise referred to, have been listed.)

BUTLER, JOSEPH. Letter to the Duke of Newcastle, 5 August 1750, Newcastle Papers, vol. xxxvii, British Museum, Additional MSS. 32722, ff. 56–7.

—— Letter to the Duke of Newcastle, 1 December 1751, Newcastle Papers, vol. xl, British Museum, Additional MSS. 32725, f. 457.

—— *Works*, ed. S. Halifax, 2 vols. (Oxford, 1874).

—— *Works*, ed. J. H. Bernard, 2 vols. (1900).

BERKELEY, GEORGE. Sermons, British Museum, Additional MSS. 39304 & 39306.

—— *Works*, ed. A. A. Luce and T. E. Jessop, 9 vols. (1948–57).

SECKER, THOMAS. Lambeth Palace Library, Secker MSS. 1483 & 1719.

—— *Fourteen Sermons Preached on Several Occasions* (1766).

—— *Eight Charges delivered to the Clergy of the Dioceses of Oxford and Canterbury* (1769).

—— *Sermons on Several Subjects*, 7 vols. (1770–1).

SECKER, THOMAS. *Works*, with a life of Secker by Beilby Porteus, 6 vols. (1811).

STERNE, LAURENCE. *Sermons of Mr. Yorick*, 7 vols. (1760–9).

—— *Works*, 7 vols. (Oxford, 1926–7).

—— *Letters*, ed. L. P. Curtis (Oxford, 1935).

WHITEFIELD, GEORGE. *A Short Account of God's Dealings with the Reverend Mr. George Whitefield* (1740).

—— *Eighteen Sermons Preached by the late Rev. George Whitefield*, ed. J. Gurney (1771).

—— *Works*, ed. J. Gillies, 6 vols. (1771–2).

—— *Sketches of the Life and Labours of the Rev. George Whitefield*, with two discourses preached in the year 1739 (Edinburgh [1849]).

—— MACFARLANE, D. *Revivals of the Eighteenth Century*, with [three] sermons by the Rev. George Whitefield (Edinburgh, n.d.).

WESLEY, JOHN. *Sermons on Several Occasions*, 3 vols. (1838).

—— *Works*, 14 vols. (1872).

—— *Journal*, ed. N. Curnock, 8 vols. (1909).

—— *Letters*, ed. J. Telford, 8 vols. (1931).

—— *Standard Sermons*, ed. E. H. Sugden, 5th. ed., 2 vols. (1961).

II *Other seventeenth- and eighteenth-century preachers referred to*

ANDREWES, LANCELOT. *XCVI Sermons*, eds. W. Laud and J. Buckeridge (1629).

ATTERBURY, FRANCIS. *Sermons and Discourses on Several Subjects*, 3 vols. (1740).

BARROW, ISAAC. *Works*, ed. J. Tillotson, 3 vols. (1700).

BULL, GEORGE. *Works*, ed. E. Burton, 7 vols. (Oxford, 1827).

BURNET, GILBERT. *A Sermon preached at the Funeral of the most Reverend Father in God John . . . Archbishop of Canterbury* (1694).

DONNE, JOHN. *LXXX Sermons*, with a life by Izaak Walton (1640).

HOADLY, BENJAMIN. *Works*, 3 vols. (1773).

LATIMER, HUGH. *Sermons*, ed. H. C. Beeching, Everyman's Library (1906).

SHERLOCK, THOMAS. *Several Discourses Preached at the Temple Church*, 3 vols. (1755).

SIMEON, CHARLES. *Horae Homileticae: or Discourses*, 21 vols. (1832–3).

SOUTH, ROBERT. *Works*, 7 vols. (Oxford, 1823).

SWIFT, JONATHAN. *Irish Tracts, 1720–23, and Sermons*, ed. H. Davis, with an Introduction and notes by L. A. Landa (Oxford, 1948).

TAYLOR, JEREMY. *Works*, ed. R. Heber, 15 vols. (1822).

TILLOTSON, JOHN. *Works*, ed. T. Birch, 10 vols. (1820).

III   *Other contemporary works*

ANDERSON, ROBERT (ed.). *A Complete Edition of the Poets of Great Britain*, 14 vols. (Edinburgh, 1792–5).

[CHURTON, RALPH]. *A Letter to the Lord Bishop of Worcester occasioned by his Strictures on Archbishop Secker and Bishop Lowth in his Life of Bishop Warburton* (1796).

COLE, WILLIAM. *The Blecheley Diary of William Cole 1765–7*, ed. F. G. Stokes (1951).

COOPER, ANTHONY ASHLEY, 3rd EARL OF SHAFTESBURY. *Characteristicks of Men, Manners, Opinions, Times*, 3 vols. (1711).

COWPER, WILLIAM. *Poetical Works*, ed. H. S. Milford (1911).

CRABBE, GEORGE. *Poetical Works*, eds. A. J. and R. M. Carlyle (1914).

FIELDING, HENRY. *The Adventures of Joseph Andrews*, with an Introduction by J. B. Priestley (1929).

—— *The History of Tom Jones, a Foundling*, 2 vols., Everyman's Library (1955).

FOOTE, SAMUEL. *Works*, 3 vols. (1830).

Gentleman's Magazine, xxxviii (1768) and lxiv (1794).

GILLIES, JOHN. *Memoirs of the Life of the Reverend George Whitefield* (1772).

GOLDSMITH, OLIVER. 'Of Eloquence', *The Bee*, no 7 (17 November 1759).

—— *The Citizen of the World*, The British Essayists, ed. R. Lynam, vol. 21 (1827).

GRAVES, RICHARD. *The Spiritual Quixote* (1810).

GRAY, THOMAS, *Correspondence*, eds. P. Toynbee and L. Whibley, 3 vols. (1935).

HAMPSON, JOHN. *Memoirs of John Wesley*, 3 vols. (1791).

HAZLITT, WILLIAM. *Works*, ed. P. P. Howe, 21 vols. (1930–4).

HERRING, THOMAS. *The Visitation Returns of Archbishop Herring, 1743*, eds. S. L. Ollard and P. C. Walker, Yorkshire Archaeological Society Record Series, vols. 71–3 (1929).

HOBBES, THOMAS. *Leviathan* (1651).

HUTCHINSON, W. *The History and Antiquities of the County Palatine of Durham*, 3 vols. (1785).

JOHNSON, SAMUEL. *Works*, ed. R. Lynam, 6 vols. (1825).

—— *Boswell's Life of Johnson*, ed. G. B. Hill, rev. L. F. Powell, 6 vols. (Oxford, 1934–50).

JONES, WILLIAM. *The Diary of the Revd. William Jones*, ed. O. F. Christie (1929).

KECKERMANN, BARTHOLOMEW. *Rhetoricae Ecclesiasticae, Siue Artis Formandi et Habendi Conciones Sacras, Libri Dvo: Methodice Adornati per Praecepta & Explicationes*, Editio tertia (Hanover, 1606).

LOCKE, JOHN. *An Essay Concerning Humane Understanding* (1690).

—— *The Reasonableness of Christianity* (1695).

—— *An Early Draft of Locke's Essay together with Excerpts from his Journals*, eds. R. I. Aaron and J. Gibb (1936).

MILTON, JOHN. *Areopagitica* (1644).

Monthly Review, xliii (1770).

PERCIVAL, JOHN, 1st EARL OF EGMONT. *Diary of Viscount Percival*, ed. R. A. Roberts, 3 vols. (1920–3).

POPE, ALEXANDER. *Poems*, eds. John Butt and others, 6 vols. (1939–62).

RYDER, DUDLEY. *The Diary of Dudley Ryder 1715–1716*, ed. W. Matthews (1939).

SMOLLETT, TOBIAS. *The Expedition of Humphry Clinker* (1771).

—— *The History of England from the Restoration to the Death of George the Second*, 5 vols. (1790).

The Spectator, ed. G. G. Smith, Everyman's Library, 4 vols. (1950).

SPRAT, THOMAS. *History of the Royal Society* (1667).

THOMSON, JAMES. *Complete Poetical Works*, ed. J. L. Roberton (1908).

THOMSON, KATHERINE. *Memoirs of Viscountess Sundon, Mistress of the Robes to Queen Caroline, Consort of George II*, 2 vols. (1847).

WALPOLE, HORACE. *Memoirs of the Reign of King George the Second*, ed. Lord Holland, 3 vols. (1846).

WARBURTON, WILLIAM. *Letters from a Late Eminent Prelate to One of his Friends*, 2nd ed. (1809).

WOODFORDE, JAMES. *The Diary of a Country Parson*, ed. J. Beresford, 5 vols. (1924–31).

YOUNG, EDWARD. *Poetical Works*, ed. J. Mitford, 2 vols. (1830–6).

2. SECONDARY SOURCES

AARON, R. I. *John Locke* (1937).

ABBEY, C. J. *The English Church and Its Bishops*, 2 vols. (1887).

—— and J. H. Overton. *The English Church in the Eighteenth Century*, 2 vols. (1902).

ARBER, E. (ed.). *The Term Catalogues, 1688–1709*, 3 vols. (1905).

ARNOLD, MATTHEW. *Works*, 15 vols. (1904).

BAGEHOT, W. *Estimates of Some Englishmen and Scotchmen* (1858).

—— *Literary Studies* (1879).

BAKER, E. W. *A Herald of the Evangelical Revival* (1948).

BARTLETT, T. *Memoirs of Bishop Butler* (1839).

BELDEN, A. D. *George Whitefield—the Awakener* (1931).

BETT, H. *The Early Methodist Preachers* (1935).

BLENCH, J. W. *Preaching in England in the late Fifteenth and Sixteenth Centuries: A Study of English Sermons, 1450–c. 1600* (Oxford, 1964).

BRASH, B. *Methodism* (1928).

BRILIOTH, YNGRE. *Landmarks in the History of Preaching* (1950).

BROADUS, J. A. *Lectures on the History of Preaching* (New York, 1899).

BROWN, W. E. M. *The Polished Shaft: Studies in the Purpose and Influence of the Christian Writer in the Eighteenth Century* (1950).

BUTLER, D. J. *Wesley and G. Whitefield in Scotland* (Edinburgh, 1898).

The Cambridge History of English Literature, eds. A. W. Ward and A. R. Waller, 14 vols. (1907–16; general index, 1927).

CANNON, W. R. *The Theology of John Wesley* (New York, 1946).

CARPENTER, E. *Thomas Sherlock, 1678–1761* (1936).

CARPENTER, S. C. *Eighteenth Century Church and People* (1959).

CASH, A. H. 'The Sermon in Tristram Shandy', *A Journal of English Literary History*, xxxi (December, 1964), 395–417.

—— *Sterne's Comedy of Moral Sentiments: The Ethical Dimensions of the Journey* (Pittsburgh, 1966).

CHANDOS, J. 'The Art of the Preacher', a series of five talks given on the Third Programme of the BBC in September and October, 1965. Unpublished.

CHRISTMAS, F. E. (ed.). *The Parson in English Literature* (1950).

CHURCH, L. F. *The Early Methodist People* (1948).

—— *More About the Early Methodist People* (1949).

240 BIBLIOGRAPHY

CHURCH, R. W. *Paschal and Other Sermons* (1895).

CLARKE, W. K. L. *Eighteenth Century Piety* (1944).

CLIFFORD, J. L. (ed.) *Eighteenth Century English Literature: Modern Essays in Criticism* (New York, 1959).

—— (ed.) *Man Versus Society in Eighteenth-Century Britain* (Cambridge, 1968).

CONNELY, W. *Laurence Sterne as Yorick* (1958).

CORDASCO, F. G. M. *Laurence Sterne: A List of Critical Studies published from 1896–1946* (Brooklyn, 1946).

CRAGG, G. R. *The Church and the Age of Reason, 1648–1789* (1960).

—— *Reason and Authority in the Eighteenth Century* (Cambridge, 1964).

CRAIK, H. *English Prose Selections*, 8 vols. (1893–6).

CREED, J. M. and J. S. BOYS SMITH. *Religious Thought in the Eighteenth Century Illustrated from Writers of the Period* (Cambridge, 1934).

CROFT, JOHN. 'Anecdotes of Sterne vulgarly Tristram Shandy', *The Whitefoord Papers*, ed. W. A. S. Hewins (Oxford, 1898), pp. 225–35.

CROSS, W. L. *The Life and Times of Laurence Sterne*, 2 vols. (New Haven, 1925).

CUNNINGHAM, B. K. *Religion in the Eighteenth Century* (1909).

CURTIS, L. P. *Anglican Moods of the Eighteenth Century* (New Haven, 1966).

DARBY, H. S. *Hugh Latimer* (1953).

DARGAN, E. C. *A History of Preaching*, 2 vols. (1912).

DARK, S. *Five Deans*. Studies of John Colet, John Donne, Jonathan Swift, Arthur Penrhyn, William Ralph Inge (1928).

DAVIES, D. H. M. *The English Free Churches* (1952).

—— *Worship and Theology in England from Watts and Wesley to Maurice, 1690–1850* (Princeton, 1961).

—— *Varieties of English Preaching 1900–1960* (1963).

DAWSON, J. *John Wesley on Preaching* (1904).

DEFROE, A. *Laurence Sterne and his Novels Studied in the Light of Modern Psychology* (Groningen, 1925).

A Dictionary of English Church History, eds. S. L. Ollard and others, 3rd ed. (1948).

Dictionary of National Biography, eds. L. Stephen and S. Lee (1885–1900).

DIXON, R. W. *History of the Church of England*, 6 vols. (1878–1902).

DOBRÉE, B. *John Wesley* (1933).

—— 'Berkeley as a Man of Letters', *Hermathena*, lxxxii (November, 1953), 49–75.

DOUGHTY, W. L. *John Wesley, Preacher* (1955).

EDWARDS, M. *John Wesley and the Eighteenth Century* (1933).

ELIOT, T. S. *Selected Essays*, 3rd ed. (1951).

ELLIOT-BINNS, L. E. *The Early Evangelicals: A Religious and Social Study* (Greenwich, Conn., 1953).

ELTON, O. *A Survey of English Literature 1730–1780*, 2 vols. (1928).

FERRIAR, JOHN. *Illustrations of Sterne*, 2nd ed., 2 vols. (1812).

FITCHETT, W. H. *Wesley and His Century: A Study in Spiritual Forces* (1906).

FITZGERALD, P. *The Life of Laurence Sterne*, 2 vols. (1864).

FLUCHÈRE, H. *Laurence Sterne: From Tristram to Yorick*, tr. from the French by Barbara Bray (1965).

FRASER, A. C. *Life and Letters of George Berkeley* (Oxford, 1871).

GILL, F. C. *The Romantic Movement and Methodism* (1937).

GLEDSTONE, J. P. *George Whitefield, M.A., Field-Preacher* (1900).

GOSSE, E. *History of Eighteenth-Century English Literature* (1887).

GREEN, J. B. *John Wesley and William Law* (1945).

GREEN, R. *A Bibliography of the Works of John and Charles Wesley* (1896).

—— *Anti-Methodist Publications issued during the Eighteenth Century* (1902).

—— *John Wesley, Evangelist* (1905).

HALÉVY, E. *A History of the English People*, 3 vols. (1934).

HAMMOND, L. V. der H. *Laurence Sterne's Sermons of Mr. Yorick* (New Haven, 1948).

HART, A. T. *The Eighteenth Century Country Parson* (Shrewsbury, 1955).

HARTLEY, L. 'This is Lorence'—*A Narrative of the Reverend Laurence Sterne* (Chapel Hill, 1943).

HASTINGS, SELINA, COUNTESS OF HUNTINGDON. *The Life and Times of Selina Countess of Huntingdon*, ed. A. C. H. Seymour, 2 vols. (1840).

HENDERSON, B. N. 'John Wesley's Last University Sermon', *Cornhill Magazine*, lviii (1935), 93–100.

HENRY, S. C. *George Whitefield, Wayfaring Witness* (New York and Nashville, 1957).

HENSON, H. H. (ed.) *Selected English Sermons: Sixteenth to Nineteenth Centuries* (1939).

HERBERT, T. W. *J. Wesley as Editor and Author* (1940).

HILDEBRAND, F. *Christianity According to the Wesleys* (1956).

HONE, J. M. and M. M. ROSSI, *Bishop Berkeley: His Life, Writings, and Philosophy*, with an Introduction by W. B. Yeats (1931).

HUGHES, H. M. *Wesley and Whitefield* (1913).

HUMPHREYS, A. R. *The Augustan World: Life and Letters in Eighteenth-Century England* (1954).

JACKSON, R. W. *Jonathan Swift, Dean and Pastor* (1939).

JEFFERSON, D. W. *Laurence Sterne*, 'Writers and their Work', no. 52 (1954).

JESSOP, T. E. 'Homage to George Berkeley', *Hermathena*, lxxxii (November, 1953), 1–12.

—— *George Berkeley*, 'Writers and their Work', no. 113 (1959).

—— and A. A. LUCE. *A Bibliography of George Berkeley*. With an Inventory of Berkeley's Manuscript Remains (Oxford, 1934).

JONES, R. F. *The Seventeenth Century* (Standford, 1951).

KEMPE, J. E. *The Classic Preachers of the English Church* (1877).

KILVERT, F. *Memoirs of the Life and Writings of the Rev. Richard Hurd, D.D.* (1860).

KNOX, R. A. *Enthusiasm, A Chapter in the History of Religion with Special Reference to the XVIIth and XVIIIth Centuries* (Oxford, 1950).

KUIST, J. M. 'New Light on Sterne: An Old Man's Recollections of the Young Vicar', *Publication of the Modern Language Association*, lxxx (December, 1965), 549–53.

LANDA, L. A. *Swift and the Church of Ireland* (Oxford, 1954).

LAWSON, A. B. *John Wesley and the Christian Ministry* (1963).

LAWSON, J. *Notes on Wesley's Forty-Four Sermons* (1929).

LAWTON, G. *John Wesley's English* (1962).

LECKY, W. E. H. *A History of England in the Eighteenth Century*, 8 vols. (1892).

LEGG, J. W. *English Church Life from the Restoration to the Tractarian Movement* (1914).

LINDSTRÖM, H. *Wesley and Sanctification: A Study in the Doctrine of Salvation* (Stockholm, 1946).

LOANE, M. L. *Oxford and the Evangelical Succession* (1935).

LUCE, A. A. 'Two Sermons by Berkeley', *Hermathena* xlvii (1932), 1–42.

—— 'Two Sermons by Bishop Berkeley', *Proceedings of the Royal Irish Academy*, xliii (1936), 271–90.

—— *The Life of George Berkeley, Bishop of Cloyne* (1949).

—— 'Berkeley's Search for Truth', *Hermathena*, lxxxii (November, 1953), 13–26.

LYLES, A. M. *Methodism Mocked: The Satiric Reaction to Methodism in the Eighteenth Century* (1960).

MACKERNESS, E. D. *The Heeded Voice: Studies in the Literary Status of the Anglican Sermon, 1830–1900* (Cambridge, 1959).

MACLEAN, K. *John Locke and English Literature of the Eighteenth Century* (New Haven, 1936).

MACLURE, M. *The Paul's Cross Sermons 1534–1642* (Toronto, 1958).

MANNING, B. L. *The Making of Modern English Religion* (1929).

MEAD, G. H. 'Bishop Berkeley and his Message', *Journal of Philosophy*, xxvi (1929), 421–30.

MITCHELL, W. F. *English Pulpit Oratory from Andrewes to Tillotson*, 2nd ed. (New York, 1962).

MITTON, C. L. *A Clue to Wesley's Sermons* (1951).

MOORE, H. *The Life of the Rev. John Wesley, A.M.*, 2 vols. (1824–5).

MOSSNER, E. C. *Bishop Butler and the Age of Reason* (New York, 1936).

NICHOLS, J. *Literary Anecdotes of the Eighteenth Century*, 9 vols. (1812–15).

NORTON, J. *Bishop Butler, Moralist and Divine* (New Jersey, 1940).

OLLARD, S. L. 'Sterne as a Parish Priest', letter in *Times Literary Supplement*, 18 March 1926, p. 217.

OVERTON, J. H. *John Wesley* (1891).

OWST, G. R. *Preaching in Medieval England: an Introduction to Sermon Manuscripts of the Period c. 1350–1450* (Cambridge, 1926).

—— *Literature and Pulpit in Medieval England: a Neglected Chapter in the History of English Letters and of the English People* (1933).

PARTON, J. *Life and Times of Benjamin Franklin*, 2 vols. (Cambridge, Mass., 1892).

PATTISON, M. 'Tendencies of Religious Thought in England, 1688 to 1750', *Essays and Reviews* (1860), 254–329.

PAULL, H. M. *Literary Ethics: A Study in the Growth of the Literary Conscience* (1928).

POLLARD, A. *English Sermons*, 'Writers and their Work', no. 158 (1963).

QUENNELL, P. *Four Portraits: Studies of the Eighteenth Century* (1945).

RAND, B. *Berkeley's American Sojourn* (Cambridge, Mass., 1932).

READ, H. 'Introduction' to *A Sentimental Journey through France and Italy* (1929).
—— *The Sense of Glory* (Cambridge, 1929).
RICHARDSON, A. E. *Georgian England* (1931).
RICHARDSON, C. F. *English Preachers and Preaching 1640–1670: A Secular Study* (New York, 1928).
RIGG, J. H. *The Living Wesley*, 2nd ed. (1891).
ROWDEN, A. W. *The Primates of the Four Georges* (1916).
RYLE, J. C. *The Christian Leaders of the Last Century* (1869).
SAINTSBURY, G. E. B. *A History of English Prose Rhythm* (1912).
—— *The Peace of the Augustans* (1916).
SANGSTER, P. *Pity My Simplicity: The Evangelical Revival and the Religious Education of Children 1738–1800* (1963).
SANGSTER, W. E. *An Approach to Preaching* (1951).
—— *The Craft of the Sermon* (1954).
SHEPHERD, T. B. *Methodism and the Literature of the Eighteenth Century* (1940).
SIMPSON, J. G. *Preachers and Teachers* (1910).
SLACK, K. *The British Churches Today* (1961).
SMITH, S. S. *Dean Swift* (1910).
SMYTH, C. *The Art of Preaching: a Practical Survey of Preaching in the Church of England, 747–1939* (1939).
—— *Simeon and Church Order: A Study of the Origins of the Evangelical Revival in Cambridge in the Eighteenth Century* (Cambridge, 1940).
SOUTHEY, R. *The Life of John Wesley*, 2nd ed., 2 vols. (1820).
SPOONER, W. A. *Bishop Butler* (1901).
STAPFER, P. *Laurence Sterne, sa personne et ses ouvrages* (Paris, 1870).
STEDMOND, J. M. *The Comic Art of Laurence Sterne: convention and innovation in 'Tristram Shandy' and 'A Sentimental Journey'* (Toronto, 1967).
STEPHEN, L. *English Literature and Society in the Eighteenth Century* (1907).
—— *History of English Thought in the Eighteenth Century*, Harbinger ed., 2 vols. (1962).

STROMBERG, R. *Religious Liberalism in Eighteenth-Century England* (1954).

STROUGHTON, J. *History of Religion in England*, 8 vols. (1878).

—— *Religion in England Under Queen Anne and the Georges*, 2 vols. (1878).

SUTHERLAND, J. R. *On English Prose* (Toronto, 1957).

—— *Preface to Eighteenth Century Poetry*, Oxford Paperbacks ed. (1963).

SYKES, N. *Church and State in England in the Eighteenth Century* (Cambridge, 1934).

—— 'The Sermons of a Country Parson', *Theology*, xxxviii (February, 1939), 97–106.

—— *William Wake, Archbishop of Canterbury, 1657–1737*, 2 vols. (Cambridge, 1957).

—— *From Sheldon to Secker, Aspects of English Church History, 1660–1768* (Cambridge, 1959).

THACKERAY, W. M. *The English Humourists of the Eighteenth Century* (1853).

TILLOTSON, G. *Augustan Studies* (1961).

TIMBS, J. *A Century of Anecdotes* (1869).

TOWNSEND, W. T., H. B. WORKMAN, and G. EARYS (eds.). *A New History of Methodism*, 2 vols. (1909).

TRAILL, H. D. *Sterne*, English Men of Letters (1882).

TRAUGOTT, J. *Tristram Shandy's World: Sterne's Philosophical Rhetoric* (Berkeley, 1954).

TYERMAN, L. *The Life of the Reverend George Whitefield*, 2 vols. (New York, 1877).

—— *The Life and Times of the Rev. John Wesley*, 4th ed., 3 vols. (1878).

UPDIKE, W. *History of the Narragansett Church* (New York, 1847).

VALLINS, G. H. *The Wesleys and the English Language* (1957).

WALKER, W. *A History of the Christian Church* (Edinburgh, 1919).

WATKINS, W. B. C. *Perilous Balance: The Tragic Genius of Swift, Johnson, and Sterne* (Princeton, 1939).

WEARMOUTH, R. F. *Methodism and the Common People of the Eighteenth Century* (1945).

The Wesleyan Methodist Magazine (1825).

WHITELEY, J. H. *Wesley's England: A Survey of XVIIIth Century Social and Cultural Conditions* (1938).

WHITTAKER, W. B. *The Eighteenth Century English Sunday* (1940).

WILD, J. D. 'An Unpublished Sermon of Berkeley', *Philosophical Review*, xl (1931), 522–36.

—— *George Berkeley*, 2nd ed. (New York, 1962).

WILLEY, B. *The Eighteenth-Century Background* (1940).

WILLIAMS, C. W. *John Wesley's Theology Today* (1960).

WIMSATT, W. K., Jr. *The Prose Style of Samuel Johnson*, 2nd ed. (1963).

WOOLF, V. 'Introduction' to *A Sentimental Journey through France and Italy* (1928).

YOUNG, D. T. *Popular Preaching* (1929).

INDEX

Main entries are in bold figures

Addison, Joseph, 6–7, 10–11, 16, 17, 70n, 216, 218, 224

Andrewes, Lancelot, 3, 12, 21, 57, 226

Anglicans, *see* Church of England

Antinomianism, 185, 194

Apocrypha, The, 48–9

Aristotle, 28, 34, 40, 45, 102

Arminianism, 17, 159, 200

Arnold, Matthew, 31–2, 34, 45

Atonement, doctrine of the, 66, 95, 100, 157, 161, 190, 191, 195

Atterbury, Francis, 10, 19, 27–9, 49, 86, 100, 216

Augustine, Saint, 57

Bagehot, Walter, 39–40, 57, 117, 118

Bangorian Controversy, 17

Barrow, Isaac, 3, 12, 24, 27, 113

Barth, Karl, 49

Bartlett, Thomas, 44

Baxter, Richard, 3

Beattie, James, 31

Beauclerk, Topham, 9

Bentley, Richard, 21, 124

Berkeley, George, 14, 19, 21, 31n, 33, 43, 49, 52, **58–88** (extant sermons, 58–9; change of emphasis in preaching, 59–62; view of the Church, 62–3; anticipates evangelicals, 63–8; compared to Butler and Swift, 68–78; pulpit notes, 78–81; prose style, 83–5; oratory, 85–7), 92, 128, 167, 190, 228.

Bermuda Project, Berkeley's, 67–8

Berridge, John, 227n

Bethesda Project, Whitefield's, 186

Bible, The, 48, 81, 85, 98–9, 129, 159–60, 178, 195–7, 218–19, 221

Birch, Thomas, 24

Blair, James, 118, 125

Bolingbroke, Lord, 187

Boswell, James, 44, 180–1

Buckingham, the Duchess of, 172

Bull, George, 6

Burke, Edmund, 31, 224

Burnet, Gilbert, 25–6, 27

Burton, Robert, 123

Butler, Joseph, 12, 14, 19, 21, 28, 29, **30–57** (popularity and influence of the *Analogy*, 30–2; popularity and influence of the *Fifteen Sermons*, 32–5; answer to Hobbes, 35–8; opinions about his prose style, 38–40; troubled devotion, 43–5; view of reason, 45–8; analysis of prose style, 49–55; orator, 55–7), 63, 69–70, 73–4, 75, 81, 90, 92, 95, 98n, 101, 110, 111, 127, 225, 228

Calvinism, 14, 17, 86, 99, 157, 165, 194, 195, 196, 198, 200, 225

Carlyle, Thomas, 4

Carmontelle, Louis, 136n
Caroline, Queen, 31
Cash, A. H., 132
Chesterfield, Lord, 136n, 171
Church of England, 2, 4, 14, 17–19, 22,
    30, 33, 44, 57, 70, 74–5, 87, 92,
    94–5, 96, 98, 113, 128, 129, 157,
    179, 180, 181, 226, 228
Church, R. W., 53–4
Churton, Ralph, 90
Cicero, 113, 162, 217, 224
Clarke, Samuel, 10, 14, 36, 118, 124n,
    125
Clement, Père, 139–40
Coleridge, Samuel T., 33
Couch, Quiller, 224
Cowley, Abraham, 218
Cowper, William, 8, 16, 43, 187–8
Crabbe, George, 8–9, 16, 21, 101
Cragg, G. R., 196
Crébillon, C. P. J. de, 123
Croft, John, 127n, 150
Cross, W. L., 9n, 119–20, 122–3, 124n,
    127, 136n, 140
Cudworth, Ralph, 36

Dante, 161
Davies, Horton, 1, 15, 93, 171, 179, 195
Davies, Sir John, 218
Defroe, Arie, 119n
Deism, 17, 19, 30, 31, 61, 71
Diderot, Denis, 123
Dissenters, 71, 74–5, 98, see also
    Evangelicalism and Methodism
Dobrée, Bonamy, 82, 221
Doddridge, Philip, 29
Dominic, Saint, 225
Donne, John, 3, 12, 13, 21, 137, 225,
    226
Doughty, W. L., 201, 214
Dryden, John, 24, 27, 126n

Eachard, John, 24
Election, doctrine of, 157, 187
Eliot, T. S., 57
Elliott-Binns, L. E., 16

Enthusiasm, 13, 15, 23, 27, 28, 48, 65,
    86, 92, 99, 156, 180, 181, 195, 197,
    198, 219
Erasmus, 147
Evangelicalism, 20, 28, 47, 63, 65, 67,
    69, 78, 84, 87, 96, 98, 99, 103, 110,
    113, 129–30, 133, 157, 161, 176,
    180, 198, 207, 219, 228, 229

Fénelon, François, 52
Ferriar, John, 123
Fielding, Henry, 4–5, 11–12, 16, 173n,
    181–2
Final Judgement, doctrine of, 190,
    204–5
Fitzgerald, Percy, 123–4
Fletcher, John, 227n
Fluchère, Henri, 120
Foley, Robert, 122
Foote, Samuel, 184–5
Foster, James, 118, 125
Franklin, Benjamin, 165, 168, 186
Friar, the medieval, 2, 164
Furly, Samuel, 215–17

Gainsborough, Thomas, 136n
Garrick David, 5, 139, 168
Gladstone, W. Ewart, 52
Goldsmith, Oliver, 8, 16, 17
Graves, Richard, 16, 181, 183–4
Gray, Thomas, 147
Greenwood, Richard, 127n, 136n,
    150–1
Grimshaw, William, 99, 227n

Hall, Robert, 118, 124n
Hammond, L. H., 120, 124–6
Hampson, J., 210
Hazlitt, William, 33
Henry, S. C., 169
Henson, H. H., 17–18
Herbert, George, 210n
Herring, Archbishop, 126–7
Hervey, James, 90, 218
Hildebrand, 225

Hoadly, Benjamin, 17, 19, 21, 100
Hobbes, Thomas, 36–7, 38, 52, 72
d'Holbach, Paul Henri, 123
Homer, 34, 163, 217
Horace, 217
Hume, David, 31, 47, 122, 170–1
Hunter, Joseph, 127n, 150–1
Huntingdon, the Countess of, 171, 172, 187
Hurd, Richard, 21, 90, 102
Hutchinson, W., 50n
Hutton, W. H., 38–9

Jackson, R. W., 72
James, Mrs. Anne, 129
Jefferson, D. W., 116
Jessop, T. E., 70, 81, 82
Johnson, Samuel, 6, 8, 9, 29, 31, 43, 44, 103, 180–1, 205, 224
Jones, R. F., 22–3
Jones, Samuel, 98n
Jones, William, 12
Josephus, 146
Jowett, Benjamin, 2
Justification, doctrine of, 191–5, 207
Juvenal, 217

Keckermann, Bartholomew, 104–5
Kennicott, Benjamin, 211–12
King, John, 208
Kingsley, Charles, 2
Kuist, J. M., 127n

Landa, L. A., 71–2, 75
Langhorne, John, 9
Latimer, Hugh, 164–5, 178, 205
Latitudinarianism, 10, 14–16, 19–20, 60, 64, 94, 129, 190, 219, 229
Laud, William, 17, 74, 94
Law, William, 19, 21, 43, 49, 196n
Lawson, John, 202
Lawton, George, 206, 215, 224
Leightonhouse, Walter, 124n
Liddon, H. P., 2
Locke, John, 14, 15n, 16, 36, 65, 133, 138, 146

Lowth, Robert, 21
Loyola, Saint Ignatius, 225
Luce, A. A., 62, 70, 84–5
Luther, Martin, 193, 195, 196, 225

Mackerness, E. D., 2
MacLean, Kenneth, 146
MacLure, Millar, 4
Magee, W. C., 2
Manning, B. L., 224–5
Methodism, 17, 20, 28, 48, 52n, 66, 100–1, 103, 133, 155, 172, 179, 182, 183, 184, 185, 189, 195, 198, 200, 201, 205, 206, 208, 210, 211, 221, 225
Middleton, Conyers, 216
Mill, James, 32
Milton, John, 4, 218
Mitchell, W. F., 3, 27, 104
Moore, Henry, 52–3n
Mossner, E. C., 30n, 36

Nelson, John, 211
Newcastle, the Duke of, 56–7n
Newman, J. H., 2, 151n
Newton, John, 99, 198, 218, 227n
Non-Jurors, 17, 18
Norris, John, 124

Ogden, Samuel, 136
Ollard, S. L., 127
Original Sin, doctrine of, 95, 157–8, 160, 190–1
Ovid, 217
Owst, G. R., 2, 164

Paley, William, 18, 21, 92n
Parker, Joseph, 24
Patrick, Simon, 24
Pattison, Mark, 12, 13, 52
Paul, Saint, 57, 76, 98, 99–100, 134, 175, 191
Pelagianism, 15, 190

Percival, Viscount, 68, 86, 91
Piracy, sermon, 5–8
Pitt, Christopher, 90–1
Pitt, William (the Younger), 32
Plagiarism, sermon, 6, 117–18, 120–6
Plato, 78, 217
Pollard, Arthur, 50
Pope, Alexander, 10, 13, 16, 70n, 86, 90, 95, 126n, 163, 181, 218
Porteus, Beilby, 101, 108
Potter, Archbishop, 44
Preaching, twentieth-century, 1; nine-teenth-century, 1–2; medieval, 2; Reformation, 3; seventeenth-cen-tury, 3–4, 21–7, 226; eighteenth-century, 4 *passim*; rational-ethical, 10–16, 30–57; polemical, 17–19, 70–5; evangelical, 20, 155–225; reform of, 21–9; proleptic, 58–88; moderate, 89–114; 'rhetorical', 115–54; rhetorical devices in, 49–55, 81–5, 110–13, 139–49, 151–4, 167, 170, 174–8, 202, 215–224; oratorical devices in, 55–6, 85–7, 149–51, 164–73, 204–9; homiletic features of, 77–81, 103–110, 136–8, 178, 203–4
Prior, Matthew, 70n, 218
Protestantism, 3, 12, 94, 190, 195, 196, 201, 225, 228
Puritanism, 4, 13, 14, 22–3, 64, 132, 226
Putney, R. D. S., 135

Quakers, 86, 210
Quintilian, 217, 224

Rabelais, François, 123, 147
Rand, B., 87n
Read, Herbert, 116, 120, 151
Reason, 13–14, 25, 45–8, 63–5, 66, 87, 92–3, 97, 103, 196, 197–9
Reid, Thomas, 31
Resurrection, 95
Reynolds, Sir Joshua, 90n, 121, 135–6
Richardson, C. F., 12

Richardson, Samuel, 16
Robertson, F. W., 2
Rochefoucauld, François, Duc de la, 52
Romaine, William, 227n
Roman Catholicism, 3, 4, 14, 16, 71, 74–5, 92
Romantic Movement, 20
Rowden, A. W., 89
Royal Society, 22

Sacheverell, Henry, 18–19, 100
Saint Paul's Cross, 4, 13
Saintsbury, George, 81–2, 119n
Sanctification, doctrine of, 194–5
Sangster, W. E., 107
Scott, Thomas, 227n
Secker, Thomas, 31n, 40, **89–114** (popularity, 89–91; conservatism, 91–2; orthodoxy, 92–6; attitude towards evangelicalism, 96–101; attitude towards The Bible, 98–100; didactic preaching, 101–2; moderation, 102–3; views on preaching, 103–8; preaching pract-ice, 108–10; prose style, 110–13), 190, 208, 228
Seneca, 162, 217, 224
Sermons, *see* Preaching
Shaftesbury, Anthony Ashley Cooper, Earl of, 36–7, 52
Shakespeare, William, 83, 218
Sherlock, Thomas, 31n, 190
Shuter, Edward, 173
Simeon, Charles, 62, 96n, 228–9
Slack, Kenneth, 189
Smart, Christopher, 43
Smollett, Tobias, 16, 181, 182–3
Smyth, Charles, 20, 164–5, 228
Society for the Propagation of the Gospel, 58, 69
Socinianism, 148n, 190
South, Robert, 3, 12, 23, 24, 27, 216
Southey, Robert, 179
Sprat, Thomas, 22
Spurgeon, Charles Haddon, 188
Stapfer, Paul, 118–19, 128, 132, 135, 146–7

Steel, Richard, 210
Steele, Richard, 16, 70n
Stephen, Leslie, 17, 32, 43, 56, 116–17,
    118, 202–3, 212–13, 215, 223
Sterne, Laurence, 5, 12, 13, 16, 21, 101,
    115–54 (attack and defence, 115–
    120; plagiarism, 120–6; country
    parson, 126–7; salient themes in
    preaching, 127–34; view of man,
    131–3; compared to Swift, 134–5;
    appearance, 135–6; approach to
    preaching, 136–8; dramatic ele-
    ment in sermons, 139–43; treat-
    ment of Biblical characters, 145–7;
    rhetorician, 147–9; orator, 149–51;
    prose stylist, 151–4), 167, 195n, 228
Sterne, Lydia, 123
Stillingfleet, Edward, 27
Suetonius, 217
Sutherland, James, 24, 55, 113, 126n
Swift, Jonathan, 11, 12, 13, 18, 21, 22n,
    43, 54, 55, 69–78, 82, 83, 100, 101,
    104n, 128, 134–5, 147, 216, 217,
    224, 227
Sykes, Norman, 30n

Taylor, Jeremy, 3, 21, 81, 137, 196n
Terence, 217
Thackeray, W. M., 116, 117, 118
Thomson, K., 86
Tillotson, Geoffrey, 226–7
Tillotson, John, 3, 10, 14–16, 19, 20,
    24–9, 36, 45, 46, 47, 52, 81, 92, 97,
    118, 124n, 125, 129, 133, 154, 190,
    205, 225, 227
Timbs, J., 7
Toplady, Augustus, 99, 198
Tories, 19
Traill, H. D., 117, 119n, 143
Traugott, John, 147
Trinity, doctrine of the, 46, 61–2, 95,
    129, 157, 190, 194–5
Trustler, John, 7–8
Tucker, Dean, 44

Updike, Ludowick, 86

Vaughan, A. J., 97
Venn, Henry, 227n
Virgil, 217
Voltaire, F. M. A., 123

Wake, William, 18
Walker, Benjamin, 87
Walker, P. C., 127
Walker, Samuel, 227n
Walpole, Horace, 89, 99
Warburton, William, 18, 21, 27
Watkins, W. B. C., 119n, 120, 130n
Wesley, Charles, 67, 189n, 200, 218,
    221
Wesley, John, 5, 20, 21, 28, 31, 43, 47,
    49, 52–3n, 55, 62, 67, 78, 96, 98,
    100, 127–8, 133, 141, 155, 157,
    167, 179–80, 181, 189–225 (varied
    talents, 190–1; doctrine of salva-
    tion, 191–5; approach to The
    Bible, 195–6; view of reason,
    197–9; ethical preaching, 200;
    influence of Standard Sermons,
    200–1; manner of preaching,
    201–6; proper length of sermon,
    206–7; abhorrence of 'gospel
    preaching', 207–8; pronunciation
    and gesture, 208–9; appearance
    and temperament, 209–10; des-
    criptions of preaching style, 210–
    212; on field-preaching, 213; view
    of preaching generally, 214–15;
    literary and rhetorical style, 215–
    224); 227, 228, 229
Wesley, Samuel (Jr.), 193
Westminster Assembly, 22
Wharton, Thomas, 147
Whateley, George, 137
Whigs, 18–19, 71
Whitefield, George, 5, 20, 53n, 55, 65,
    67, 99, 101, 155–88 (most contro-
    versial preacher, 155–6; major
    theme in preaching, 157–9; atti-
    tude towards The Bible, 159–60;
    concept of heaven and hell, 161–2;
    view of the clergy, 163; style of
    preaching, 163–7; extraordinary

Whitefield, George—*contd.*
voice, 167–8; acting ability, 168–170; reactions to his preaching, 170–4; rhetoric, 174–6; raconteur, 176–8; compared to Wesley, 179–180; attacked, 180–5; defended, 185–8), 194, 195, 197, 198, 204, 213, 214, 223, 224, 227, 228

Wilkes, John, 9
Wilkins, John, 22, 25
William and Mary, 18

Williams, C. W., 195
Wollaston, William, 52, 124n
Woodforde, James, 16
Woodhouse, John, 130n
Woolf, Virginia, 152
Wordsworth, William, 20

Yeats, W. B., 88
Young, D. T., 201
Young, Edward, 64, 124n, 218

DATE DUE